CW00763135

DEVON PUBS

Kingston

DEVON PUBS

A PICTORIAL RETROSPECTIVE

ANDREW SWIFT &
KIRSTEN ELLIOTT

AKEMAN PRESS

Published by AKEMAN PRESS
www.akemanpress.com

© Andrew Swift & Kirsten Elliott 2015

ISBN 978-0-9560989-8-6

All rights reserved. No part of this publication may be reproduced, stored in a retrieval system, or transmitted, in any form or by any means, electrical, mechanical, photocopying, recording or otherwise, without the prior permission of Akeman Press.

Front cover: The Bridge Inn, Topsham

Back cover: The White Hart Inn, Spreyton, now the Tom Cobley Tavern

Title page: The Dolphin Inn, Kingston

Printed through SS Media Ltd, Rickmansworth, Hertfordshire WD3 1RE

Contents

MISCELLANEOUS SECTIONS

Alfresco drinking outside the Union Inn at Holbeton in the 1920s

Introduction

This book has been over a decade in the making, and what started off as a celebration of Devon's pubs has increasingly adopted the tone of a lament. The pub – be it in city, town or village – is one of this country's greatest institutions, but it is an institution under threat as never before.

The photographs in this book span around a hundred years – from the 1860s to the 1960s – and record not only a vanished way of life, but in many cases pubs that have called last orders for ever.

While travelling around the county to research this book, time and again we came upon pubs that had recently closed or been converted to other uses. When it came to making final revisions prior to publication, many others had to be added to the tally. It seems inevitable that more will have joined their ranks by the time you read this. It is not only pubs that have reached a point of no return that close; often it is thriving and much-loved pubs that go, not because they are no longer viable, but because there is more money to be made converting them to something else. The roots of this state of affairs go back a very long way. We look in more detail at the history of brewing in the county and the light this sheds on the current plight of the county's pubs at the end of the book.

The sight of abandoned, boarded-up pubs has become as defining an image of the current decade as the sight of abandoned railway lines was of the 1960s. Fifty years hence, will people wax misty-eyed at the thought of Britain's lost pubs as they do now for the age of steam?

The loss of community pubs is, of course, part of a wider social change. Looking at the scenes of rural, town and village life gathered together here, it is hard to resist the feeling – despite our awareness of the hardships and privations those who gaze back at us often suffered – that a continuity and sense of place stretching back centuries have been lost forever. Many villages once populated by families whose roots went back generations are now given over largely to holiday lets or second homes.

Where communities have managed to maintain a sense of identity, it is through adaptation and opposition to the forces working to destroy it. In many rural communities, with no shop, no school, no post office, no bus service, the pub is the last bastion of community life. When it too closes, the danger is that the community will dwindle to just another collection of houses. As Hilaire Belloc wrote over a century ago, 'when you have lost your inns ... you have lost the last of England'.

Thankfully, there is, amid the doom and gloom, still much to celebrate – superb traditional free houses such as the Bridge Inn at Topsham and the Tom Cobley Tavern at Spreyton, both the subject of special features, as well as many others. The history of Devon's inns is rich, diverse and colourful; if the journeys into the past that follow inspire you to explore – and defend – what remains of that heritage, we will have achieved what we set out to do.

Andrew Swift & Kirsten Elliott
September 2015

Researching Pub History

Compared to other areas of historical research, pub history is largely neglected. This neglect is remarkable, given the centrality of inns and pubs to the social, cultural, commercial and economic life of the communities they have served. Perhaps it is because local history, with its roots in eighteenth- and nineteenth-century antiquarian study of the ecclesiastical, aristocratic and genteel aspects of provincial life, has shied away from the often insalubrious and gritty life of institutions which served not only the well-to-do but also those regarded as the undeserving, improvident and inebriated poor. Until well into the twentieth century, local dignitaries – who often doubled as local historians – fought to quell the influence of pubs and reduce their number. They can hardly have been expected to dignify them with historical enquiry.

As a result, much of what follows is based on original research – with all the pitfalls and caveats that entails. One of the problems is that so much of what passes for pub history falls into the realms of legend or anecdote. None of this can be discounted, of course, as much of it will have a basis in fact, however elaborated, garbled or misconstrued it may have been over the centuries. Where we have been able to put historical flesh on anecdotal bones we have done so; where we have not, we have, while relaying stories handed down from hand to mouth, resorted to equivocations such as 'it is believed that' or 'it is said that', in the hope that others may take up the challenge of getting to the root of the matter.

It is also not surprising, given the ubiquity of spirits on their premises, that ghosts figure largely in the annals of so many pubs. We have, however, bar the odd digression here and there, decided to restrict our enquiries to what may be termed natural history, leaving the supernatural to those better qualified to deal with it.

Ploughing such an untrodden field as pub history can be hit and miss. For some pubs we have turned up a wealth of information, far too much in some cases to include in a survey such as this. For other pubs, with a history almost certainly no less fascinating, we have turned up virtually nothing. We have resisted the temptation to make up this deficiency with lists of landlords, reports of petty infringements of the law, minor misdemeanours, or descriptions of friendly-society meetings and the like. Fascinating as such minutiae may be when they concern a pub you know well, repetition of it ad infinitum would, we felt, make for information overload.

Finally, we should pay tribute to the photographers and postcard publishers without whose images this book would not have been possible. Although many of the images have survived the years remarkably well, others have not, either fading or being scuffed, torn or otherwise damaged in the interim. Although efforts have been made to enhance them, the quality of some remains fairly lamentable. They have nonetheless been included because of their historical value.

All images – except the painting of the Bridge Inn at Topsham on the back cover – are from the Akeman Press archive ... and, in case you are wondering why your favourite pub is not featured, it is because we did not find an archive photograph of it. Perhaps in volume 2 ... who knows?

56302. The New Inn, Abbotsham.

Abbotsham

The New Inn was a row of cottages before becoming an inn. It once belonged to the Anchor Brewery of Barnstaple, but, when that closed in 1918, it was bought for £700 by Hancock's of Wiveliscombe. Hancock's merged with Arnold's of Taunton in 1927 and this postcard was published shortly afterwards. Today, renamed the Thatched Inn and recently extended, it is one of the most popular free houses in North Devon.

Abbotskerswell

The Two Mile Oak, on the road from Newton Abbot to Totnes, has changed little since the photograph below was taken a century ago. Inside, wooden floors, oak beams, a log fire and beers from the barrel maintain continuity with the past. It was first licensed in 1703, having previously been a farmhouse.

Alswere

This view of Alswere near South Molton dates from around 1910, and shows the smithy and the White Hart Inn – the commercial and social hubs of the village. Today, both have been converted to private houses.

Appledore

The Coach & Horses in Appledore is renowned not only for its music sessions but also for its food, and is as snug and friendly a local as you are likely to find anywhere. It is also one of Appledore's oldest buildings, possibly dating from the fifteenth century. It belonged to the Anchor Brewery in Barnstaple until 1918, when Hancock's of Wiveliscombe bought it for £300. In this photograph from the 1920s, the landlord and landlady stand proudly at the door.

The Royal George on Irsha Street has one of the most enviable locations in Devon. Set at the water's edge, it overlooks the confluence of the Taw and Torridge estuaries, and is one of Appledore's most popular hostelries (although, after being advertised for sale in 2014, it was reported temporarily closed in summer 2015). The Prince of Wales, however, which can be seen to the left of it on this mid-twentieth century postcard, is no more, having been converted to a pair of private houses.

The Bell Inn stood on New Quay Street opposite a slipway leading down to the estuary. Long one of Appledore's most popular hostelries, it was converted to three residential units in 2005.

Another of Appledore's lost pubs is the Globe on Market Street, which had a rather splendid sign. Although the building has survived, it is now known as Globe House.

Ashburton

'This Ashburton is a poor little town – bad was the best inn,' wrote Celia Fiennes in 1685. She could have been referring to the Exeter Inn, which is said to have been built as a church house around 1130 and rebuilt in 1585. Until it was removed in 1965, a horse passage led through the inn, whose low beamed ceilings give ample evidence of the medieval origins of one of South Devon's most popular traditional hostelries. It belonged to the Kingskerswell Brewery until 1927, when the tenant, WE Halse, bought it for £1000. Legend has it that Sir Walter Raleigh was arrested in the inn in 1603, and in 2012, to commemorate the event, a trompe l'oeil mural of Raleigh looking through a window was painted on the building next door.

ASHBURTON POP

'I was born at the Rose and Crown public house on the old bridge, in the borough town of Ashburton, 1765; where a good woollen-manufactory has been carried on; and it has produced a great character, or so, for learning; and has been famous for a beverage, called Ashburton Pop, as London is for porter. I recollect its sharp feeding good taste, far richer than the best small beer, more of the champagne taste, and what was termed a good sharp bottle. When you untied and hand-drew the cork, it gave a report louder than a pop-gun, to which I attribute its name; its contents would fly up to the ceiling; if you did not mind to keep the mouth of the stone bottle into the white quart cup, it filled it with froth, but not over a pint of clear liquor. Three old cronies would sit an afternoon six hours, smoke and drink a dozen bottles, their reckoning but eight pence each, and a penny for tobacco. The pop was but twopence a bottle. It is a great novel loss to the town; because its recipe died with its brewer about 1785.'

Reminiscences of Captain John Cook, from *William Hone's Table Book*, 1828

On the corner of West and North Streets was the Rose & Crown. When it closed in 1969, it was taken over by the Churchward family, who 32 years earlier had acquired the Sun Inn next door and converted it to a grocer's. The Rose & Crown became part of the grocer's as well; today that grocer's is a Spar supermarket, with the rare distinction of occupying not one but two old inns.

The London Inn on West Street dated from the fifteenth century, but by the time this postcard was published in the early 1900s it had been renamed the London Hotel. In 1981, a brewery was established upstairs. Later relocated to the old stable block, it lasted until 1997 when a fire brought its career, along with that of the inn, to an untimely end. Although the building was restored, it is now a Moorish restaurant.

On North Street was the Globe, seen on the left in the 1930s. Although a relative newcomer among Ashburton's inns, it was one of the best appointed, with balls, dinners and other social occasions held in its function room. The photograph below was taken in August 1938, when Devon was hit by a series of devastating storms. On 12 August 1938, the *Exeter & Plymouth Gazette* reported that Buckland Bridge in Ashburton had been swept away and 'the Globe Hotel had water up to the bar counters.' The Globe closed in 1949 and is now an antique shop.

Here, on a postcard from around 1906, we see three of Ashburton's lost hostelries in a row – the Golden Lion, the Golden Lion Tap and the Red Lion. The Golden Lion was built in the late eighteenth century as a townhouse for a wealthy surgeon called Nicholas Tripe. After becoming an inn around 1795, it quickly gained a reputation as the haunt of political mavericks. In 1825, William Barons, a staunch Tory, became its landlord. In the 1837 election campaign, with the Golden Lion operating as the Tory HQ, the 'principles of fair contention' were, according to the *Western Times*, 'entirely abandoned by the Tories'. One Liberal supporter was kidnapped and hidden away in the Golden Lion, while another had his drink spiked before being carted off and dumped on Dartmoor.

A more recent landlord was Alan Hope, friend and supporter of Screaming Lord Sutch, founder of the Monster Raving Loony Party. After the party's annual conference was held at the Golden Lion in 1984, Hope became party chairman. Elected to the town council, he later became Loony Mayor of Ashburton, and, after Screaming Lord Sutch's death in 1999, he became leader of the party. The inn closed when he moved to Hampshire a few months later and is now an hotel.

With its splendid set of Assembly Rooms (out of view to the left), elegant façade and fearsome lion with paw on globe (a slighting reference to the Globe in North Street, perhaps), the Golden Lion was, in its heyday, one of South Devon's top inns. And, like all the best inns, it had a tap – somewhere for the coachmen, ostlers, servants and hoi polloi to drink, leaving the inn for the gentry. The Golden Lion Tap can be seen to the right of the inn, with a sign for the stables on its wall. It was demolished shortly after this postcard was published, to make way for a fire station. The site is now occupied by a car park.

Beyond it can be seen the Red Lion, the oldest of the lot and the most recent casualty. Dating from the sixteenth century, if not earlier, it was remodelled in the early nineteenth century, retaining many original features. Since closing in 2009, it has been converted to four apartments and a retail unit.

Ashill

Ashill, tucked away down country lanes east of Uffculme, has seen many changes since this group of children lined up for the camera around 1910, but the New Inn – now renamed the Ashill Inn – remains a traditional local at the heart of the community. Dating from 1835, it replaced a building destroyed by fire, and was originally a beerhouse.

On 25 August 1849, the *Exeter & Plymouth Gazette* reported the landlord's attempt to obtain a full licence:

> William Salter of Ashill, Uffculme, applied for an alehouse licence. He said his house was on the high road, about two miles from Uffculme, and two miles from Collumpton [sic]. The population of the locality was about 200.
>
> Mr Drewe asked the applicant if he had not been convicted of keeping a disorderly house.
>
> The applicant said he couldn't deny that there was something about 19 years ago.
>
> Mr Drewe: 'But wasn't there something about two years ago?'
>
> The applicant hemmed and hawed – and the result was that he admitted that he had been brought before the Bench by a summons.
>
> Mr Drewe: 'I believe your son is a constable of the parish – and I hope he does his duty.

The licence was refused, 'the Bench observing that no case of public want had been made out'. A year later, Mr Salter's second attempt to get a full licence, reported by the *Gazette* on 7 September 1850, was accompanied by 'a testimonial, signed by the vicar and churchwardens, and other inhabitants':

> Mr Huyshe said the applicant should have gone to the schoolmaster to have written out the testimonial more orthographically, for there were many mistakes in the spelling.
>
> The applicant said the nearest public house was two miles distant. There was a great trade doing in Ashill – three shops and two master carpenters.
>
> Mr Huyshe: 'They will be much the worse for this, depend on it.'

Despite Mr Huyshe's opposition, the application was granted.

Aveton Gifford

The King's Arms at Aveton Gifford lies at the head of the Avon estuary and is now known, appropriately, as the Fishermen's Rest. This distant view of it dates from around 1905. The packed barge in the foreground is setting off for the annual Wesleyan Sunday School trip to Bantham.

Until recently, there was another pub in Aveton Gifford, a traditional local called the Taverners in the heart of the village. Until 1962, it was known as the Commercial Inn, but was renamed after a company of actors who performed there. The Taverners,

founded by the actor Henry McCarthy, and supported by the Brewers Society, regularly brought classic drama, including plays by Chekhov, Shaw and Shakespeare, to around 50 pubs across the country. Sadly, any hopes that the Taverners might become a permanent arts venue for the South Hams have been dashed, for the final curtain has come down on its career as a pub and it is now apartments.

Avonwick

The Avon Inn at Avonwick has changed little since this photograph was taken almost a century ago, although the stables on the right have gone to make way for a car park. After a few years as an upmarket food destination, new owners have pledged to turn the Avon Inn back into a traditional community pub, with an emphasis on real ale, live music, hog roasts and barbecues.

Awliscombe & Weston

This unassuming cider house, from which Christmas greetings were sent around 1907, stood amid cider orchards alongside the River Otter in the village of Weston. Today, extended almost beyond recognition, it has been transformed into one of East Devon's busiest hostelries, the Otter Inn. Where orchards once stood is an enormous car park, with family-friendly gardens running down to the river.

Axminster

There has been an inn on the site of the George at Axminster for centuries, but in 1760, after the previous building was damaged by fire, it was rebuilt and renamed in honour of the coronation of George III. This postcard shows it around 1910. Since then, the section to the right of the archway has been demolished to widen the road. The George closed in 2008.

Axmouth

Until its estuary silted up in the fourteenth century, Axmouth had one of the busiest harbours in Devon, with around 14 inns. Although its glory days are long gone, two inns remain. This is the Ship, built to replace a thatched building which burnt down on Christmas Eve in 1880.

Axmouth's other inn is the Harbour, a thatched, low-beamed building dating from the seventeenth century. On 5 February 1926, the *Western Times* reported that the magistrates had debated whether or not to renew its licence, but eventually agreed to do so on condition that proper sanitation was installed. In 2011, it was taken over by the team that runs the Wheelwright at Colyford. The Harbour may not have changed much externally since the photograph above was taken in the early twentieth century, but a regular from back then, wandering into the inn today and expecting it to look as it does in the photograph below would be in for a big surprise.

Aylesbeare

Apart from gaining an extension at the back and a new porch, the Blue Anchor has changed little since this postcard was published in 1908. Later renamed the Aylesbeare Inn, this popular and welcoming local closed in 2013 and its future is uncertain.

Bampton

Bampton, described in Murray's 1851 *Handbook* as 'a small secluded town embedded among hills in a singularly beautiful country', is one of the oldest towns in Devon, dating back to Saxon times, with a fair founded by royal charter in 1258. The White Horse, seen here in the 1920s, was for years Bampton's premier inn. More recently, it has been closed for long periods, the last of which began in 2010. Since then, the function room at the back has been converted to a dwelling, but despite rumours of the pub's reopening, a visit in November 2014 found little sign of activity.

Bampton has long been famous for its pony fair. Many of the ponies were sold in the stables behind the Tiverton Hotel, seen here on a postcard from the 1930s. In 2006, after a period as the Seahorse, it was renamed the Quarryman's Rest, recalling the men who worked at a nearby quarry. New owners took over in 2013, and with its sofas, log fires, real ale and a popular restaurant, it is busier than ever.

The Exeter Inn lies in the Exe valley just south of Bampton. Since being acquired by new owners in 2009, it has gained a reputation for its food, beer and friendly atmosphere. Built as a farmhouse in the late fifteenth century, it was already over 400 years old when this postcard was published around 1930. Since then the road has been realigned to create a forecourt and car park in front of the inn.

Bantham

One of the best-known pubs in the South Hams is the Sloop at Bantham, possibly dating from the fourteenth century. Since this postcard was published around 1910, the slate on the first floor has been replaced by render, a single-storey bay has been added on the right and the lean-to extension on the left has been raised to three floors.

Barnstaple

A 1920s view from the steps of Barnstaple Town station of the Castle Hotel, with Barnstaple Fair in full swing. The fair moved across the river in the 1960s, the station closed in 1970 and the school on the left has been replaced by a telecom building. The pub survives, however, and, after a spell as the Monkey Island, is now the Watering Hole.

Barnstaple claims to be the oldest borough in England, with a charter granted by King Athelstan in AD930, and until recently it had an inn befitting such illustrious ancestry. The Three Tuns was the oldest and most famous pub in town. Despite many changes, it remained the sort of place you could imagine Elizabethan merchants gathering, the sort of place John Gay – who went to school across the road – might have come to glean material for his *Beggar's Opera*. Cosy, dim, noisy, wood-panelled, with seats tucked away in a passageway at the back and a bar upstairs if things got too lively, this was not some twee reconstruction aimed at tourists, but an honest-to-goodness, take-it-or-leave-it pub, where people met to indulge in those twin delights – good beer and good company.

Nobody knew how old the Three Tuns was. A building was first recorded here in 1415 when John Hunt bought it for £8 from Thomas Walshe. It was rebuilt as a shop in the mid-fifteenth century, but by 1704 it had become an inn. The eighteenth century saw it

refronted, and in the nineteenth new windows were installed on the ground floor. In Victorian times, it opened at six in the morning so that locals could drop in for a penny tot of rum and a halfpenny screw of tobacco on their way to work. Every year a special ale was brewed for Barnstaple Fair, using a secret recipe handed down from generation to generation, with water drawn from an ancient lead pump in the yard.

In 1946, it was refronted again, in Elizabethan style, and the interior was remodelled accordingly. So successful was the makeover – seen on the two postcards opposite – that few people suspected it to be anything other than what it appeared – a perfectly preserved example of Tudor England, and one of the most atmospheric pubs in the country. Today, although the building survives, it is a branch of Pizza Express.

Barnstaple suffered more changes in the twentieth century than anywhere else in North Devon, with many of its historic inns falling victim to the bulldozer. On the

left is the Mermaid, which stood at the west end of the High Street, next to the North Gate. The North Gate was demolished in 1842 and the Mermaid has now followed it into oblivion.

The building opposite the Mermaid, on the corner of High Street and Boutport Street – now a charity shop – can be seen on the right in the photograph below. Next to it stood the Green Dragon, which closed in 1934 when its licence was transferred to a new Green Dragon at Sticklepath on the outskirts of Barnstaple. It was subsequently demolished and new shops were built on the site.

Continuing along Boutport Street, you would have come to the Poltimore Arms, facing the bottom of Vicarage Street. When advertised to let in 1873, it was described as a 'newly built and excellent public house ... with stabling, courtlage, etc, a large room, over 50 feet in length, suitable for a club room, or for sales by auction, etc.' Today, an access road to a multi-storey car park runs through the site.

The Horse & Groom, on the north side of Boutport Street, met a similar fate. Demolished before the Second World War to widen Queen Street, a new Horse & Groom was built on part of the site. It is still open, but is now known as the Olive Branch.

A little way along Queen Street, on the left-hand side, on the corner of Azes Lane, was the Globe. Queens House now occupies the site.

Continuing along Boutport Street, you would have come to the Queen's Hotel on the corner of Wells Street, a particularly pleasing example of Victorian pub design – which makes it even more regrettable that the modern retail unit that now occupies the site is one of the ugliest buildings in a town served more than usually ill by the developers.

Heading across the Square and along Taw Vale, you would have come to the Taw Vale Tavern, the tap for the Taw Vale Brewery. The entrance to the brewery yard was through the archway, with the tavern to the right of it. After the brewery closed, it was used as a distribution depot by Starkey, Knight & Ford. Apartment blocks now occupy the site.

Not all of Barnstaple has been so comprehensively redeveloped. The suburb of Pilton – once a separate borough – is especially delightful, with its main street, climbing towards the priory church, lined with old buildings. Two of them, the New Inn and the Chichester Arms, are seen above in the 1920s. The New Inn closed around 1971 and was converted into two houses – The Maltings and Oriel Cottage – but the Chichester, recently refurbished as the Green Man Bar & Bistro, is thriving. The renaming celebrates a medieval carving in the church which has also inspired an annual green man festival.

At the bottom of Pilton's main street is the Reform Inn, seen opposite in the 1920s. It looks much the same today, except that the ground floor has been painted white and a large window has been inserted into the end bay to match the other two. Originally a two-storey thatch and cob building called the Gardeners Inn, it was renamed to celebrate the passing of the Reform Act in 1832. It belonged to Ilfracombe parish church until sold to Taw Vale Brewery in 1878. Despite the change of ownership, a malthouse at the back continued to be used until the inn was rebuilt in 1892. In 1889 the Taw Vale Brewery was taken over by Arnold, Perrett & Co of Wickwar, Gloucestershire, which in 1896 disposed of the tied houses to Starkey, Knight & Ford. In 1962, Starkey, Knight & Ford were taken over by Whitbread's, and the Reform later became a free house. In 1996 the Barum Brewery opened on the premises, reviving a long and distinguished tradition; in January 1753, a correspondent in the *Gentleman's Magazine* wrote in praise of Barnstaple ales claiming that they were 'as good as Derby ales, though not quite so famous'. The selection of Barum beers on tap in the Reform still allows drinkers to confirm the validity of that assertion today.

Beaford

An early twentieth-century view of the Globe at Beaford, with two touring bikes propped against the wall. The architraves and lintels surrounding the door and windows are now painted white – a striking contrast to the dark local stone – but otherwise the scene is little changed. The Globe is believed to date from around 1790, but may incorporate an older building. This popular community pub was taken over by new owners in July 2014 and has already received glowing reviews for its menu, ambience and welcome.

IN PRAISE OF THE VILLAGE INN

What an element of cosiness, hospitality, picturesqueness is introduced into the village by the inn! ... I know some villages from which the squire has banished the hostelry, and poor, forlorn, half-hearted places they seem to me. If there be a side to the village inn that is undesirable, I venture to think that the advantage of having one surpasses the disadvantages. What the squire has done in closing the inn he hardly realizes. He has broken a tradition that is very ancient. He has snapped a tie with the past.

At the village tavern squire and attorney and doctor were wont to meet, and not infrequently the parson appeared there as well. That condition of affairs is past ... It is now too late to revert to old habits, but I have a hankering notion that it would have been, perhaps, on the whole, better if the gentle classes had not 'cut' the tavern, and instead have taken their ease there, in sobriety and kindly intercourse, yeoman, squire, and farm labourer, on the one level of the tavern floor, round the blaze of the one hearth warming all, drinking the same generous liquor, and in the one mellowing atmosphere of tobacco smoke.

Sabine Baring-Gould, *An Old English Home and its Dependencies*, 1898

Beesands

The Cricket Inn at Beesands opened in 1867 to serve the fishermen who lived and worked in this remote spot. This early twentieth-century view of Beesands may seem idyllic, but the village has witnessed more than its share of tragedy. One Sunday afternoon in 1942 a German bomb fell near the inn, destroying two houses, killing seven people and seriously injuring many more. In 1979, the village was evacuated for three days when a storm threatened to engulf it. In 2001 the beach was sealed off when a child discovered detonator wires sticking out of one of boulders shipped in from Sweden to protect Beesands from the sea. Bomb disposal experts subsequently carried out controlled explosions of gelignite charges that had failed to go off in the quarry where the boulders came from. 2001 also saw the Cricket Inn, long regarded as one of the least changed hostelries in Devon, acquired by new owners. A complete refit followed, and in 2010 a large restaurant opened in an adjoining building. It is deservedly popular, but for those who miss the old Cricket Inn, Henry Williamson's description of a visit there in 1933 will evoke a wistful sigh:

> The landlord gave me a small glass of sweet visitors' cider to taste, which I sipped and returned with thanks, ordering for myself a glass of scrumpy, otherwise hard or farmhouse cider. Two old fishermen sitting there drank with me, together with the landlord, and then it seemed that we had known each other all our lives … More cider; a lunch of bread-and-butter and bananas … A beer bottle of unusual shape and size stood on a shelf above the landlord's head. He said it was one of four bottles of beer, brewed by the late King Edward, which had come from the Rothschild cellars at Tring … On other shelves were stuffed pheasants, one of them an imperfect albino, with bottles of spirit containing a snake and a viper. It seemed to be part of a past age, and I made up my mind to return and stay there some time, to go out with the fishermen.

Bere Alston

An evocative Edwardian view of Fore Street in Bere Alston, with the Victoria Inn on the right. Long closed as an inn, until October 2000 the building housed a bakery. Today it is home to the Victoria Bookshop.

Bere Ferrers

A mid-twentieth-century view of the Plough Inn at Bere Ferrers – now the Olde Plough – with its superb view over the estuary of the Tavy. This splendid sixteenth-century inn, with its flagstone floors, old beams and hearty welcome, has hardly changed since this postcard was published. It remains one of the most popular traditional pubs in the Plymouth area.

The seventeenth-century Passage Inn stood on the east bank of the Tamar, from where there was a ferry to Calstock. In the nineteenth century, a shipyard opened nearby, and the grounds of the inn were developed as pleasure gardens for daytrippers who came up from Plymouth by paddle steamer. One of the steamers can be seen in the postcard below, showing the railway viaduct under construction. Although the viaduct blocks the view of the inn, the shipyard next to it can be clearly seen. The railway opened in 1908, taking away much of the Passage Inn's passing trade. The shipyard closed in 1923, and, although the inn struggled on for a few more years, it was clearly unviable. In 1927, when the landlord applied for an extension for Calstock Regatta, he explained that regatta day and one or two bank holidays were the only occasions he did much trade. The inn closed in 1934 and became a farm, but, although the ferry service was withdrawn the following year, it was later revived and continued until the 1960s.

Berrynarbor

The Globe Inn in Berrynarbor may have started life around 1280 as a church house, before being converted to a row of cottages, one of which became a beerhouse. The beerhouse later expanded to take over the other cottages. There was also an inn called the Unicorn a few doors along on Pit Hill. In 1891, however, the Rector of Berrynarbor persuaded Mr Basset of Watermouth Castle, who owned both buildings, that there was

no need for a licensed house in the village, and both beerhouse and pub were closed. Following complaints from residents and visitors, there was a change of heart and it was agreed that one of them should reopen. As the Globe was better equipped than the Unicorn, it was granted a full

licence on the understanding that the Unicorn would remain closed. It was a wise move, as anyone who knows the Globe will affirm. This rambling, traditional local, with log fires, lime-ash floors and a well under the darts area, is now known – with some justification – as Ye Olde Globe, and has changed remarkably little since these postcards were published early last century.

Bickington

TOBY JUG INN, BICKINGTON, SOUTH DEVON

This picture of a bar adorned with Toby jugs and horse brasses may not seem that exciting, but, for those who remember the Toby Jug at Bickington, it is heartbreaking. The Toby Jug wasn't a particularly noteworthy or special pub, unless, that is, you lived in Bickington. This was, for many people, the hub of their community. It was built in the 1830s as the Jolly Sailor, possibly because its first landlord had nautical connections, possibly in honour of William IV, the Sailor King. It stood on the old road from Exeter to Plymouth, but, when a new road opened in the 1970s, it went from being a roadside hostelry on the busiest road in Devon to an isolated pub on a back road used by locals. By then renamed the Toby Jug, presumably because one of its landlords had a passion for Toby jugs (witness the postcard), it soon settled into its new role. By the late 1990s, however, its regulars were growing increasingly concerned at what they saw as attempts to run it down. In 2003, Heavitree Brewery (which despite its name had stopped brewing beer in 1970 to concentrate on running pubs) claimed it was no longer viable and closed it. Four years later, they submitted plans to build a house on the site. Its former regulars did not take this lying down, forming the Save The Toby Jug Action Group (STAG), urging the council to issue a compulsory purchase order, and attracting the attention of the national media. In 2007, there were signs of a change of heart, as workmen moved in to spruce the place up. They were soon followed by squatters, however, and by the time of their eviction in March 2008 the inn was in a worse state than before. The workmen did not return.

Today, it stands deserted at the top of the village. Tiles have fallen from its roof, the signboard has disappeared, flower baskets hang crooked and empty. Its two rooms – visible through grimy sash windows and a layer of dust – have been stripped of their fittings. From the porch, a bedraggled piece of tinsel flaps in the wind. Hopes of it reopening seem farther away than ever. By the look of it, the time when this once loved but abandoned building will have reached the point of no return cannot be that far away.

Bideford

A battered photograph of Bideford quay from across the bridge in 1864, showing four inns in a row – the Steam Packet & Railway Hotel, the Newfoundland Inn, the King's Arms and the Three Tuns. Only the King's Arms remains open. The Steam Packet & Railway and the Three Tuns have been replaced by new buildings, while the Newfoundland has been largely rebuilt.

This is the Newfoundland after it was renamed the Old Ship, taking full advantage of its links to Charles Kingsley's *Westward Ho!* It closed around 1930 and the right-hand side became tearooms. In 1942, it was badly damaged by fire and rebuilding drastically altered its appearance. The parapet was removed to reveal the gables, plate glass windows were inserted on the ground floor and the stables on the left were demolished, to be later replaced by an unsympathetic bit of infill. It reopened as the Rose of Torridge tearooms, but is now a fish and chip shop.

The King's Arms, dating from the mid sixteenth century, is seen here in the 1920s. Today, painted white, with the stones around the doors and windows picked out in black, and greenery trailing from boxes at every window all summer long, it presents a very striking picture. Inside, old beams, a wide range of ales and good food make it one of Bideford's most popular pubs.

Just around the corner from the King's Arms, at the bottom of the High Street, was one of Bideford's more colourful pubs, the Talbot, which closed in 2010. It is seen here a century ago, when it was William Talbot's wine and spirit vaults.

One street back from Bideford Quay is the White Hart, seen here in the 1920s, and still one of Bideford's best-kept secrets. A back-street boozer in the best sense of the term, this welcoming hostelry, with an open fire and an excellent selection of local ales (including one brewed especially for the pub and named after a much-missed pub dog), is a popular bolthole for locals and visitors alike.

Although the railway arrived in Bideford in 1856, it was never extended westward to Clovelly or Hartland, which continued to be served by stagecoaches until the early twentieth century. Here some intrepid travellers line up outside Bideford's New Inn in the Market Place around 1905. Although the New Inn remained one of the town's top hostelries after the demise of the coaching trade – later changing its name to the Old Coach Inn – it closed around 2004 and has been converted to residential units.

Just up the hill from the New Inn was the Old Ring of Bells. Next door, with part of its name visible in this 1920s photograph, was the New Ring of Bells. Both were there by 1830, both were later rebuilt and both relied on the nearby market for much of their trade. The New Ring of Bells, now renamed the Anchor, is still open, but the Old Ring of Bells has been converted to flats.

Also converted to flats is the Torridge Inn on Torridge Hill, which closed in 1989. On 16 August 1855, when the lease was advertised in the *North Devon Journal*, it was described as

> that long-established, commodious, and well-accustomed inn ... with very extensive stabling, lock-up coach house, lofts, etc. The house contains, on the ground floor, two parlours, bar, kitchen, wash house, brewhouse, and well-arranged and convenient domestic offices; on the first floor, a large sitting room and five bedrooms; on the second floor, a large room 60 feet by 14 feet, used as a club room, and three bedrooms. There is an abundance of hard and soft water, and an excellent underground cellar.

In this 1920s postcard another pub, the Globe, can be seen on the right. It was demolished around 50 years ago to widen the road.

Continuing up the main road out of Bideford, you eventually come to the appropriately named First In Last Out. Still open today and little changed since the photograph on the right was taken in the 1920s, it remains a friendly community pub with good value food and a couple of ales on draught.

Leaving Bideford in the other direction, the first pub you came to after crossing the bridge was the Swan. It too is still open and has changed little – externally at least – since the photograph below was taken in the 1920s. In February 2011, however, after a major refurbishment, it reopened as the Riverbank Bar Bistro.

As you continued past the Swan, with shipyards on your left, you would have seen a string of pubs on your right. Today, the shipyards are gone and the pubs have all closed. The last to go was the Ship on Launch, seen here in the 1920s. It is now home to a firm of financial advisers.

Bigbury

Two views of the Royal Oak at Bigbury in the 1920s. Long one of the most popular pubs in the South Hams, in 2012, after going into receivership, it was bought by the owners of the St Moritz Hotel in Polzeath. Fifteen months after reopening, however, it closed in November 2013. A 300-signature petition was sent to South Hams District Council, calling for it to be declared an Asset of Community Value. The owners objected on grounds of the pub's non-viability, and the application was rejected. However, the owners have since intimated that they might be prepared to open the public bar for the use of locals, and in July 2015 were granted permission to build four houses on part of the car park.

Half a mile north of Bigbury lies the hamlet of St Ann's Chapel, with an inn that has had a succession of names. These two postcards show it as the Pickwick Inn, but until 1929 it was the Hare & Hounds. More recently, it has been known as the Old Chapel Inn – appropriately enough, as the building incorporates the fifteenth-century chapel that gave this settlement its name, as well as an adjoining cottage dating from the seventeenth century. After a chequered career, it closed in 2009, but in 2012, after a complete refurbishment, it reopened as the Pickwick, serving Italian food which has received glowing reviews.

Bishop's Tawton

The Chichester Arms in Bishop's Tawton near Barnstaple, built of cob and thatch in the fifteenth century, was rebuilt after being gutted by fire in 2005. Nevertheless, it still looks much as it did when this postcard was published in the early twentieth century, while inside flagstones underfoot and low weathered beams overhead remain the order of the day.

Just along the street is the Three Pigeons, seen here in the 1920s. In 2009 it closed for a five-month refit, but after reopening soon became re-established as a traditional community pub, with an emphasis on pub games, live music and real ale. Sadly, it closed in 2012 and in 2015 permisison was granted to convert it to a house.

Bishopsteignton

The Commercial Inn – now renamed the Bishop John de Grandisson after a fourteenth-century Bishop of Exeter whose palace was nearby – has changed little since this postcard was published in the early twentieth century. In 2013 it was sold by Heavitree Brewery, and it is now a free house with six real ales.

The Manor Inn, down on Fore Street, was originally known as the Union Inn, but has long since closed and been converted to a private house. It is seen here in happier days, when children could still play safely in the street.

Down at the other end of Fore Street, the Ring of Bells is not only still in business but looks far smarter than it does on this Edwardian postcard. This curiously skewed building is now only part of the pub. Its doorway has been converted to a window and the entrance is now in the far larger building off to the left.

Blackawton

The George at Blackawton was originally the Church House Inn. It has suffered at least two fires in its history and looks very different to what it did when this postcard was published over a century ago. With two beer festivals a year and an annual worm-charming festival, the George is firmly established as one of the most popular pubs in the South Hams, and in 2015 expanded to make more room for community events.

The Commercial Inn, just visible behind the thatched cottage in the previous postcard, is seen here around 1908. No longer tile-hung, but still with that characteristic porch, it is now the Normandy Arms Country Pub and Restaurant. Its renaming is a reminder of the evacuation of this part of the South Hams in 1943 for troop exercises prior to the Normandy landings on D Day.

THE MARKET RETURNS TO BLACKAWTON

This town with all its privileges was handed over to the church centuries ago. Its fairs and markets were allowed to fall into desuetude and its dwellings into decay until recently, when a few enterprising farmers conceived the project of a revival. A committee was formed, subscriptions were invited, and a fund raised. The amount being found ample, a day was fixed for reopening a market free to all owners of stock on 26 September 1860, to be continued on the last Wednesday of every month.

As the morning dawned the national flag waved in graceful movement on the square, massive and ancient church steeple, the splendid peal of bells chimed forth their cheering notes, and the sun rose encouragingly. The pens previously formed were ready to receive the bleating flocks, and the station was fixed for an array of horned cattle.

At eight the market opened, presenting a goodly number of first-rate sheep and fine bullocks. The day was not one on which a very numerous attendance of buyers could be expected on account of the several markets and fairs in many of the surrounding districts. Prices, however, were well sustained, and all parties were well satisfied with this opening day.

Triumphal arches of evergreen, surmounted by flags, graced the entrance on the Dartmouth side of the town at the Commercial Inn, where a goodly assembly did justice to a liberally served market dinner, under the catering of the hostess and the superintendance of the host, a son of the respected postmaster and parish clerk. The George, in the heart of the market, was rendered attractive by the liberal providings of the host, Mr Hoskins, who had penned a remarkable ewe with a male and female lamb, her second product of the like, having had born to her two families in the space of six months and a fortnight. This pen attracted much attention, and on the whole as a revival, the market gave great promise of future progress.

A sumptuous dinner was provided by Mr and Mrs Ellis of the Dartmouth Arms*, where the committee have their headquarters. A respectable gathering of 24, under the encouraging presidency of Mr Cholwich, did ample justice to the inviting repast. Cider was the leading beverage, and splendid plum puddings, for which the hostess is celebrated, seemed to sweeten and satisfy every taste ... Then followed a health to the committee, with thanks for their commendable and successful endeavours to revive a market for cattle and agricultural produce in a town, the locality of which and the many roads converging into it as their centre, rendered it eminently available to both buyer and seller. The chairman assuring the company that the maiden endeavours of the committee being so encouraged by the success of the day should stimulate them to renewed exertions to advance the market in favour of buyers and sellers until Blackawton should become that great place of resort it had been, in ages past, for a long continuance. The church bells continued their lusty peals during the day.

Western Times, 29 September 1860

The Dartmouth Arms on Church Hill, also known as the Dartmouth Inn, is now Dartmouth House

Blackmoor Gate

In May 1898, when the narrow-gauge railway from Barnstaple to Lynton opened, the station seen on the left was provided at an isolated crossroads known ominously as Blackmoor Gate. Two months later, a fortnightly livestock auction was established nearby. It soon became one of the busiest auctions in North Devon, even though the nearest pub was over a mile and half away. Eventually, in 1917, a licence was granted to the landlord of the Fox & Goose at Parracombe to run a bar there on auction days. In 1930, the hotel seen below opened. It was granted a hotel licence the following year, but when the owner applied for a full licence in 1936, the landlord of the Fox & Goose engaged a barrister to oppose the application. It was nevertheless granted, and the hotel soon became popular with daytrippers and partygoers alike. The hotel burned down while being refurbished in 1970 and a car park now occupies the site. Blackmoor Gate station, however, which closed in 1935, is now the Old Station House Inn.

Bow

Although refronted in the late eighteenth or early nineteenth century, behind the façade of the King's Arms at Bow lurked a much older building. The inn was originally in the adjoining building (out of sight in this Edwardian postcard view), where the future Charles II stayed in 1643. In 2005, after the King's Arms closed, planning permission was granted for it to be converted into two dwellings.

The nineteenth-century façade of the White Hart – embellished with half timbering in the twentieth – also masks a building dating back at least 400 years. When advertised for sale in the *Exeter Flying Post* on 5 March 1862, it was described as having a 'commercial room, bar parlour, seven bedrooms, two kitchens with cellars, brewhouse, stables and yard'. It also had a garden behind and an orchard across the road. The White Hart is still open, retains many original features, and is known for its traditional hospitality, good food and local beer and cider.

Bradninch

The Castle in Bradninch was built in 1835, at the same time as the town hall next door, and once had its own steam brewery. The Castle is still noted for the range and quality of its beers, as well as the welcome extended to regulars and visitors alike. Although essentially unchanged, the Castle has been painted grey with white quoins and architraves since this postcard was published over half a century ago.

Heading down Fore Street from the Castle, you would once have come to the King William, its name suggesting it started out as a beerhouse in the 1830s after the passage, by William IV's government, of the Beerhouse Act. Later rebuilt in grand style, it is now a private house.

Bradworthy

From the outside, the Bradworthy Inn, seen here a century ago when it was the Bradworthy Hotel, may look eighteenth century. Walk through its front door, though, along a corridor flanked by elegant reception rooms (one now given over to pool), past a staircase with a handsomely-carved balustrade, and you suddenly find yourself stepping back several hundred years as you enter what was originally the church house and is now the heart of this resolutely traditional village inn.

Branscombe

The Masons' Arms, seen above and at the top of the following page around 1910, was originally a ciderhouse amidst a row of cottages. It now occupies the whole row, along with extensions at the back, and its fine selection of beers and ciders is

complemented by a popular restaurant. It is said that the inn was named after the masons who built Exeter cathedral, using stone from nearby quarries. The building, along with much of the village, was owned for centuries by the dean and chapter of the cathedral.

At the top of the village is the Fountain Head, seen below around 1920, with the last working blacksmith, Jimmy Loveridge, standing outside the forge next door. The forge is now part of this gloriously traditional inn, and two gable windows have been inserted into its repitched pantile roof. But, apart from that, and apart from the porches that now frame the two doors, the scene has changed remarkably little. The stream that gave the inn its name still runs past the door, and the flagstone-floored bar still looks the sort of place farmers might have called into for a pint while their horses were being shod. Sitting here today, quaffing ale brewed at the nearby Branscombe Vale Brewery, tucking into splendid home-cooked food, and enjoying conviviality and conversation unmediated by piped music, it is easy to see why many regard this as one of Devon's finest inns.

The Three Horseshoes opened in the 1830s on the lonely turnpike road high above Branscombe. This mid-twentieth-century view shows it at an untypically quiet moment, as it was always a busy establishment – until 2000, when permission was granted to convert it to residential use. Five years later, an application to build nine houses on the site was rejected, and since then this once handsome building has sunk into a staggering state of neglect, covered in vegetation and looking like something out of a dystopian fairy tale. In July 2014, however, it was reported that it had been put up for sale.

Bratton Clovelly

The Clovelly Hotel in Bratton Clovelly, seen here in the mid-twentieth century, was originally the Packhorse – indicating the form of transport most commonly used in remote areas such as this. Now renamed the Clovelly Inn, it remains a traditional village pub, with a good selection of real ales, home cooked food, and a fireplace with the date of 1789 carved into its lintel.

Bratton Fleming

Villagers pose for the camera outside the White Hart in Bratton Fleming, high in the foothills of Exmoor. Since this photograph was taken, the inn has seen many changes – slates gone from the wall, a storey added to the extension fronting the road and a large conservatory built. It remained a popular amenity, however, until, in December 2012, after changing hands, it closed. Locals banded together to save their pub, and North Devon District Council declared it an Asset of Community Value. The owner lodged an appeal against the decision, but it was upheld in November 2014. In July 2015, he intimated that 'a tea room-cum-café, a shop and a scaled-down pub' could open in part of the building, but villagers still hope to see it restored to its former glory.

CIDER COMES TO DEVON

The cider orchard is another source of income to the Devonshire farmer ... An orchard produces 10 to 15 hogsheads an acre, the selling price of which at present is 25s to 30s a hogshead, and the cost of preparing it 5s to 8s. As much as 150 hogsheads are produced on some farms, half of which is consumed by the farm labourers. Lysons, in the *Magna Britannia*, remarks: 'I find no mention when Devonshire first became noted as a cider country. Orchards are not mentioned in Domesday, and I have not met with any incidental mention of them in records of the two or three centuries succeeding to throw any light on the subject.' It is now generally considered that orchards and the manufacture of cider were first introduced into Devonshire by the monks, probably during the thirteenth century, and it appears to have been clearly proved that cider was the ordinary drink of the labourers on the manor of Axmouth as early as the year 1286, and that the orchards were first planted there by one of the abbots of 'Montburg' in Normandy, to whom the property then belonged. The parish of Buckland Monachorum was early celebrated for this drink, and the orchards there doubtless originated with the Cistercians, who colonised Buckland Abbey ... in the year 1278. The wages of labourers vary from 12s to 18s per week, with three pints or two quarts of cider daily, the men bringing in every morning their wooden bottle to receive their day's allowance.

James Caird, *English Agriculture in 1850-51*

Brendon

A coachload of holidaymakers outside the Rockford Inn at Brendon around 1910. Billed as 'Little Switzerland', the area round Lynton and Lynmouth was justly popular in the Edwardian era, and the only way to get around, unless you were prepared for some serious walking, was by coach. Bowling along through glorious countryside atop a coach on a fine summer's day with the sea glinting in the distance must have been a delight. The Rockford Inn, set amid classic hunting, shooting, fishing and walking country, is still thriving today, offering refreshment and accommodation in the most alluring of settings. The building on the extreme left in the view above has been demolished to make way for a car park, but otherwise little has changed. Inside, the inn still has a traditional ambience, although there have been a few changes since the postcard below, showing the long bar, was published in the 1940s.

The Staghunters at Brendon has long been one of the most popular hostelries on Exmoor. Not surprisingly, given its name and location, it has been a centre for hunting and other outdoor pursuits for generations, although a rather curious letter from a lady called Margaret to her sister Beatrice in New Zealand, published in the *Exeter & Plymouth Gazette* on 21 August 1924, suggests an unsuspected level of sophistication:

My dear Beatrice, You will see by the address that I have left London with its noise and bustle, and am staying in such lovely surroundings on Exmoor.

I fear this letter will be late because the last two nights, instead of writing to you, I have been to an excellent variety entertainment ... You have heard of Marge and Leslie Howard Gordon, who wrote The Borderer for Julia Neilson and Fred Terry, and other well-known plays and books. They live at Brendon and some time ago started a Dramatic Society, called 'The Brendon Players'. They are a most talented company, and ... Mr and Mrs Totterdell, the host and hostess of the Stag Hunters, kindly lent their hall, which is fitted with a stage and electric light ... The programme opened with a piano solo by Cyril Richards, a bright looking schoolboy, who was well applauded. He was followed by Miss Ethel Groves, a dainty maiden with a charming voice. Next a comedy. 'A Sister to assist 'er', brilliantly acted by Mrs Gordon and Mr Savill. Miss Dorothy Kellaway sang 'Felix' and the whole audience joined heartily in the chorus. Mr Jonathan Richards delighted everyone with his Devonshire readings. I only wish you – in far away New Zealand – could hear him, for you could then know what the real Devonshire dialect is like, and how musical it can sound ... In Part 2 of the programme ... came the grand finale, a melodramatic incident in one act, 'The House of Fear', specially written for the occasion ... The audiences showed their appreciation by giving the performers rounds of applause ... Both evenings concluded with a dance at which Mr Tom Ash and Mr D Graham played on their accordions so well that everyone had to dance whether they wanted or not.

Brentor

The Brentor Hotel stood beside the turnpike road from Tavistock to Lydford, which opened in 1762, and was first recorded, as the Herring (or Herring's) Arms, in 1827. Originally part of the Langstone estate, in 1895 it was sold to Mr Newcombe of Thomas's Hotel, Devonport for £1,650. It was renamed the Brentor Hotel around 1928. When Henry Williamson visited in 1934 – around the time this postcard was published – he sang its praises, but warned that, 'if you are not used to the hard Devon cider, be careful not to take more than a pint.' The Brentor has been closed for over a decade, and, although its current owners have pledged to reopen it, concerns continue to be raised over its future.

Bridestowe

Bridestowe's Royal Oak Inn, with a sundial bearing the date 1714, is seen in the distance in this Edwardian view. Since this well-appointed and commodious inn closed around 2000, it has become a bed and breakfast establishment called Royal Oak House. The archway on the left, which leads into the churchyard, is Norman and originally formed part of a chapel dismantled in 1828.

The archway can also been seen in this view of the White Hart. According to the *Western Times* on 11 December 1893, when an application was made to transfer the licence, it was 'objected to on the grounds that the house was much out of repair'. A temporary transfer was granted to allow 'repairs to be carried out in the meantime to the satisfaction of the superintendant'. On this postcard, published around 15 years later, it still looks to be in urgent need of attention. A century on, not only is it still open, but it looks far smarter, maintaining its place as the hub of the community.

The Fox & Hounds, on the turnpike road east of Bridestowe, was virtually new when this postcard was published in the early twentieth century. It had previously occupied the smaller building to the left. The Fox & Hounds has been run by the same family for almost 40 years, and a warm welcome, especially for walkers who stagger in off the moor, is assured. A particularly striking feature of the interior is a mural of a foxhunt painted by a German prisoner of war in the 1940s.

Brixton

The ever popular Foxhound at Brixton has been catering for travellers and locals since the eighteenth century. Although its name was long thought to be connected with hunting, a local historian has come up with an alternative explanation, concerning a clipper called the Foxhound which in 1785 ran a party of smugglers to ground in a nearby creek. They were tried in a room above the inn, and the clipper's commander was rewarded with the lease of the inn, which he renamed the Foxhound. Today it is one of the county's top real ale pubs, with a splendid, ever-changing selection of brews, and also serves up excellent home-cooked food.

Broadhembury

The Drewe Arms at Broadhembury dates from around 1400 and may originally have been the church house. It was called the Red Lion until around 1920, when it was renamed after the Drewe family who lived at the nearby Grange. As can seen from this 1920s postcard, however, a red lion still stands atop the sign of this welcoming and atmospheric inn.

Buckfastleigh

The King's Arms was built around 1820, when the coaching trade – even though nobody knew it at the time – had but a short time to run, and it was built in grand style, with its own assembly rooms next door. The view of the King's Arms above dates from around 1910, when it was still safe for dogs to wander in the street.

By the time the photograph below was taken in the mid-twentieth century, the assembly rooms had become a bank. Today, they have been converted to a house. In 2014, the King's Arms was sold to its present owner, and, as a free house, is now more popular than ever. The photograph also shows a pub across the road, to the right of the building with first-floor bays. Known as the Valiant Soldier, it was first recorded as a pub in 1813. Whitbread closed it in 1965, but allowed Mr and Mrs Roberts, who had run it since 1939, to rent the property. They later bought it from the brewery, on the understanding that they could not reopen it as a pub. Mr Roberts died in 1969, but, although his wife stayed on, the bar remained as it was on the day the pub closed. When Mrs Roberts moved to a nursing home in 1997, local residents, realising how unique this time capsule was, persuaded Teignbridge Council to buy it. A year later it opened as a museum, which, as time goes by, provides an ever more fascinating reminder of a time when beer cost one and fivepence ha'penny a pint. The only thing missing is the beer; due to the restrictive covenant placed on the pub by Whitbread, alcohol cannot be served.

Budleigh Salterton

The Feathers in the High Street is one of Budleigh Salterton's oldest inns, dating from the sixteenth century, although, as can be seen from this early twentieth-century photograph, it has since been rebuilt and refronted. Long known as the Feathers Inn, it was renamed the Feathers Hotel around 1904, but, while continuing to offer quality accommodation, it is still very much a traditional pub at the heart of the community.

Burgh Island

Burgh Island – a part-time island which you can walk to at low tide – was settled by monks in the fourteenth century, and the building which forms the core of the Pilchard Inn is believed to date from around 1336. After the monks left, the island became the haunt of smugglers, one of whom, Tom Crocker, is said to haunt the inn. His ghost featured in an episode of Lovejoy, in which the eponymous antique dealer discovered treasure hidden behind a wall in the inn. In the early twentieth century, the landlord of the Pilchard was George Chirgwin, a music-hall artist known as 'The White Eyed Kaffir' who appeared as a black-faced minstrel in a tight body suit and unfeasibly tall top hat, with a white diamond painted over his right eye. In 1929, the island, formerly owned by the Dukes of Cleveland, was bought by a property

developer called Mr Nettelsold, who proposed building a large hotel on it. Despite protests from local residents the development went ahead. On 3 February 1931 the *Western Morning News* reported that an application for an 'on licence' for the hotel had been made at Yealmpton licensing sessions:

Sir Reginald Blaker ... said that the application was made on behalf of a Mr Nettelsold, who, however, was blind, and had decided to install Mr Wm Alfred Lott as manager ... Mr Nettelsold had made improvements to the Pilchard Inn in keeping with the countryside of Devon, such as oak beams. A new hotel had been planned at a cost of £40,000. It was intended to cater for a holiday, and not for chance visitors. There would be 34 bedrooms, with electric lights, and the hotel would be capable of taking some 60 people. Nearby a cove had been dammed to make a bathing pool, this alone costing

The Pilchard Inn before and after the alterations of 1931

£1,000 ... It was proposed to have a special causeway, worked with caterpillar tractors, from the mainland to the island. On the mainland there would be a building capable of accommodating 30 cars. As far as the Pilchard Inn was concerned, they wanted it to remain to cater for that class who would not be staying at the hotel ... Supt Hannaford offered no objection, but he hoped it would not be the thin end of the wedge to close the Pilchard Inn. He estimated that 3,500 people visited Burgh Island in the summer. The justices granted the application, the chairman remarking that it was subject only to guests or persons taking meals. He stated that at no time would the justices allow the licence of the Pilchard Inn to lapse.

Designed in sumptuous art-deco style, in its heyday the hotel attracted the likes of Agatha Christie, Noel Coward and Winston Churchill. Meanwhile, with the growth of private motoring, the popularity of the Pilchard Inn continued to increase. With one of the most stunning locations anywhere, it was, not surprisingly, high on many people's list of favourite pubs. Since new owners have acquired the island, however, the Pilchard's main bar is reserved for hotel guests, and much of the island is out of bounds.

Inside the Pilchard Inn in the 1930s

The Bathing Pool and Hotel in the 1930s

Burlescombe

The Red Ball at Burlescombe, on the old main road from Exeter to Taunton, was built as a coaching inn in the eighteenth century. By the time this postcard was published in the early twentieth century, however, it had been rebuilt, although the splendid sign may have come from the original building. Less than a mile from the inn is Whiteball Tunnel, built by the Bristol & Exeter Railway in the 1840s. During its construction, the inn became a magnet for thirsty navvies. CW Green, a local historian, recorded a story from a local resident called William Doble concerning one particularly notorious incident:

> The last time the Culmstock bounds were beaten was about 1844. Cider had been stored at the Red Ball for the thirsty beaters, and the navvies at the tunnel getting wind of it, went in a body and drank it. A battle ensued in which the navvies came off best. The inn was almost wrecked; the defeat, however, was no disgrace to our fathers, there were doughty pugilists and men of tough mettle in the parish then, and they did not take their beating lying down; only numbers overpowered them. Jimmy Jones, a crippled shoemaker of Culmstock, was said to be the only man who returned to the village with a whole skin; he saved himself by hobbling upstairs and hiding under the landlord's bed. My uncle described it as a battle royal – the blood flying in all directions.

After the railway opened, the coaching trade ended and around 1854 the magistrates downgraded the Red Ball from a fully licensed house to a beerhouse. In 1870, they withdrew its licence altogether, although the landlord appealed and it was later reinstated. With the return of road traffic in the twentieth century, the Red Ball was rebuilt as a roadhouse, but it has now been delicensed once again and is home to Wychanger Barton Saddlery.

Butterleigh

The New Inn at Butterleigh – now renamed the Butterleigh Inn – is one of the most popular country pubs in Devon. Built around a 400-year-old longhouse at the heart of a peaceful mid-Devon village, it has been considerably extended since this photograph was taken in the 1920s, and its brickwork has been covered in render. The Butterleigh Inn is famed not only for its selection of local ales and home-cooked food, but also for its relaxed ambience and traditional welcome.

Chagford

The Three Crowns in Chagford dates from the thirteenth century and was originally the home of the Whiddon family. Seen here on a postcard from around 1904, the Three Crowns has seen few external changes in the last hundred years. Inside, however, time and the deadly hand of the pub improver have taken their toll, ripping out old fittings and installing a sports bar and other accoutrements of the modern hospitality industry. In 2012, after being taken over by St Austell Brewery, however, the Three Crowns reopened after a rather more sensitive refurbishment.

A VISIT TO THE THREE CROWNS IN 1904

The ride to Chagford on the coach is not dashing, the horses have many hills to pull up, and the driver's tender care, combined with the heavy brake, prevents them from going down again too quickly. The setting sun had prepared such a gorgeous spectacle in our honour that we should have been satisfied that evening with even a slower pace. We came just within sight of Kes Tor, the west directly facing us, when behind the roundest hill in sight, the sun popped down looking like a huge orange globe; then every sort of colour and shade of red, blue, green, and purple, at once spread over the hills of the moorland in the background, while the fertile valleys before us grew blue and misty as we gazed down into them.

We were almost at the end of the eleven miles, before the town showed itself lying in a wide basin among the hills, a little bunch of white houses, and a tall church tower giving back answering colours to the brilliant sky. Our last hill was very steep, and, as we clattered down into the narrow town street, we got a peep of the near-by furze-grown moor, making a rough park for an old manor-house.

The most fashionable hotel in Chagford is the Moor Park, but it had no room for us, so we went on up the mounting street and over the market-place, to the Three Crowns, 'a beautiful old mullioned perpendicular inn', so Charles Kingsley wrote of it.

Since I had last been here, a new landlord and a good scrubbing, although both somewhat modified the picturesque appearance of the interior, had worked wonders for the greater comfort of guests. The musty smell of centuries had fled before hot water and soap, new paper and fresh furniture.

The house was built by Sir John Whyddon, a worthy of the time of King Henry VIII. It was his town mansion. He was a gentleman of enterprising instincts; in fact, a self-made man. Born in Chagford, of a respectable family, but one hitherto totally without fame, Sir John's youthful ambitions took him to London, a most perilous journey when Henry VII was still king. Young Whyddon studied law, rose to be judge of the King's Bench, became Sir John, and had the unspeakable honour of being the first judge who rode to Westminster on a horse; previous to that eventful occasion, mules had been considered quite good enough for dignitaries of the law.

The old house, with its iron-barred, deep-mullioned windows set in stone frames, its thick walls, and stone floors, has sheltered in its young days fine ladies and grim men-at-arms. On one of the stone benches still within the entrance porch, there sank down, shot to death for his loyalty to the Stuarts, Sir Sydney Godolphin, a gentle young Cornishman, more poet than soldier.

The thatched roof, green and brown with creeping moss, hangs thick above the rough gray stones of the walls; while here and there about the windows cling pink clusters of climbing roses. The Three Crowns has been used as an inn for over a century. The old innkeeper who preceded the present host, was noted far and near throughout Devon in his early days for the excellence of his entertainment. Sorrow over the unhappy marriage of a favourite son drove him and his excellent wife to habits fatal to their business ... The poor old hostess has died of excesses, and the old innkeeper, so many years host of the Three Crowns, has been succeeded by the new young landlord, whose bright little wife has tidied up the ancient inn. It now boasts a bathroom, electric lights in the sitting-room, and owns neither stuffed birds nor battered porcelain cups as decoration.

Josephine Tozer, *Among English Inns*, 1904

There has been an inn on the site of the Ring o' Bells in Chagford since the fifteenth century, although it has twice been rebuilt after being destroyed by fire. This traditional local has been put to a variety of uses over the years. A stannary court once met in an upper room, while another room was used as a coroner's court and mortuary. The buttery doubled as a holding area for prisoners en route to Okehampton Assizes and a butcher also operated in part of the premises until the 1930s.

The Mid Devon Foxhounds meeting outside the sixteenth-century Sandy Park Inn in the early 1900s. Turning right on entering the inn today, you come into a traditional low-beamed, matchboard-panelled locals' bar with a cosy snug beyond. Turning left, you come to an award-winning, candlelit restaurant. It is this combination of traditional and modern, chic dining and convivial imbibing, which makes the Sandy Park such a perennial favourite among Devon's inns.

Challacombe

'At Challacombe,' wrote Henry Williamson in 1933, 'there used to be a genuine old English inn, where one sat on adze-hewn forms before a fire of roots and sticks. Sitting there eating sandwiches you felt that you really were away from the circumstances of ordinary life. So few people came here that sometimes in summer the beer went sour; but with craft this could be poured outside without distress to landlord or guest.' Two years later, he wrote of it again:

> In this moorland village I know a grand old pot-house ... Pink and blue chamber-pots, with hundreds of fine cracks in them: oak forms polished by trousers like old sacks and hands like old roots: a hearth where roots of trees smouldered. Few visitors came here, besides the regulars, the shepherds and moor-men. On three occasions when I came here on three successive summers the beer was sour, but I managed to pour it away discreetly on the dock-root growing under the wall by the threshold outside. Here I rested one night, when my hunter went lame and foundered after a long run with the staghounds; here I walked on a rainy day with Zeale, in the week of the otter hunt at Weare Giffard ... After bread-and-cheese and ale we decided to walk, and so we continued along the rough road to the County Gate between Devon and Somerset.

For Williamson to wax misty-eyed over an inn with beer so rank it had to be poured away, it must have been something special, and this early postcard view gives an idea what it was like when he visited. Modern visitors can take comfort that the Ring O'Bells at Challacombe not only looks much the same today but was recently voted North Devon Pub of the Year – so no need to nip outside to dispose of your beer. There has been one other change: it is no longer called the Ring O'Bells. Since the 1970s it has been known as the Black Venus, renamed – so it is said – after a local breed of sheep.

Chawleigh

In 1869 the London Inn in Chawleigh, on the old road from Exeter to Barnstaple, burnt down. It was rebuilt by the Earl of Portsmouth, the local landowner, as the Portsmouth Hotel. It is seen here when owned by St Anne's Well Brewery in the 1930s. Today, renamed the Earl of Portsmouth, it is a thriving free house, serving the local community and a popular place to dine. It looks very different, however, the quoins and architraves round the door and windows having been painted black and the stonework white.

CIDER AT HOLLACOMBE

'This year, for reasons economical and otherwise, I pitched my tent in a little Devon village between Exeter and Barnstaple, ten miles from Dartmoor forest, and at least five miles from any railway station. Its name ... is Hollacombe, and it is situated in a beautiful combe or valley, the wooded sides of which slope down to the banks of a little trout stream which runs down the middle ... There is not even a public house, nor even a beershop, within a distance of two miles. The universal beverage is cider, real Devonshire cider – as different to the liquor sold in London as is the finest champagne to gooseberry wine. There is probably no better drink for a hot day than cider, for it exhilarates without stupefying; but it cannot be called sweet. The juice of the apple, after being expressed by an operation called 'pounding', ferments, and its sugar becomes changed to alcohol; but chemical action does not end here. A second fermentation is invariably allowed to take place, and this converts a portion of the alcohol into acetic acid; in fact a certain amount of acidity is considered a sine qua non of good cider. The farm labourer carries his day's allowances to field in a sort of miniature cask, known to him as a 'firkin', which may hold from a quart to a gallon, and with this he moistens his frugal dinner, and quenches his thirst as occasion may require.'

Pall Mall Gazette, 20 August 1886

Cheriton Fitzpaine

The Half Moon at Cheriton Fitzpaine as it looked in the early twentieth century, with petrol pump and phone box on the forecourt, and corrugated iron in place of thatch. The roof is now tiled, the forecourt has been cleared and the sixteenth-century building now stands resplendent in a very pleasing shade of pink.

Cheriton Fitzpaine has another excellent inn, the fourteenth-century Ring of Bells, with its thatched roof, inglenooks, exposed beams and open fireplaces. On 15 May 1925, the *Western Times* reported that, 'at the auction of Parish Charity property held at the Ring of Bells, the tenants in most cases bought their own property, the Ring of Bells going to Hancock's (brewers).' In 2011, after 26 years at the inn, the owners announced they were retiring and placed the Ring of Bells on the market. It subsequently closed, but, after extensive refurbishment, new owners opened it in 2014, since when reports suggest that it is well worth a visit.

Christow

The Artichoke Inn in Christow, parts of which are believed to date from the twelfth century, is said to have taken its name from the Jerusalem artichokes brought back by Crusaders. Be that as it may, it has been a focal point of the community for centuries. In the nineteenth century, Christow was famous for bellringing matches. On 28 October 1837, the *Western Times* reported that, 'after the ringing, a good old English dinner was provided by the worthy landlord of the Artichoke Inn, of which nearly 100 ringers and numerous other persons partook.' Skittle matches were also popular. On 20 July 1833, the *Western Times* reported that, 'on Tuesday, a party of the fair sex took possession of the skittle alley at the Artichoke Inn, Christow, where they played a most manly game; a party of young gents, happening to pass, joined them, and the ladies being divided played so well that a public match is contemplated and expected with great interest.'

Not all customers were so welcome, or so well behaved, as this report of the trial of an intoxicated underwear fetishist from the *Western Times* for 30 June 1871 reveals:

> Henry Searle, hawker, 60, was charged with stealing a chemise, the property of Anna Lanyon; also a pair of drawers, the property of Mary Hemens, at Christow on the 3rd of June ... Mrs Cornish resided with her son, who kept the Artichoke Inn, Christow, and also a mangle. On the day named she mangled the articles mentioned, and put them in two flaskets [baskets]. Prisoner came to the house at about ten in the morning and stayed there some hours, and from his suspicious movements he was searched by a farmer who happened to be in the house, and the articles mentioned were found on him. Prisoner was very drunk at the time ... and did not know what he was about. He admitted a previous conviction. Sentenced to six months' hard labour.

After many years in the ownership of Heavitree Brewery, in 2013 the Artichoke was bought by Samuel Key, a local man who, after renovating the property, reopened it in September 2014, since when it has received accolades for the quality of its food, beer and wine.

Chudleigh

The Lion Inn stood on the corner of New Exeter Street – originally known as Culver Street. This postcard of it dates from between 1906 and 1913, when John Withycombe was the landlord. Rebuilt after the fire of 1807 which destroyed much of Chudleigh, by 1939 the Lion was in a poor state of repair, like several of the adjoining properties, and the council, keen to redevelop the site, withdrew its licence. It was demolished in 1962.

Opposite the site of the Lion, on the corner of Clifford Street, is the Ship, which has hardly changed – apart from a striking mural being painted on its wall – since this postcard was published over a century ago. First recorded in 1811, tragedy struck eleven

years later when a soldier fired his pistol to try to clear soot from the chimney, but shot the landlady instead. Such untoward excitement is thankfully a thing of the past in this traditional and popular pub.

The Plymouth Inn, facing Chudleigh church, was largely rebuilt after the fire of 1807. The previous building is said to have dated from around 1730, although it has been suggested that an inn may have stood here since 1158. In 1956, it was renamed the Bishop Lacy after a fifteenth-century Bishop of Exeter who had a palace nearby, and remains one of Chudleigh's most popular inns, with an excellent selection of beers.

The Clifford Arms was opened around 1793 by John Weston, who had been in the service of Lord Clifford at nearby Ugbrooke. After it was badly damaged in the fire of 1807, he moved the Clifford Arms to a property further along Fore Street before reopening it on its original site ten years later. In 1972, it was renamed the Old Coaching House. On 15 December 2011, it was once again gutted by fire. Despite fears it would never reopen, nine days later the undamaged function room bar and kitchen reopened as a bar and restaurant. Plans were soon drawn up to refurbish the rest of the inn, and a new bar and restaurant called the Phoenix opened in February 2014.

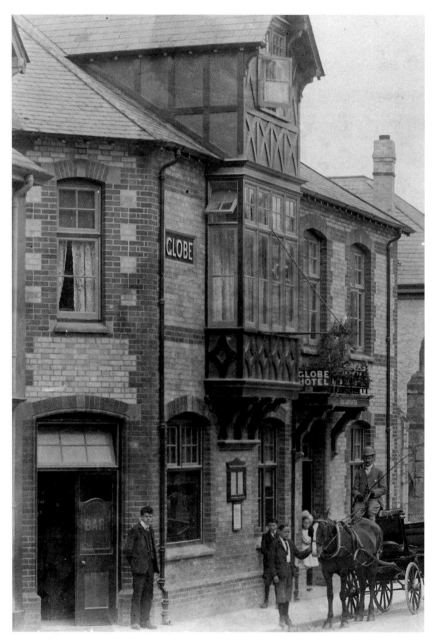

The Globe on Fore Street opened as the Maltster's Arms some time before 1830 and acquired its present name in 1835. When advertised for sale in 1879, the premises included a malthouse, brewhouse, stables, coach houses, blacksmith's shop, skittle alley, piggery, seven bedrooms, dining, commercial and smoking rooms, a bar, bar parlour, two kitchens, two storerooms and three-quarters of an acre of land. In the 1890s, it was extensively remodelled and acquired the new façade seen here. Over a century on, it looks much the same, and is especially popular with sports fans.

Chudleigh Knighton

The Anchor at Chudleigh Knighton occupied a very old building, but the earliest record of it being an inn dates from 1824, when part of it was demolished to widen the road. Long one of the most popular pubs in this part of Devon, new owners bought the freehold in 2011, and it was going from strength to strength when, on 4 March 2015, a devastating fire reduced it to a charred shell. The village had lost its community hub; the owners had lost everything. Villagers rallied round to help them after they were forced to move into a caravan, and, although they want to rebuild and reopen as soon as possible, they have to wait for insurance to be sorted before they can proceed. We can only hope that this terrible impasse will swiftly be resolved and this superb local rise again.

Churchstow

Some claim that the Church House at Churchstow was built by monks from Buckfast around 1254, others that it dates from around 1510. Among its noteworthy features are an enormous fireplace, a deep well and a spiral staircase leading to a projecting lava-

tory. In the early 1700s, the east end collapsed; to stabilise the building two tenements were built against it using the fallen stone. Almost 300 years on, the Church House is still standing and still popular.

Clayhidon

The Half Moon at Clayhidon has been an inn since at least 1787, when a licence was granted to Thomas Salter. It was almost certainly in existence long before that, and may have started life as a church house. The old pathway to the church, which led through the inn, is still used once a year on Rogation Sunday. The inn has been extended since this photograph was taken in the 1920s, but it remains a welcoming and traditional hostelry, with a log fire, fine ales and a reputation for traditional food.

Clyst Honiton

The photograph below shows the Exeter Inn at Clyst Honiton in the mid-twentieth century. Today it is adorned with cartwheels, recalling the stagecoaches

that once provided much of its custom. It is more modern forms of transport that bring customers here today. With a lorry park across the road and Exeter International Airport nearby, it remains a busy place. The photograph beneath it, dating from around 1910, shows the inn from the other direction, with the Duke of York – still open and still popular – a few doors along.

Clyst St George

Located beside a busy junction between Exeter and Exmouth, the St George & Dragon at Clyst St George is one of the best-known inns in the county. Dating from the nineteenth century, it was converted to a roadhouse in the 1920s, when the distinctive half-timbering was added. This postcard shows it in the 1940s, when the road was a lot quieter than it is today.

Clyst St Mary

Although the half-timbering on the St George & Dragon survives, that on the Half Moon at nearby Clyst St Mary, seen here in the 1940s, has been removed, and shutters now flank the windows. Until 1968, the main road ran past the Half Moon, but the 700-year-old bridge, just west of the inn, is now closed, and traffic uses a by-pass. The Half Moon, however, remains a popular traditional pub at the heart of the community.

Not so Clyst St Mary's other pub, the Maltster's Arms, seen here a century ago, which closed in 2008. Less than two years later, in February 2010, insult was added to injury when its fixtures and fittings were moved to the Blackmore Theatre in Exmouth. There they formed the set for a production of *Jeffrey Bernard is Unwell*, and, for a few nights only, the memory of the Maltster's lived on, courtesy of one of the twentieth century's best-known tipplers. Permission for conversion to flats was granted in 2009.

Cockwood

Overlooking the harbour at Cockwood, near Starcross, is the 450-year-old Anchor Inn. Seen here in the mid-twentieth century, its superb location and reputation for fish have made it so popular that it has recently expanded into the old village hall on the left, doubling its capacity.

Just up from Cockwood harbour is the Ship, a family-run pub believed to date from 1640, with good food, real ale and views across the village green. It still looks much as it did when this group of locals lined up outside it a century ago.

Colyford

The road past the White Hart at Colyford is much busier than it was when this postcard was published in the mid-twentieth century, and, to prevent customers walking out onto it, the doorways seen here have been converted to windows, and the entrance moved to the side. Colyford is one of the oldest boroughs in Devon, with a licence to hold a fair granted in 1208, and part of the White Hart is believed to have originally been a chapel beside the ford over the River Coly.

Colyton

Colyton is particularly rich in early-nineteenth-century Greek Revival buildings, including the Colcombe Castle Inn in the Market Place, seen here in the 1920s. It takes its name from the seat of the Courtenay family, which stood half a mile west of the village.

Church Street in Colyton, with the long-closed White Hart on the left. The building survives as White Hart Cottage.

The Gerrard Arms on St Andrew's Square in Colyton started life as a beerhouse run by a blacksmith called John Bull. Although officially known as the New Inn, it was (according to the obituary of one of Bull's descendants in the *Western Times* on 12 July 1915) generally referred to as the Flying Pig. By the late 1860s, however, it had been taken over by a butcher called John Harding, renamed the Gerrard Arms and granted a full licence. In 1869, John Harding left to pursue his trade as a butcher and the Gerrard Arms was taken over by John Harris, son of the landlord of the nearby Dolphin Inn. He continued as landlord until the 1890s, but by the time of the 1901 Census his widow, Annie Harris, was the licensee. It is her name that appears above the door on this Edwardian postcard, which shows the inn in its rebuilt state after being badly damaged when the thatch caught fire. Today, its brickwork has been painted white, dormer windows have been inserted in the roof, and the archway through to the yard has been glazed to form part of the pub, but the Gerrard Arms remains one of East Devon's most popular traditional hostelries.

The Globe Inn on Dolphin Street in the 1920s. Now called the Kingfisher, it has been stripped of its render to reveal the rubble stone and brick beneath, but remains a resolutely traditional inn, popular with locals and visitors alike.

At the end of King Street was the Lion Inn. It burned down on 10 November 1908 and a pair of semi-detached houses – one called Old Lion House – was built on the site.

Combe Martin

Combe Martin has one of the longest village streets in the country, and among the inns that once lined it were two called the George & Dragon. To avoid confusion, they were known as the Top George and the Bottom George. The Bottom George is still doing a roaring trade, but the Top George, seen on the left in this Edwardian postcard, closed in 2007 and has since been converted to flats.

Kings Arms, Combe Martin

One of Devon's more bizarre inns, the Pack of Cards at Combe Martin was still known – officially at least – as the Kings Arms when this postcard was published around 1910. It is said to have been built around 1690 by George Ley of Marwood to celebrate a phenomenal win at the gaming table, on a site 52 feet square, with four floors, 13 doors on each floor, 52 stairs, 52 windows, and looking like a house of cards. It has had some colourful regulars over the years, including the actor Terry 'What an absolute shower' Thomas. It was officially renamed the Pack of Cards – having long been called that by all and sundry – in 1933.

Down by the sea is the Dolphin, seen here in the 1920s. Today, it has been transformed by the insertion of large windows, which command superb sea views. Add to that a selection of well-kept beers and a restaurant noted for seafood, and it is not surprising that the Dolphin is one of Combe Martin's most popular pubs.

Combeinteignhead

Coombe Cellars at Combeinteignhead has one of the finest locations in Devon, but for centuries this was a wild and lawless spot where only fishermen and smugglers dared tread. The cellars, where fishermen brought their catches to be dried, smoked or salted, were ideal for storing contraband. By the mid-nineteenth century, however, it was a popular destination for daytrippers. On 25 May 1861, the *Western Times* reported that 'the inhabitants of this little village, which is situated on the banks of the Teign between Newton and Teignmouth, and which has acquired a reputation for its bivalves, held a regatta on Tuesday. Crowds of holiday-seekers from Teignmouth, Newton and the surrounding villages flocked in to see the sports, which consisted of rowing and sculling matches. A band was in attendance, and dancing was kept up with spirit, and all went off well.' Coombe Cellars is as popular today as it was when these postcards were published over a century ago, and, apart from a conservatory taking the place of the awning-shaded patio seen below, there have been few external changes.

Tea Gardens, "Coombe Cellars", Teignmouth. Part of Tea Terrace.

Cornwood

The Cornwood Inn first appeared in *White's Directory* for 1850 as the Tavistock Inn, with James Doddridge as landlord. By 1866, however, it had become the Cornwood Inn, run by William Vivian. Between 1889 and 1950, it had only two licensees – John Glover, a well-known breeder of black pigs, whose name can be seen over the door in this photograph, and William Sandover, who took over in 1920. It still looks much the same as when these children posed outside it over a century ago. After a temporary closure, it reopened in September 2013, and is once again proving popular with locals and visitors alike.

Countisbury

A coach pauses outside the Blue Ball at Countisbury after completing the gruelling 1 in 4 climb from Lynmouth. The inn has been extended at either end since this postcard was published in the early 1900s, but the central range looks much the same. After a brief spell as the Blue Boar and then the Exmoor Sandpiper, this traditional inn has reverted to its original name, and remains a popular centre for exploring the Exmoor coast.

Crediton

A view of the Oat Sheaf Inn in the 1920s with a Starkey's lorry drawn up outside. The Oat Sheaf opened sometime before 1803 and was rebuilt in the 1870s. In 1989 it was refurbished as the Exchange, and later became the Corner House before closing in 2010 and being split into three parts. One part became an Indian restaurant, the main building was converted to flats and the beer garden was sold as a development site.

Croyde

The Manor House Inn at Croyde – now renamed the Manor – has changed little since this photograph was taken around 1910. It remains a family-run traditional pub, with the stream still burbling along on the other side of the road.

A picture of rural tranquillity, with the Carpenter's Arms dozing in the heat of a summer's afternoon 60 years or more ago. That was before surfing came to Croyde. The Carpenter's Arms is now Billy Budd's, the wall on the right has gone for road widening and the cottages in the distance are all shops. Billy Budd's is an essential part of many people's experience of Croyde and, after a few hours' hard boarding, its servings of pizzas, chilli and nachos, washed down with cold beer, must seem very welcome.

Cullompton

Cullompton was one of Devon's most important wool towns and remains a busy place today, with many historic buildings. This Edwardian postcard features one of its most popular pubs, the Bell on Exeter Hill, dating from the seventeenth century, and once known as the Three Chimneys. Although the buildings on the left have been sacrificed to road widening, the Bell and the cottages on the right look much the same today.

When we called at Cullompton's White Hart in 2008, we were met by a disheartening sight. Not only was it closed; it was clearly in a bad way. The porch was damaged, the sign had fallen off its bracket and the paint that had been hastily applied to the ground-floor windows raised fears that the building was being systematically gutted. It seemed that the White Hart had joined the long roll call of Devon's lost inns. Happily, however, we were proved wrong, and it reopened shortly afterwards. It subsequently closed again, but in May 2014, after a more thoroughgoing refurbishment, it was reopened by the Mayor of Cullompton, and now looks even better than it does in this mid-twentieth century view.

Further along, on the other side of the road, was the Dolphin. Although not as grand as the White Hart, it had a yard at the back, with stabling for eight horses. In 1926 – around the time this photograph was taken – the magistrates tried to close it down. Although they were unsuccessful on that occasion, they eventually succeeded. Jimmyz Bookmakers now occupies the building, while the inn's name lives on in Dolphin Court, reached through the archway at the side.

This was the view from Cullompton station around 1905, with the Railway Hotel & Posting House on the left. Originally a beerhouse called the Red Cow, the opening of the railway in 1844 prompted its landlord, William Burton, to apply for a full licence. The magistrates turned down his application in 1848, but he applied again the following year, promising to provide stabling, and this time was successful. After the station closed in 1964, the Railway Inn was renamed the Weary Traveller and today is busier than ever, with a large ground-floor extension, live music, discos, big screen TVs, pub bingo and a popular carvery. The cottages in the distance are still there as well, although they are now dwarfed by a three-storey apartment block, with a large Tesco's across the road.

Culmstock

Culmstock station closed in 1963, but the Railway Hotel – seen on these two early twentieth-century postcards – survives. Later renamed the Culm Valley Inn, it acquired a reputation as an unashamedly traditional – if somewhat eccentric – country pub with top-notch food, fine wines, well-kept real ales and resident dogs. In July 2014, Richard Hartley, who had owned it for the previous 13 years, left, and regulars – including some local calendar girls – mounted a campaign to save it. It was listed as a community asset, acquired by new owners, and, after a refurbishment, reopened in December 2014.

The location of the Ilminster Inn in Culmstock, opposite the church, suggests it may originally have been a church house. It has seen many changes since the photograph below was taken in the 1920s, with the Gothic archway on the left demolished, a new

façade replacing those double doors and the railings in the distance removed to make way for a car park. In the 1980s it was renamed the Ilminster Stage, but has since closed, and is to be converted to a private house.

Dartington

The Cott Inn at Dartington, believed to date from around 1320, was originally a row of three cottages. The origin of its name is a matter of some debate. Although the likeliest explanation would seem to be that cott is an abbreviation of cottage, the story goes that the first landlord was one Johannes Cott, a Dutch woollen merchant. As the track that mules and packhorses, laden with wool, took to Totnes ran past the Cott, this may well have been the case. Among those rumoured to have stopped at the inn are Charles I, Daniel Defoe and William of Orange, and in 1625 troops returning from an unsuccessful expedition to Cadiz are said to have been billeted here. All of which indicates that

it has been around a very long time. The top postcard shows the Olde Cott, with the packhorse track running beside it, in the mid-twentieth century. The view has hardly changed today, although the entrance is now on the other side of the building, where there is a large car park. The other two postcards show the public and lounge bars in the 1930s. There have been many changes since, including the removal of much of the screen to create an open-plan layout, but the character of this ancient and very popular inn has been preserved.

Dawlish

The Grand Hotel, originally known as the Royal Albert, stood opposite Dawlish station, the canopy of which can just be glimpsed on the right. The single-storey extension, which housed a lavishly-appointed bar and billiard room, and had a bust of Albert in a niche on the corner, was added in 1878. This evocation of Edwardian elegance, with a carriage bowling up to the station, appears on a postcard from around 1908. By the 1970s, the Grand had found a new role, as one of the town's top music venues, but it was later demolished to make way for an apartment block.

The London Hotel on the Strand, seen below on a postcard from around 1905. When it was offered for sale in 1908 – described as 'an old coaching house' – it was acquired by the council. They demolished part of it to widen the road, built a new façade, and put it back on the market. They seem to have had little confidence that anyone would want to take it, for they added that, 'if not required for the purpose of an hotel, the

site would be a very valuable one for the erection of first-class business premises'. Their lack of conviction was not misplaced, and the building was demolished to make way for those 'first-class business premises'.

The Teignmouth Inn in Dawlish was there long before the railway, and, as the closest inn to the foreshore, it was natural that bodies washed up by the sea should be taken there for identification. On 22 September 1846, the *Western Times* reported the death of a man who

> had been at work for the South Devon Railway at a sea wall, and returned too late with a horse and cart; the tide surrounded him, and he endeavoured to leap upon a rock, but failed, and lost his life. The horse and cart got to shore. The body was taken to the Teignmouth Inn.

On 19 July 1849, the *Exeter Flying Post* reported another fatality:

> On Saturday about noon, Mr John Chichester, who recently entered upon the occupancy of the Teignmouth Inn, met with his death whilst bathing. How the accident was occasioned can only be conjectured. It appears that he went to a place on the rocks known as 'the groin', and jumped into the sea; whether his head pitched upon a portion of the rock, or he was dashed against it by the heavy swell that was in the water, the wind blowing briskly from the east, no one can tell, but he was washed on shore in a few minutes and when taken up was quite dead. He leaves a widow and three children to deplore his loss.

His widow, Mary, stayed on at the inn for another 13 years, building on its reputation as one of the best-run establishments in Dawlish. There were, however, occasional upsets, as this report from the *Exeter & Plymouth Gazette* of 30 July 1859 indicates:

> A lady named Mrs Amy Cook, a visitor from London, and at present occupying apartments at Mrs Chichester's, of the Teignmouth Inn, has been robbed of her purse, containing £100 in bank notes and gold. No clue has yet been ascertained as to the thief.

In 1862, Thomas Curtis took over the inn, and it is his name that can be seen on it in the photograph above. In the photograph on the opposite page, taken during conversion of the GWR from broad to standard gauge in 1892, the Teignmouth

Inn can be seen dwarfed by the new buildings that had sprung up around it. It can also be seen how, thanks to the redevelopment of the area, it extended much further into the road than the buildings on either side. By this time a row of three buildings, called Parade Cottages – hidden from view by the buildings in front – had been built alongside the Teignmouth Inn. The original inn – an increasing obstacle as traffic steadily increased – survived until it was demolished for road widening. The Teignmouth Inn still survives, however, as a friendly, lively hostelry (with one bar decorated with frogs), having moved into Parade Cottages.

HENRY WILLIAMSON IN DAWLISH

After lounging about the place and glancing at the books in a shop, I went on, coming to the Teignmouth Inn on the road out of Dawlish … and drank a pint of beer. While I was sitting there by myself another man came in and had half a pint, remarking to me that we were going to have rain. I asked him why he thought that and he replied, 'Look at the colour of the sea'. We peered together out of the window, and the sea was the colour it had been for the last three or four days, owing to the great surge upon the foreshore, which had disturbed the silt in the sand, and had broken up some of the cliff bases. I did not, however, wish to contradict him, so I said I hoped it would not rain. 'Ah,' said he, 'we will get it before nightfall, you mark my words.' He then remarked cheerfully to the landlord that he had come up from another inn where it was crowded and very comfortable. The tactful and scientific fellow then left for the other inn, and I left after him, remarking to the landlord that I thought his inn was most comfortable. I hope the reader will not think that the above account is intended solely to prove what a superior fellow the writer is; but it is now a fortnight since I was there, and it has not yet rained.

From *On Foot in Devon*, 1933

The South Devon Inn on Strand Hill in Dawlish was originally known as the Butcher's Arms. It was kept by a butcher called Mr Lammacraft who died around 1855, leaving the inn in trust for his infant son. The trustees allowed the licence to lapse, but the landlord of the Mariner's Compass on Park Street, a Mr Holder, took it on and spent a great deal of money turning it into a 'first-class inn'. When he applied for a licence, however, it was refused. Only one person had objected, but that person was the Rev Martin, curate of Dawlish, who considered it would be a 'nuisance'. At this, a memorial was presented to the magistrates, signed by 'the most respectable inhabitants of Dawlish, and also the principal innkeepers of the town', testifying to Mr Holder's good character and 'praying that the licence be granted'. Which it duly was, and the Butcher's Arms, renamed the South Devon Inn (after the South Devon Railway), reopened in October 1857. The view above dates from around 1905. It has

hardly changed today, although standing in the road is a good deal less popular. The cottages on the right, which bear the date 1539, are among the oldest in Dawlish, and the inn itself dates from around 1750. It remains one of Dawlish's most popular pubs, with regular beer festivals.

The view on the right shows two of Dawlish's oldest hostelries, the Railway Inn and the Exeter Inn, over a century ago. Both nearly disappeared in the 1930s: the licence of the Exeter Inn was referred to the compensation authorities in 1935, that of the Railway Inn four years later, both on grounds of redundancy. Following appeals, both licences were renewed. The Railway is still going strong today, but the Exeter closed in 2012, and in 2014 permission was granted to convert it to three residential units.

Half a mile back from the sea, clustered around the parish church, is what remains of Dawlish's old town centre. This Edwardian postcard shows the Red Lion, hub of community life for centuries, and still remembered by many as a superbly old-fashioned pub. It closed in the 1980s and was demolished in 1991 to make way for Red Lion Place.

In the early 1880s, Mount Pleasant, above Dawlish Warren, was the venue for the Mount Pleasant Races, while tea gardens and this superbly ramshackle inn attracted excursionists from far and wide. The Mount Pleasant Inn, first recorded in 1756 but almost certainly much older, was popular with smugglers as well. Contraband was hidden in nearby caves dug into the hillside and lanterns were hung in the windows of the inn, letting smugglers know when it was safe to come ashore. Today, the inn, along with the area around it, has been transformed. Chalet parks, caravan sites and funfairs extend in all directions, and the inn has been expanded almost beyond recognition.

Dean Prior

For centuries, Dean Prior lay isolated in bucolic quietude deep amid the network of narrow lanes south of Buckfastleigh. Today, its peace has been rudely shattered by the A38 Expressway which slices though the parish, passing just yards from the church where the poet Robert Herrick was vicar over three centuries ago. Herrick was the great bard of pleasure and rustic merrymaking, which included the quaffing of 'stout beer ... which drowns all care'. Here is one of his descriptions of the round of country pleasures:

> For sports, for pageantry, and plays,
> Thou hast thy eves, and holydays:
> On which the young men and maids meet,
> To exercise their dancing feet:
> Tripping the comely country round,
> With daffodils and daisies crown'd.
> Thy wakes, thy quintels, here thou hast,
> Thy May-poles too with garlands graced;
> Thy Morris-dance; thy Whitsun-ale;
> Thy shearing-feast, which never fail.
> Thy harvest home; thy wassail bowl,
> That's toss'd up after Fox i' th' hole:
> Thy mummeries; thy Twelve-tide kings
> And queens; thy Christmas revellings:
> Thy nut-brown mirth, thy russet wit,
> And no man pays too dear for it.

Another of his poems described what could happen when these rustic festivities drew to a close. It may well strike a chord with present-day readers:

Near the dying of the day
There will be a cudgel-play,
Where a coxcomb will be broke,
Ere a good word can be spoke:
But the anger ends all here,
Drench'd in ale, or drown'd in beer.
Happy rusticks! best content
With the cheapest merriment;
And possess no other fear,
Than to want the Wake next year.

The postcard opposite shows what was once Dean Prior's pub – the Rose & Crown. White's *Directory* for 1850 lists George Cole as its landlord, but it closed around 1867 and became a private house. It was later the home of James Thorpe, an artist and writer who discovered the village while on a walking tour in the early 1900s, and lived there until 1949.

Denbury

The Church House Inn in Denbury, south-west of Newton Abbot, has changed little since this postcard was published around 1910 – except that it has now been converted to two private houses. It belonged to the feoffees of Denbury, who in 1929 sold it at auction to St Anne's Well Brewery of Exeter for £1,325. It eventually passed to Whitbread's, who closed it in the 1960s. The structure on the left, by which one man and his dog have paused to pose for the camera, is an eighteenth-century water conduit, sited next to the inn, perhaps, to provide an alternative to beer and cider.

Dittisham

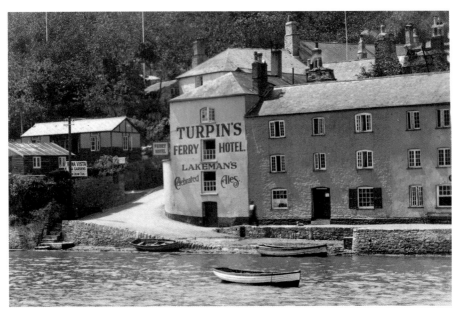

A 1920s view of the Ferry Hotel at Dittisham, originally known as the Passage House Inn and now renamed the Ferry Boat Inn. With ferries running from Greenway and Dartmouth, this traditional, unspoilt pub, with a choice of four real ales and barbecues on the beach, attracts an eclectic mix of customers, from yachties to locals, and has a location to rival that of the Royal George at Appledore. The photograph below shows the Greenway Ferry in 1949, with the Ferry Hotel in the distance.

Doddiscombleigh

Hidden away between the Haldon Hills and the Teign Valley lies the village of Doddiscombsleigh. Although a mere six miles from Exeter, it feels like a place where the scene depicted on this Edwardian postcard could be recreated without too much difficulty. You'd have problems finding the New Inn, though. One of its landlords (it's only had five since it first opened in 1838) was in the habit of locking himself and his cronies in and shouting 'nobody in' if anyone knocked at the door. So regular was the occurrence that the name stuck and the New Inn is known as the Nobody Inn to this day. Dating from the seventeenth century, if not earlier, and possibly built as a church house, its low ceilings, soot-blackened beams and assortment of antique furniture give it a timeless quality. Yet the old-world charm of the original building – its thatch now replaced by slate – is set off by large extensions to left and right, as well as at the back, and what was once one of the most exclusive inns in Devon is now one of the most popular. As well as local ales and locally-sourced food, it has a 250-strong wine list, with around the same number of single malts ranged behind the bar. The inn's name may be one of the most memorable in Devon; it is also one of the least appropriate.

Dolton

The Ram's Head at Dolton, between Winkleigh and Torrington, has changed little since this mid-twentieth century postcard was published. This friendly, family-run inn with a popular restaurant dates from the seventeenth century, if not earlier. Although it was remodelled and extended in the nineteenth century, it still retains many original features such as bread ovens and open fireplaces.

Drewsteignton

When English Heritage listed the Drewe Arms in Drewsteignton in 1967, they described it as 'a completely preserved nineteenth-century public house'. As indeed it was. In 1891, Alfred Mudge took over the New Inn, which had recently been renamed the Druid's Arms. He not only ran the inn, but also operated a twice-weekly carrier service to Exeter. In 1910, Julius Drewe, a wealthy businessman, acquired 450 acres of land nearby, on which he commissioned Sir Edwin Lutyens to build Castle Drogo. At his instigation the inn was renamed the Drewe Arms in 1913. In 1919, Alfred gave up the inn to become a farmer, and the licence was transferred to his brother Ernest, who, along with his 24-year-old wife Mabel, had been running the Royal Hotel at Crockernwell. The postcard opposite shows the inn in the 1930s with Ernest Mudge's name over the door. He died in 1951, but Mabel was determined to stay on. She was still there in 1993, when *A Walkers' Guide to the Pubs of Dartmoor* described what visitors to the Drewe Arms could expect to find:

> There is no bar as such, just one small room, with the beer and cider being tapped in a kitchen-like room at the back. The front room has simple seats and a brick floor, and is decorated with old advertisements and photographs. The atmosphere is very informal and the locals often wander through to the back to help themselves to drinks. Although it is beginning to look a little run down, it is well worth a visit, as it must be one of the few remaining examples of this kind of pub left unchanged. To go into it is like stepping back in history.

The following year, Mabel retired at the age of 99. Villagers stepped in to save the Drewe Arms and reached an agreement with Whitbread to run it as a trust until new tenants took

over in 1996. Since then, although the historic core of the inn has been preserved more or less intact, other rooms have been opened up for the use of customers. Early in 2013, the Drewe Arms closed when the licensee left after a rent increase demand from Enterprise Inns, which now owns the inn. It reopened in September 2013 and has since received warm reviews.

ALFRED MUDGE RECALLS THE DREWE ARMS

Mr Alfred Mudge of Bowden Farm, Drewsteignton has many happy memories of the old coaching days and nights on the open roads, with the clean wind swinging through the traces, swathes of rain mingling with the protesting jolts of the carriage, and the rhythmic clippety-clop of the horses' hooves as they dashed pell-mell through the darkness. An interesting story of his life as a carrier from Drewsteignton to Exeter many years ago was narrated by him to our staff representative at Okehampton a few days ago.

His eyes dancing, he dropped the boot he was cleaning, and one knuckled hand smacked against the palm of the other when the interviewer communicated his errand.

'Ay, they was the happiest days o' me life, sor,' spoke up 77-year-old Mr Mudge, and Mistress Jessie Mudge, his better half, sensing his excitement, must come rushing forth, prim bonnet askew, and look at him so very understandingly wifelike that I fully expected her to kiss his grizzled cheek, tanned to a leathery hardness by many a hard ride under broiling sun and bleak wind.

'Ay, they was happy days,' he repeated. ''Twas how I picked up me missus at Cheriton Cross.'

Here, 'missus' blushed, very becomingly I thought, but stood her ground and admitted shyly that it was so. 'Many's the time I've sat beside Alf in the van,' she stated. Was there ever a more perfect theme for a romantic plot than this.

Mr Mudge was born and bred in Drewsteignton, and he revealed that, according to an American gentleman who had taken the trouble to trace their antecedents, the family dated back to 1600.

His father, Mr William Mudge, also of Drewsteignton, was, in his days, the local 'strong man' and regularly carried home full sacks of potatoes and manure from near where he was employed at the lime quarries.

Mr Mudge rented the Drewe Arms from Mr Norman Pring of the City Brewery Co, Exeter, and carried on business from there to Exeter for 25 years. Twice a week (Tuesdays and Fridays) it was a common sight to see him bowling along the highway, whip a-flourish and a pair of mettlesome steeds scurrying up the dust clouds as he left to and from the city with his passengers – departing sober and sedate, but returning at great pace and with many a lusty 'Yoicks' and 'Tallyho', for ... 'Beer's beer, ain't it?' opined Mr Mudge, with a wicked wink at his wife.

Then, in addition to his trade as a carrier, Mr Mudge kept posting stables, catering for weddings, funerals and dinners. On one occasion, his wife had to cope with three dinners in one day – the City Brewery, St Anne's Well Brewery, and another firm.

Mr Mudge explained that the Drewe Arms had rather a peculiar history. It was at one time known as the New Inn, under Squire Ponsford, but when sold the new owner, a Mr Marks, altered the name to the Druid Arms. In turn, Mr Pring purchased it and it was later rented by Mr Mudge, who was asked by a prominent member of the Drewe family whether he had any objections to the inn being called the Drewe Arms. Mr Mudge had not. Special deeds were drawn up and signed and the alteration effected. 'Anyhow, it made no difference,' said Mr Mudge, 'I never sold no more beer, nor no less.'

From the *Devon & Exeter Gazette*, 25 January 1935

Just along from the Drewe Arms in Drewsteignton was the seventeenth-century Old Inn, seen here around 1905. Although still known as the Old Inn, 'old' now means 'former', as it has been converted to a restaurant and guest house.

Dunsford

The Royal Oak in Dunsford, seen here around 1920, has changed little. When the lease of the inn, 'with the excellent garden, orchard, meadow and every other convenience,' was offered for sale in June 1861, the building had 'five rooms on the ground floor, with large club room and six bedrooms above'. There were also 'brewhouses, cellar, night-stall stable, linhays, cow-houses, piggery, etc.' The inn was part of a working farm until the 1960s, and a host of animals still roam the beer garden at the back. Inside the split-level, multi-roomed pub, there is an excellent selection of real ales and home-cooked food, making the Royal Oak a perennial favourite with young and old alike.

East Allington

When this postcard was published around 1905, East Allington was a tight-knit farming community. The Fortescue Arms, on the left, served ale and cider to men working on the land, and travelling shops such as the one seen here were a lifeline for people who rarely set foot outside the village. Today, houses have been built on the fields in the distance, few people work on the land and many cottages are holiday homes. At least the Fortescue Arms is still open, and, after a brief spell as a gastropub, is back to being a popular and traditional community pub.

East Budleigh

The King's Arms, seen here on the left, dates from the sixteenth century, but did not become an inn until the nineteenth century. Now renamed the Sir Walter Raleigh after East Budleigh's most famous son, this traditional, friendly free house has changed little since this postcard was published in the early twentieth century.

The Rolle Arms, named after the family who owned nearby Bicton Court, opened in 1845 on the site of a malthouse. This imposing building has changed little in the 70 years or so since this postcard was published. It remains a popular meeting and dining place, with skittles, cricket and football teams, and live music.

East Prawle

Henry Williamson, whom we met drinking cider with fishermen in the Cricket Inn at Beesands, eventually left them to continue his walk around the coast. Footsore and weary, with the clouds gathering in the west, his description of that walk soon drifted into the third person, giving it that quasi-hallucinatory quality familiar to the lunchtime cider drinker:

> There was, according to the map, a footpath round Start Point. But now the traveller was many hours behind his schedule; and although the white lighthouse built below the headland looked attractive in the sunlight, he took a path that led up over the fields and down past a farmhouse and barns with weathered slated roofs, standing within trees about a hollow.
>
> No cattle dog jumped up from slumber and rushed forward barking. The place seemed quiet and tranquil, and even the hens did not cluck ...
>
> It was already four o'clock. Should he go inland after passing the next little valley and have tea at the village of East Prawle? … The sun was already hidden by grey clouds from the south-west, and it was too late to reach Thurlestone that night, or even the next night.
>
> By Sharpers Head he turned inland and walked up a steep field, and so to a row of cottages. The field seemed badly tilled, with many weeds growing; the inhabitants had pitched many old broken bottles and plates over the wall into the field. Hoping that the village itself would be better, he went on round the lane and came to it. No one seemed about. The cottages looked as though they had not been lime-washed for many years.
>
> He walked round the village for a while, trying to make up his mind to knock at the door of one or another of the two inns, and ask for tea. A church was marked on the map, and this turned out to be a chapel. Opposite the chapel two men were talking in a dim space seen through an open door, where nets and a ladder and other gear hung. He talked awhile to an elderly man of happy disposition, who was mending a trammel which he said was used for catching bait for his lobster pots. The fisherman had been born in the little panelled bedroom just over his head, and he had slept for more than 60 years in the same bed in which he had been born. Few men could say the same thing about themselves, eh? And very happy he

had been, too; his source of happiness being connected with the chapel yonder. The traveller nodded; said good-bye; and went into the Providence Inn, meaning to ask for tea, but when he got there he decided to have a small glass of beer, and to go on his way almost immediately.

The sky was becoming duller, and he sat there beside a deserted bagatelle board, in the silence of a small room with its tightly closed window. He sat for three-quarters of an hour, and then got up, said good afternoon to the air, and went outside, enquired the way to East Portlemouth, and set out quickly, hoping to get warm.

The Providence Inn, in which Williamson sat with his solitary glass of beer, is seen above on an early twentieth-century postcard. He would find even less of a welcome there today, for it closed in 2008 and is now a holiday let (complete with bar football and pool tables).

Happily, East Prawle's other pub, the Pig's Nose – originally known as the Union – is still very much in business. Nobody knows how old it is, but it has seen more than its share of smuggling over the centuries, as well as providing a haven for shipwrecked mariners. The most lurid episode in its history came on 4 December 1872, when, after colliding with another vessel, an Italian sailing ship, the Maria Theresa, ran aground near East Prawle. Some of the crew remained with the ship, but five took shelter in a room at the Union Inn. In the early hours of the morning, one of them ran amok, attacking his shipmates. After they had managed to escape, the landlord, assisted by some coastguards, tried to apprehend him. He attacked them with a knife and ran off in the direction of the coastguard cottages. He subsequently attacked several other people, including the wife of one of the coastguards, before fatally wounding himself on a tuck stick as a group of men tried to restrain him.

Visiting East Prawle today, it is hard to conjure up the terrors of that dark December night. Hard too to find any trace of the grim, run-down, faintly spooky village Henry Williamson found in 1933. This is second-home country par excellence, with the price of the quainter cottages comparable to property prices in London. All the more wonder then, that the Pig's Nose is still a traditional Devon pub, with nicotine-stained walls, old photos of the village, piles of pig paraphernalia and a box of pigs' noses on the bar

for dogs. There is also superb food courtesy of an Italian chef, although the Pig's Nose is about as far away from a gastropub as you can get. The atmosphere, friendliness and mix of clientele in the Pig's Nose have made it one of the most popular pubs in South Devon – all down to Peter and Lesley Webber, who have owned it for over a decade. And, as an added attraction, regular gigs are held in the hall adjoining the pub – featuring bands such as Wishbone Ash, The Animals, The Boomtown Rats and The Yardbirds – a legacy of Peter's former career in the London music business.

The postcard above shows the Pig's Nose in the 1950s, when it was a Simonds' house, while the photograph below dates from a decade later, with Flower's Keg Bitter, Watney Red Barrel and a 'Mabel, Black Label' bar towel adding up to an ale drinker's worst nightmare. Happily, this is one place where things have gone backwards, with local beer now served from barrels behind the bar and even the till predating the one seen here by the best part of a century – although a pint now costs considerably more than 3/10!

Eggesford

Eggesford station, midway between Exeter and Barnstaple, opened on 1 August 1854. Just over a year later, on 13 October 1855, the *Western Times* carried the following announcement:

FOX & HOUNDS INN, EGGESFORD STATION

G Edwards, in respectfully announcing that he has entered upon the above inn, which is situated within a short distance of the Eggesford station, on the North Devon Railway, begs to inform the nobility, gentry, and the public generally, that post horses and carriages can be procured at the shortest notice.

A few weeks later, on 15 December 1855, the *Western Times* reported that

the first periodical sale ... came off on Monday last, at the Fox & Hounds Inn, close to the Eggesford station of the North Devon Railway, and we are happy to say that the results exceeded the most sanguine expectations of the friends of the project ... The sale was advertised to take place at eleven o'clock in the forenoon; but the auctioneer, Mr JM Letheren, thought it desirable to await the 12.35 down train, when the sale commenced immediately ... Mr Letheren, in his opening address, informed the company that this periodical sale was projected by the Earl of Portsmouth, in order to develop more fully the benefit of the North Devon Railway to that particular locality, by enabling the breeders, graziers, and agriculturalists of the district, to bring their stock to a station which was well situated for a large agricultural market ... After the business was over, a substantial dinner was provided by Mr Edwards of the Fox & Hounds Inn, for more than 100 individuals. Mr Luxton took the chair, and the dinner was followed by a good deal of spirited speaking.

Eggesford station remains the railhead for a large area, while the Fox & Hounds remains a centre for country pursuits. Since the postcard above was published in the early twentieth century, the outbuildings on the left have been replaced with an extension, more than doubling the size of the inn.

Exbourne

The sixteenth-century Red Lion has changed little since this photograph was taken in the 1920s. It proudly proclaims itself to be one of only two pubs in Devon with no draught lager. This gives a good idea what to expect at this superbly traditional hostelry: beer from local brewers, cider from up the road, food from local suppliers, a lively mix of locals and visitors (and their dogs), three beer festivals a year and a pantomime at Christmas. An archetypal, magnificently unspoilt and much cherished village pub.

Exebridge

On the banks of the Exe, just below its confluence with the Barle, is the seventeenth-century Anchor Inn, dating from the seventeenth-century. RD Blackmore stayed here while writing *Lorna Doone*, and, drawing on the inn's associations with the highwayman Tom Faggus, included it in the novel. The Anchor still has a Tom Faggus Bar, and its riverside setting attracts not just anglers but also those who want a break in one of the most unspoilt parts of Devon.

Exeter

The Bude Hotel was originally known as the London Inn and dated back to 1358. It stood on the corner of Sidwell Street and Paris Street, and in the mid-eighteenth century was the starting point for a coach service to London. In 1788 the Prince of Wales had dinner there, further enhancing its reputation. In 1790, to avoid confusion with the New London Inn, which had just opened, it was renamed the Old London Inn. In 1848, due to loss of trade following the arrival of the railway, it underwent – according to a report in the *Exeter & Plymouth Gazette* for 14 October – 'considerable improvement and alteration by a convenient contraction of its extent'. Half of the building became a chemist's shop, while the remaining half was renamed the Bude Haven Hotel. The change of name reflected a change of role. The coach service to London had ended when the railway opened in 1844, and the inn became the starting point for the Bude mailcoach. Around 1878, there was a final change of name, to the Bude Hotel. The postcard above dates from around 1906 when Walter Norman was the landlord. The photograph on the right shows Robert Hamlin Dymond, who succeeded him in the 1920s. In 1933, the city council acquired the building and demolished it to widen the road.

The Royal Museum Hotel in Queen Street opened in 1868. On 13 March, the *Exeter & Plymouth Gazette* announced that 'the bar and smoking room are now open, and supplied with none but the very best and genuine articles; prime Old, Mild and Burton Ales,' and that 'the internal arrangements of the hotel will be complete in a few days.' By 22 May, the paper could announce that 'private gentlemen or families will find in this hotel all the quiet and comfort of home, good attendance and moderate charges.' Unfortunately, it proved somewhat quieter than anticipated, so much so that by August the following year it was offered for sale by auction. Shortly afterwards Alfred Hughes, the landlord, was declared bankrupt. The hotel had a life of less than 60 years, for in 1924 it was acquired by the council to widen the road. It was demolished two years later.

The Dolphin stood on the corner of Market Street and Preston Street, in one of the most historic parts of the city. It dated from Tudor times, first appearing in a document of 1578. When it was advertised for sale in June 1844, it consisted of a 'large room, bar, tradesman's room, four parlours, ten bedrooms, kitchen, cellars, large yard, skittle alley, lock-up warehouses (one of which is occupied by the Great Western Railroad Company), and granary'. The advertisement added that 'the comforts, convenience and extent of trade at the above house is too well known by travellers in the western counties to need any further comment.' The photograph on the previous page dates from sometime between 1924, when J Matthews took the lease, and 1931, when the licence was transferred to a newly-built pub called the Dolphin on Burnthouse Lane, The building survived until 1941, when, after being badly damaged in a bombing raid, it was demolished. Augusta Court, a modern apartment complex, now stands on the site.

MURDER AND MAYHEM AT THE DOLPHIN

Francis Pengelly, an Exeter apothecary, was the owner of the Dolphin at the beginning of the seventeenth century, and gave it in charity to trustees for certain benevolent purposes ... Once in 1725 the Dolphin happened to remain unlet for a week, and was kept open by the trustees. Their accounts show that during this short period there came carriers from Moreton, Yeovil, Ashburton, Totnes and Okehampton, with 56 packhorses amongst them. The regular charge was sixpence per night for each horse.

A century before this the Dolphin ... was frequented by guests of a higher class. Amongst the documents preserved in our Guildhall record room are some lengthy depositions of witnesses on a charge of murder supposed to have been committed by some of these.

It appears that on a January night in the year 1611 there was staying at the Dolphin Sir Edward Seymour of Berry Pomeroy ... Sir Edward was seated in an upper chamber playing at cards with some friends when the party was joined by Master William Petre, a member of a distinguished family ... and by John and Edward Drewe, then of Killerton.

These three young gallants, already flushed with wine at the Mermaid and at the Bear in South Street, drank a pot or two of beer, and some more wine with Sir Edward Seymour at the Dolphin. Perhaps they were in too quarrelsome a mood to be very acceptable company, for, after tarrying there an hour and indulging a rude practical joke on the tapster, they remounted their horses, dropped in at a few more taverns, and finally rode out of the city through the east gate.

Here Will Petre spurred on at a reckless pace up the broad highway of St Sidwell, and was soon lost in the darkness. The Drewes gave chase, but stopped at St Anne's Chapel and shouted to their companion by name. Receiving no answer, they groped their way to a house where a light was burning, but the woman of the house had seen nothing of Will Petre. They rode on to his house at Whipton House, and there found his horse standing riderless at the gate.

Edward Drewe deposed that 'he took the horse by the bridle, and with his foot as he sate on horseback, knocked at the gate, whereupon a servant of the house came forth and opened the gate. He (Edward Drewe) then willed him to take of him his master's horse, and then the servant demanded where his master was.' Drewe, contenting himself with the answer that he thought he would come by and bye, rode on with his brother to his home at Killerton.

The dawn of Sunday morning shewed the dead body of Will Petre lying by the causeway near St Anne's Chapel, with a ghastly wound on the head. The hue and cry was raised, and the two Drewes were taken as they lay in their beds and brought before the city justices on the charge of murdering their friend.

Some of the witnesses testified to a quarrel between Edward Drewe and Will Petre, but, though the papers do not disclose the issue of the trial, there is no doubt but what it must have ended in the discharge of the accused. It is but an old version of a tale since repeated, with variations, a thousand times – a tale of drinking, quarrelling and violent death.

From the *Western Times*, 7 April 1902

The Antelope beerhouse stood on the north side of Holloway Street, wedged between Lansdowne Terrace and Holloway Street Schools. First recorded in 1866, it was closed by the licensing authorities in 1935 as part of a campaign to reduce the number of public houses in Exeter. The site is now occupied by a single-storey extension to the house on the corner of Lansdown Terrace.

The Exonia Vaults at 8 South Street, first recorded in 1878, was destroyed by bombing in 1942. Modern shops now stand on the site.

The Port Royal on St Leonard's Quay, opposite the entrance to the Exeter Canal, was first recorded as a tavern in 1844 although the building is almost certainly older. On 7 September 1850 it was hit by a whirlwind: a four-masted schooner moored alongside it was lifted 15 feet out of the water before being dropped back down again, as customers looked on. From 1864 to 1982, the Port Royal was the headquarters of the Exeter Amateur Rowing Club; when they moved out, their clubhouse was replaced by a large function room. This photograph dates from around 1910; although the building is still recognisable today, the front door has been blocked up and a fascia board stretches the length of the frontage. The wooden slipway in front of the pub has also given way to a flight of steps. Changes to the Port Royal pale into insignificance, however, compared to what has happened to the other buildings in this photograph: all have been demolished and replaced by a cluster of modern flats and houses.

The Elephant & Castle stood on the corner of Codrington Street and Summerland Street. It was first licensed on 9 September 1858 and destroyed by bombing in 1942.

According to legend, Sir Francis Drake declared that, 'next to my own shippe I do most love that old Shippe in Exon, a tavern in Fyshe Street, as the peple call it, or as the clergy will have it, St Martin's Lane.' Although historians have cast doubt on this, this ancient hostelry has played its part in Exeter's history. During the siege of Exeter in the Civil War, the royalist commander, Captain Benet, wrote, 'I have quartered my men at the Ship in St Martin's Lane, an excellent place with good wine, victuals and forage.' In 1719 the inn came under attack from a mob who believed that some clergymen in alliance with the Whig government had taken refuge there. They threatened to burn it down, and only dispersed when the militia intervened.

The postcard opposite shows Dick Johns, landlord of the Ship between 1907 and 1917, standing outside the inn, and was sent by him as a Christmas card to friends in Holsworthy in 1910. At this time, the Ship only occupied No 3 Martin's Lane; an antique dealer called Henry Overmass occupied Nos 1 and 2, and his sign can be seen behind Mr Johns. However, a report in the *Exeter & Plymouth Gazette* on 4 April 1911, a few months after this photograph was taken, not only indicates that the Ship originally occupied all three buildings but sheds some fascinating light on its history:

> Exeter is rich in architectural antiquities, and occasionally these are added to by discoveries during restorations. Mr C Cole is one of Exeter's keenest architects in preserving any antiquities he may find in the practice of his profession. Several interesting things have been discovered by Mr Cole during the restoration of No 1, Martin's Lane. There is evidence that, originally, both Nos 1 and 2 were portions of the old Ship Inn, and that the timbers of a ship were used in the construction of the premises. The roof is in the shape of a bow, and the oak beams which support the roof are shaped like those of the bow of a ship, and have holes in them similar to the trunnion holes of a ship's timbers. It is fairly certain the holes were not cut for the purpose to which the timbers were applied in the structure of the house.
>
> In one of the rooms, Mr Cole discovered, under layers of plaster, an ancient fireplace of early sixteenth-century work. It has a drop-centre arch. Under this there was, presumably, a moulding, which, however, was cut away previous to the fireplace being covered with plaster. The moulding was supported by a stone lintel resting on stone corbels. The fireplace itself is of Thorverton or volcanic stone, but the upper part is of mixed Heavitree and Pocombe stone. A similar fireplace was uncovered in No 2, Martin's Lane some time since. Both are now being preserved, and are, as near as possible, shown in their original state. In the front of No 1 an ancient fascia board was discovered. This, of course, has also been preserved, and can be seen from the outside. Between the panels are figures of men and women, the former with an arm each in a sling.

The Ship subsequently expanded back into Nos 1 and 2 and survived the Second World War, but its interior was comprehensively revamped in 1964 and again in 1994, when a Russian paid £2,700 for the fittings which he exported to Kaliningrad to recreate an English pub. In the photograph on the right, taken in August 1938 a man with a briefcase stands indecisively outside the Ship, pondering whether to venture in.

A Great Western express passes the Cowley Bridge Inn in the 1920s. The inn predated the railway and was originally a farmhouse, before opening as the New Inn in the mid-1700s. It was first recorded as the Cowley Bridge Inn in 1807, with William Humphrey as landlord. It was a well-appointed establishment, as this report from the *Exeter & Plymouth Gazette* for 22 May 1841 indicates:

> On Tuesday morning last, the right worshipful the mayor, with the high sheriff, aldermen and council, and officers of the corporation, accompanied by the bluecoat boys, made their annual perambulation of the bounds of the city, observing the customary forms. The party, after the fresh air and exercise, enjoyed a sumptuous breakfast at Bowden's Cowley Bridge Inn, the far-famed potted eels of this suburban resting place, with other etceteras, forming part of the handsome and substantial repast.

Its tranquillity was soon to be shattered by the arrival of the railway. On 4 November 1843, the *Exeter & Plymouth Gazette* reported that 'the works at Cowley Bridge ... which the heavy rains on Monday had caused to be discontinued during Tuesday, were resumed with increased activity during Wednesday'. It went on to describe the 'spirit-stirring industry' of 'the alterations going on in the Cowley Bridge road, preparatory to the projected deviation of the junction with the Crediton road from the present point at the Cowley Bridge Inn, by means of bridges which span in succession the River Exe and the railway line'. The railway opened on 1 May 1844, and, just over a year later, the *Western Times* reported that a party from St Petrock's church in the High Street had 'dined at the Cowley Bridge Inn, where they picked their teeth after dinner, and gazed at the flying trains as they shot along, and cogitated on the changing character of all things mundane.'

The inn has always been subject to flooding. On 16 January 1866, the *Western Times* reported that 'the marshes on each side of the Exe, from Cowley Bridge to St David's station, were one grand and stormy lake ... At the Cowley Bridge Inn, the outhouses and stabling were knocked away, and the cattle rescued with difficulty; much beer was lost in the cellar.' When the inn was offered for sale in 1879, it was described as 'an eligible freehold property, situated in the main thoroughfare leading to Crediton and Tiverton.' On the ground floor were a 'bar, bar parlour, large smoking room, kitchen, pantry and all other necessary offices'. Upstairs was a 'large dining room, five bedrooms and a large attic over', while at the back was a yard with 'stables, coach house, cow shippens, a garden with pleasure house, and skittle ground'. After being extended and largely rebuilt around 1900, it continued as an inn until 2008 when Heavitree Brewery sold it to David Jim, who opened it as the Thai Shanghai restaurant. But flooding remained an ever-present threat. In 1960, diehard drinkers had stood on benches to keep their feet dry as the waters rose, and in 2012 David Jim saw floodwaters sweep through his newly-refurbished restaurant three times. He left two years later, and the lease was taken by Ken Bowden and Carolyn Mearns, who reopened it in 2015 under its original name, the New Inn, restoring one of Exeter's most historic and popular pubs to the community.

DOUBLE LOCKS HOTEL, THE CANAL, EXETER.

South of the city, alongside the ship canal, stands the Double Locks Inn. The locks themselves are among the longest in the country, and the canal, built in the 1560s, is one of the oldest. When it was modernised in 1828, a lock keeper's cottage was demolished to make way for the inn, which included accommodation for the lock keeper and stables for the horses that towed the boats. It also hosted civic functions. On 14 May 1842, for example, the *Exeter & Plymouth Gazette* reported that 'the members of the council of Exeter on Tuesday made their annual excursion to Turf, in order to examine the state of the canal. The civic body embarked at the Quay at ten in the forenoon, and returned to the Double Lock Inn at three to dinner.' This Edwardian postcard presents an idyllic scene, with rowing boats, punts and the pleasure boat Otranto sailing through the locks. It was the growing popularity of the canal that led the landlord, Mr Hannaford, to apply, in 1913, for a licence to serve alcohol on Sundays, which he had allowed to lapse several years earlier. Despite a 932-signature petition in favour of the application and the support of the council, it was opposed by the police, who argued that it would 'attract the wrong people' and 'promote immorality on the banks'. The magistrates granted the licence, however, and today the Double Locks is busier than ever, especially on summer Sundays, with beer and cider festivals and an annual dog show. .

First recorded in 1889, the Railway Inn on Cowick Street was next to St Thomas's station, just beyond the bridge on the north side of the street. After it closed in March 1939, it became a hostel for evacuees. It was demolished in 1970.

Just along from the Railway Inn, near the corner of Buller Road, was the Turk's Head, which dated from before 1730. In 1866, it was described as having 'extensive stabling, yard, covered alley and brewhouse, with walled garden'. In 1898, the owners rebuilt it, but claimed that 'a sufficient part of the building had not been taken down to render the house a new building, and consequently it did not come under the council's by-laws.' The council agreed, but local residents saw this as 'jobbery' and held meetings protesting against collusion between the inn's owners and the council. When council elections were held in 1900, the 'Turk's Head question' was one of the most pressing issues in this part of the city. Despite the controversy, the rebuilt inn survived until 1972, when it was pulled down to make way for a car park.

Shortly before Exeter Corporation closed the tramways in 1931, four trams are seen lined up outside the Ropemakers Arms on Blackboy Road. Opened as a beerhouse by a ropemaker called James Hill sometime before 1850, the Ropemakers got a full licence in 1881. In 1987, it was renamed the Bowling Green in honour of the Belmont Bowling Club across the road, and is one of the most popular community pubs on the east side of the city.

The Victoria in Pennsylvania, opened as a beerhouse in the 1860s when the area was developed. On 3 September 1869, the *Exeter & Plymouth Gazette* reported that the landlord, James Brewer, had applied for a full licence, but had been turned down because 'the houses in the neighbourhood were occupied by private families who would not be likely to go to a public house either for beer or spirits, although it was likely, from its position, to be frequented by a certain class of customers.' When he reapplied the following year, however, the licence was granted. Carr & Quick of the West of England Brewery in Queen Street owned it for many years, but in 1925 it was sold to Starkey, Knight & Ford, who replaced the ground-floor façade seen here with one featuring green ceramic tiles. The Victoria – with a row of plaques recording the annual drinking dry of the pub by the University of Exeter – is still a lively and very popular pub today.

The Village Inn lies on the west bank of the Exe in the old village of Exwick. The building is believed to have been the manor house, which was sold in 1830 and opened as an inn called the John Bull two years later. It was renamed the Lamb around 1848 and became the Village Inn in 1987. An article from the *Western Times* for 25 May 1885 provides a glimpse of how important inns like the Lamb were to village life in days gone by:

> It will be remembered that two or three years since, on the occasion of the new iron bridge across the river near St David's station, Mr Facey of Manchester was engaged in supervising its construction. The unfailing courtesy extended by that gentleman to all who had occasion to cross the river while the works were in progress was so marked that the villagers determined to give him a substantial proof of their appreciation of his conduct. On the completion of the work they accordingly presented him with a handsome walnut writing desk and fittings, and Mr Facey left with the expression of many good wishes for his welfare. Some work undertaken for the London & South Western Railway Co at their works at the junction of Lion's Holt, has again brought Mr Facey into the neighbourhood, and a supper took place at the Lamb Inn on Friday as a kind of social reunion, at which that gentleman met many of his old friends ... After full justice had been done to a capital spread served in excellent style by the host (Mr H Hayman), song and toast whiled away the evening in a very agreeable manner.

The inn has changed considerably since the postcard above was published around 1910. The bay windows have been removed, live music sessions and Sky sports have taken the place of more traditional entertainments, but it still remains at the heart of the community.

WHIPTON.

WHIPTON VILLAGE ROAD. 25673.

Over on the east side of Exeter, there is another Village Inn in the old village of Whipton, which until 2005 was known as the Whipton Inn. The two postcards above, dating from around 1910 and 1950 respectively, provide a fascinating record of how this part of the city evolved in the twentieth century. In the first, the inn is hidden behind the houses on the left, which had gone by the time the second was published. Since then, further changes have rendered the scene almost unrecognisable. The post office and shop on the left have acquired a new façade; the left-hand side of the inn has been extended forward, and the building beyond the inn has been replaced. Beyond that, the Half Moon Inn has survived, but the buildings beyond it have been demolished to widen the road and create a beer garden.

Exminster

The Exeter Canal originally joined the Exe opposite Topsham. In 1827, it was extended a further mile and a half downstream, where the estuary was wider. At the opening ceremony on 14 September 1827, barges conveyed civic dignitaries to the new sea lock at Turf, where they were greeted by a volley of cannon. Next to the lock stood the newly-built Turf Inn, seen above with two ships moored alongside it in the early twentieth century. From the start, many of those who visited the Turf Inn were there for pleasure rather than business. On 24 July 1841, a notice appeared in the *Exeter & Plymouth Gazette*:

TURF INN, HAVEN BANKS
One Mile from Topsham

William Lewis begs to inform his friends and the public, that he has succeeded his father in the above inn, and that he has refurnished the same, and hopes, by strict attention, to merit a share of public favour. Steaks or chops provided at the shortest notice. Whitebait when in season; teas, coffee, cream, etc. Spirits, beer, ales, etc. Porter of the best quality. The sitting rooms command some of the finest scenery in Devonshire. Sitting rooms and bedrooms to be let by the week or month.

On 23 June 1860, another notice appeared in the *Western Times*:

JH Edwards respectfully informs his friends and the public in general that, in succeeding to the business of the Turf Inn, he has determined during the summer months upon making the grounds in the neighbourhood of his establishment a place of healthful and delightful resort for the inhabitants of the old city. Spaces have been appropriated for the exercise of the old English games, quoits, skittles, bagatelle, etc, etc; and the household arrangements for the supply of the choicest liquors, tea, coffee, junkets, and refreshments of every kind in their season, including WHITEBAIT and shellfish, will be found not only to be of the first class but charged at the lowest possible remunerative rates.

Whitebait was obviously a key attraction, as three years later, on 17 June 1863, Mr Edwards placed a notice in the *Exeter Flying Post* describing the Turf as 'the celebrated whitebait house', informing visitors that 'the whitebait season has just commenced', and

adding that 'tea, with whitebait' was available 'at any hour of the day'. The gardens can be seen to advantage in the Edwardian postcard on the left, with the trees planted in the mid-nineteenth century reaching maturity.

Despite its superb location and continued popularity, the inn nearly disappeared in the 1970s. Commercial traffic along the canal had virtually ceased and the building was dilapidated. Exeter City Council, who owned the inn, closed it and there were fears it would be demolished. In 1979, however, Exeter Maritime Museum managed to get it listed, and it was restored and reopened. The present owners have been at the Turf since 1990, and today it is one of the most popular and best-loved inns in Devon. The views – and the gardens – are as glorious as ever, and its distinction of being one of the few mainland inns in Britain inaccessible by car only adds to its appeal.

Fairmile

The Fairmile Inn, seen here around 1910, stood on the old road from Exeter to London, and has, like many an old coaching inn, been a victim of re-routing. The road that took traffic away from the old A30, though, was built in the teeth of fierce opposition. It was here that Daniel Hooper – better known as Swampy – and a group of protestors took to the trees and burrowed their way into a warren of tunnels to halt the bulldozers in their tracks. The road eventually got built – after the Under-Sheriff of Devon had sent in an army of climbing and tunnelling experts to evict the protesters – but the legacy of their action can still be felt today, with no government seemingly prepared to stir up another hornet's nest by extending the new road eastward through the Blackdown Hills. The Fairmile Inn closed in 2003 and has been converted to flats.

Fenny Bridges

A couple of miles east along the old A30 is the Greyhound, which, despite the loss of passing trade, has fought back with a vengeance. After being closed for nearly three years, with its thatched roof ragged and moss-covered, and all the indications of being another old inn ripe for redevelopment, it was rethatched, refurbished and reopened in January 2012 as a family-run free house. Since then it has won many plaudits for its food and hospitality, re-establishing itself as one of the most popular inns in east Devon. The photograph above was taken in the 1930s, since when the building has been transformed, largely due to extensive rebuilding after a disastrous fire in 1968. Fortunately the changes have been sympathetic, retaining the character of this centuries old building.

An Edwardian postcard of the tap room in the Greyhound. Antiquated even then, today it seems like a vision of a lost age.

Fremington

The New Inn at Fremington, west of Barnstaple, has changed little since this postcard was published a century ago, apart from having the render stripped from its ground floor to reveal the rubble stone beneath. The windows, though, are unchanged and something very much like that rustic porch still survives. SW Arnold & Sons, the Taunton brewery whose sign can be seen on the wall, merged with William Hancock & Sons of Wiveliscombe in 1927, and eventually was absorbed by Usher's.

Frogmore

The road through Frogmore is no longer the peaceful backwater seen in this mid-twentieth century postcard, but the Globe Inn is still one of the most popular in the South Hams. Although no longer slate hung, it still boasts two traditional bars, open fires, flagstone floors, real ale and local cider.

Georgeham

Georgeham is one of North Devon's most delightful villages, hidden away in a wooded combe just inland from the Atlantic coast. Its most famous resident – who now lies buried in the churchyard – was Henry Williamson. In 1935, he waxed lyrical about its two pubs – the Lower House, 'where the best eggs and bacon and tomatoes in the West Country were cooked for supper', and the Higher House, 'where, after a pint or two of scrumpy, songs were roared in the yellow oil-light, while we sat on benches more crowded than starlings at roost on the National Gallery building in London'. Those were their unofficial names – the Lower House was the King's Arms and the Higher House was the Rock – and both are still open. The King's Arms was actually renamed the Lower House for a few years after being refurbished as a gastropub in 2006, but has since reverted to its old name. Today it is a friendly and welcoming pub with a reputation for food, but in the churchyard is a reminder of less convivial times – the grave of PC Walter Creech, age 31, killed in the King's Arms in 1883 by an elderly drinker whom he had been summoned to subdue.

The Rock was originally two cottages, and, despite being knocked through and extended, still retains a cottagey atmosphere. At one time, it was owned by the Anchor Brewery in Barnstaple. When the brewery closed in 1918, the Rock was bought at auction for £338 by Hancock's Brewery of Wiveliscombe. Despite its reputation as one of North Devon's top dining pubs, the main bar of the Rock is still very much a meeting place for the village, its walls adorned with photographs of Henry Williamson drinking and chatting with regulars.

Early twentieth-century postcards of the King's Arms (above) and the Rock (below)

THE DESERTED VILLAGE

When Henry Williamson left London on his Norton motorcycle in 1921, he headed west, to Georgeham, a village he had known from boyhood. It was not just the dust of London he wanted to shake off his feet; he wanted to come to terms with four years of trench warfare and make a living as a writer. He had little money, and the cottage he rented for four pounds a year – with no water, no heat, no light and no drains – suited him perfectly. Indeed, the lack of creature comforts was a bonus, for it brought him closer to the creatures – and the natural world – that would form the theme of so much of his work.

The village Williamson came to, and whose day-to-day life he chronicled in a series of books, was a tight-knit community, but it was a community under threat. The young and ambitious were leaving, swapping life on the land or in dying rural trades for the bright lights, clean houses and opportunities to be found in towns and cities.

By the mid-twentieth century, the decline was even more marked. In 1954, WG Hoskins published what still remains the best introduction to Devon's history and character. Called simply *Devon*, it included a paean to the county's small inland towns, those

> silent little places with their peeling plaster, where cats bask on sunlit window-sills and prostrate dogs hardly bother to stir as an occasional car makes a detour around them in the road; the silence of a summer afternoon broken only at vast intervals by the short pang-pang of the church clock; the sun on the bleached blinds of the draper's shop, the wasps crawling wearily over the dried-up buns in the bakery and the sticky jars of sweets. No more three-day fairs, no more brisk markets every week for corn and cattle, sheep and provisions; no more cloth merchants and weavers, no more tin-miners and copper-miners; no more masons and quarrymen, ostlers and coachmen; no more the ring of the smithies up and down the street, the great stamping horses and the glossy cattle: but only the dusty black cats, the comatose dogs and the eternal wasps.

Despite the signs of decay, most of the things that sustained community life – schools, pubs, shops, railway stations, post offices – still survived. Most people had roots going back generations. What incomers there were tended to live in bungalows at the edge of the village rather than in the tumbledown cottages at its heart.

Visit Devon's villages and small towns today, though, and, as likely as not, you will find the buildings that once sustained the community turned into second homes or holiday lets. Often it is their names alone – Old School, Old Chapel, Old Bakery, Old Post Office, Old Smithy, and, increasingly, Old Inn – that hint at their erstwhile functions. Some places have been luckier than others. Williamson's cottage may have been knocked through into the one next door and fitted with mod cons as a holiday let, but the two pubs he frequented are still in business. Elsewhere, pubs are closing at an unprecedented rate, leaving more and more communities without a social hub for the first time ever. Creeper-clad cottages – spicker and spanner than ever before – may evoke wistful sighs for a time that never was, but the vision they represent is one of a bleak emptiness summed up in the words of 'Country Life', Show of Hands' bitter lament for the destruction of the rural community:

> The red brick cottage where I was born
> Is the empty shell of a holiday home
> Most of the year there's no-one there
> The village is dead and they don't care
> Now we live on the edge of town
> Haven't been back since the pub closed down
> One man's family pays the price
> For another man's vision of country life.

George Nympton

There has been an inn called the Castle at George Nympton for a very long time. On 21 April 1836, for example, the *North Devon Journal* announced that a timber sale was to be held there. The present building, however, is of more recent vintage. Until recently, its attractive brickwork had been covered in white paint, but, after a long period of closure, this was removed as part of a major refurbishment, and the Castle reopened at Easter 2015. Since then, it has not only won praise for the quality of its food and beer, but has also re-established itself at the centre of the community.

Goodleigh

The New Inn still looks much as it did when this postcard was published in the 1920s, although the cottage adjoining it has been replaced by a modern building. When it was advertised for sale in the *North Devon Journal* on 26 July 1855, it was described as a well-accustomed and capital inn situate in the village of Goodleigh, within 2½ miles from Barnstaple ... The premises are in excellent repair, and well adapted for carrying on an extensive business, having large club, tithe and hunting meetings held regularly, and adjoining turnpike roads leading to many populous towns and villages, and is the only inn in the neighbourhood ... For viewing, apply to the proprietor, Mr John Goss, Goodleigh.

Over 150 years on, the New Inn remains a defiantly traditional free house, with home-cooked food, real ales and a friendly welcome.

Halberton

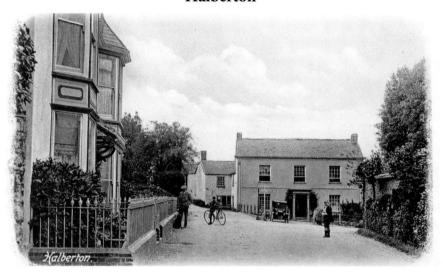

The New Inn & Railway Hotel at Halberton, seen here in the early twentieth century, was, after a spell as the Welcome Inn, renamed the Barge to celebrate the restoration of the nearby Grand Western Canal. Halberton's other pub closed years ago, but, despite the Barge's popularity and a village population of around 1500, in 2011 the owners applied to knock it down and build six houses on the site. The inn had been owned by a Torquay-based pubco called Peninsula Inns, which went into administration in 2009. It was subsequently acquired, along with around two-thirds of Peninsula's pubs, by a newly-formed company called Enlighten Inns, founded by Peninsula's former finance director. The planning application argued that because 'the village is now mainly populated by commuters from Tiverton or further away in Exeter ... it is becoming very difficult to make a profit from this business and it is a concern as to how the business can afford future investment to both grow and improve the profitability of the business.' Local residents were not impressed and organised a campaign to save their pub, gaining the support of the local MP and persuading Mid Devon Council to turn down the application. An appeal was subsequently dismissed in May 2012, and in 2014 the Barge was acquired by new owners who plan to extend the range of real ales, open an American-style smokehouse, and rename it the Hickory Inn. In July 2015, they won the top prize of £10,000 in a competition organised by PRS for Music to improve music facilities at the pub. Quite a turnaround!

Hallsands

Life in the village of Hallsands was never easy. Its inhabitants – some 128 by the mid-nineteenth century – eked out a precarious living from the sea, catching pilchards, or, when the pilchard shoals deserted the coast, turning to crabbing instead. The London Inn, first recorded in 1784, was the hub of village life, a warm, convivial haven from the roaring winds and raging waves. In 1887, however, dredgers began scooping out the banks of shingle offshore to provide hardcore for new docks at Keyham, and the delicate balance of life on this unforgiving coast was knocked irrevocably off kilter.

It soon became apparent that the holes created by the dredgers were not filling up again, but, despite protests that the beach protecting the village from the sea would be swept away if the dredging did not stop, it carried on. By 1900, it was clear that the beach was indeed disappearing, and on Friday 6 March 1903 the following report appeared in the *Western Times*:

> The encroachment of the sea with serious effects upon the village of Hallsands, near Kingsbridge, has created a feeling of deepest consternation among the inhabitants. The recent south-westerly gale was disastrous in its effects, and property has been seriously damaged. The cliff upon which the fishermen's cottages stand is undermined, and portions are continually being washed away. On Sunday morning a house collapsed, though fortunately it had been vacated some days before, otherwise there is no doubt a fatality would have occurred. A large linhay which was close to the cottage has quite disappeared. The London Inn is threatened, and the foundations are giving way ... The road leading to the village is undermined, and has been declared unfit for traffic, and the quays have been washed away. Indeed the cause of alarm among the villagers is well founded, and unless steps are taken promptly and a breakwater constructed Hallsands will cease to exist.

On 22 September 1903, the *Western Times* reported that an easterly gale had 'demolished the greenhouse, cellar and kitchen of the London Inn, and played havoc with several other houses'. The problem with the inn, as the two postcards opposite show, was that, while part of it was built on solid rock, part was built on compacted shingle which was sucked out by the action of the sea. The landlord, a naval pensioner from Saltash called George Lobb, who had only been at the inn for a few months, gave a graphic account of what happened:

> When the greenhouse collapsed, two coastguardsmen and two fishermen came to assist me to remove the things in the bedroom. While we were in the room the roof came down upon us and we all had a narrow escape. Then the gable gave way, tearing away the stove and nearly blinding us with dust. It was with the greatest difficulty that we grasped things to prevent us falling into the surf. My wife also had a very narrow escape. We had arranged to have tea as usual in the kitchen. Mrs Lobb was sitting down when the wall gave way, but not in her customary place, otherwise she would certainly have fallen and perished in the surf.

On 2 November 1903, the *Western Times* reported that work had started on a 'sea wall ... in front of the great gap beside the London Inn', but it was too late to save the inn itself. With the rest of the building now declared unsafe, George Lobb moved the bar to an adjacent stable and continued trading there. When the licence came up for renewal the following February, however, the chairman said that 'the bench were extremely sorry, but in the circumstances they could not renew the licence, as there

was really no house to licence. It was extremely hard for the landlord, and if another house had been obtained he personally would not have hesitated to grant another licence. He himself considered that the way the people of Hallsands had been treated was abominable.'

In May 1904, Alice Spital, the owner of the inn, issued a writ against the dredging company for damages which was settled out of court a few weeks later. She used the money to build the Hallsands Hotel, high above the village, which opened in 1907 and was demolished, just short of its centenary, in 2006.

Hartland

'Hartland,' wrote Henry Williamson in 1933, 'attempts to advertise itself as 'Farthest from Railways' and until a few years ago it was even more primitive than it is now. The word primitive is used in an approving sense, for this is one of the few places in old England which remains old England. The day to see it is Saturday, when the market is on. The inns are then open all day, cattle wander about the streets with almost the same expression in their eyes as that of their masters in the inn.' He called in at 'a snug little inn, with a table bagatelle, on which we played when we had scraped the clogging

ash from the runway of the steel balls. The wood fire burned brightly in the grate, cattle mooed outside. Rattle and trot of feet in the narrow street, men's boots clamping on the lime-ash floor as they came in for a chat and a laugh and a drink.' Although he did not say which inn he visited, it may well have been the New Inn or the Anchor, both of which are still open today. The high wall seen in the 1920s photograph of the New Inn (on the left) has made way for a car park, with a new housing estate in the background, while the appearance of the Anchor has been transformed since the postcard below was published by the stripping of render from the ground floor and chimney. The Anchor is the tap for the nearby Forge Brewery, while the New Inn (now renamed the Hart) has featured in the Michelin Guide.

The sixteenth-century West Country Inn stands high on Bursdon Moor, offering refreshment and accommodation to travellers heading over the border to Cornwall. Stagecoaches en route from Barnstaple to Bude once changed horses here and there was an annual fair where farmers from the surrounding area met to buy and sell livestock. The inn's extensive stables have long been converted to a bar but the remains of a smithy can still be seen across the road. The photograph above dates from the early 1900s. Since then the road has been widened, the cottages to the right incorporated into the inn and all the doorways seen here blocked up, with a new entrance on the left. The evocative photograph below shows the bar of this popular West Country Inn in the 1930s.

Hatherleigh

'Lor' bless 'ee, zur, the George 'tweren't never built, 'twas washed up by the Flood,' is what the old ostler would reply if you asked him when the George was built at Hatherleigh, in the heart of rural North Devon. Such antiquity is not, however, claimed by the proprietor, but certainly parts of the building, the main walls of which are 2ft 6in thick, must date back some 700 years. The picturesque upper courtyard, approached under the archway from the street, was restored just prior to the war, while from the ruins of the old brewhouse and lofts, where once the Annual Rent Audit dinners were held and the coachmen used to sleep, has sprung the present Jubilee (or Coffee) Room, with its splendid oak beams and original open fireplace, on which the new wing of the hotel abuts. In one corner of the yard stands an ancient granite brew-trough, where once good malt, hops and yeast went to make fine ale. Today, however, the old trough merely collects the rainwater, standing as a silent tribute to two things – ale and rain – which have helped to make the England we all know. The George fronts on the Market Place, once known as George Hill, and on the left of the entrance archway under which the coaches used to be led, lies the dining room which leads through to the 'old bar', now the lounge, with panelling down one side of the room and an antique fireplace at one end.

This account comes from *A Book of Inns* by William Luscombe, published in 1947, and, until a few years ago, was a pretty good description of one of Devon's oldest inns. A couple of days before Christmas 2008, however, fire ripped through the building, reducing it to a smouldering ruin. It was as though the heart had been ripped out of the town. The George was not only the most historic building in Hatherleigh – and one of the most historic in Devon – it symbolised the strong community feeling of this little west Devon town and provided a living link with times long gone. Perhaps the saddest and most incomprehensible thing of all is that this fire was no accident but due to arson, for which a former chef was jailed for six years. Scottish & Newcastle, who owned the building, decided that the George should be rebuilt as quickly as possible. Local people were asked for photographs of the interior and every

effort was taken to make the new inn as close to the original as possible. Modern building regulations, however, precluded such features as three-foot-thick cob walls, with the result that the new George is more spacious inside, but, from the Square, and in many places inside the inn, it is possible to believe that you are looking at a refurbished rather than a rebuilt building. But, although it is a very impressive achievement, it is a tragedy that it had to be done at all. The two photographs here, dating from the mid-nineteeenth and the mid-twentieth centuries, are a reminder of what was lost.

Almost 170 years earlier, on 23 January 1840, a fire broke out at the back of the London Inn, opposite the George. It was destroyed, along with several adjoining buildings, but soon rebuilt. The photograph above shows the rebuilt inn in the early twentieth century after it was renamed the London Hotel. Later still it became the Havelock Arms, but today, with its balcony gone and licence long since surrendered, it is known as Plumlee House, with no sign of ever having been an inn.

A little way up from the George was the New Inn, now the Tally Ho! In October 1899, when it was put up for auction, it was described as having 'five bedrooms, bar, tap room, bar parlour, sitting room, kitchen, two cellars, store room, dairy, wash house, stable, yard enclosed with folding gates, corn store, wood house, stables with loft over, skittle alley, cow house, pig and poultry houses, wc and kitchen garden, now and for many years past in the occupation of Mr W Brook'. On the evening of 11 June 1923, sparks from a passing steamroller landed on the roof, starting a fire. Volunteers clambered onto the roof to remove the thatch and douse it with water, and, with the help of the town's new fire engine, it was eventually extinguished. The Tally Ho! remains one of the most popular meeting places in west Devon – a traditional community pub with live music, good food and beer, and a friendly welcome.

Down on Bridge Street was the Royal Oak, seen on the left in the 1920s. Although it seems to have avoided catching fire, it has not escaped closure. Last orders were called around 1980 and the building now houses an insurance company.

Hawkchurch

Hawkchurch was in Dorset until boundary changes in 1896 brought it into Devon. The Old Inn is believed to have started life as a Church House, being rebuilt, according to a datestone, in 1543 or 1547, and again after a fire in 1806. It has changed little, however, since this postcard of it was published a century ago and remains a popular village inn, offering real ales and traditional food, along with accommodation.

Haytor

The Rock Inn at Haytor was built in 1826 by George Templer, shortly after he built a tramway to carry stone from his nearby granite quarries to a wharf on the Stover

Canal. Two years later, the inn was offered to let 'together with the stables, coach house, brewhouse, and all other convenient outhouses ... with about 12 acres of land thereto adjoining ... The inn is distant about five miles from the market towns of Newton and Ashburton; about half a mile from the extensive Haytor granite quarries, and immediately adjoining the valuable Haytor iron mine lately discovered, on both of which a number of workmen are actively employed.'

Early entertainment at the inn was, not surprisingly, of a fairly robust character. On Monday 10 July 1830, a wrestling match was held there, at which, it was promised, 'the first best man will receive £5; the second best £1 10s; and the third best 15s'. The advertisement added ominously that 'several Cornishmen have promised to attend'. Efforts were soon being made to attract tourists, however. On 31 May 1834, Samuel Southey placed an advertisement in the *Western Times* to 'inform his friends and the public' that he had fitted up the Rock Inn and 'made it replete with every convenience. The house is pleasantly situated, and commands delightful views of Haytor Rock and the surrounding country. Every attention will be paid in keeping a well-supplied larder, choice wines and spirits, and the utmost care will be taken in the stabling department.'

The quarries and tramway closed by 1858, but the Rock Inn is still a popular stop-off point for visitors to this fascinating part of Dartmoor. The Rock's reputation for fine wines, fine dining and well-appointed rooms may be far removed from the quarrymen and wrestlers who patronised the inn in its early years, but Samuel Southey would undoubtedly approve of its current ambience.

Hele

Hele station on the Bristol & Exeter Railway opened in 1844, was renamed Hele & Bradninch in 1867 and closed in 1967. Beside it stood the Railway Hotel, seen here in the 1920s. Despite being a considerable distance from both Hele and Bradninch, it was a busy place. In 1940, plans were drawn up to extend the bar 'because the game of darts had grown so considerably in popularity'. Around 1960, it was renamed the Devon Valley Hotel and is now known as the Crossways Tavern. As well as hosting pool, darts and skittles leagues, it caters for wedding receptions and other functions, and provides apartment-style accommodation.

Hemyock

The Star Inn on the Square in Hemyock is yet another inn destroyed by fire. On 14 June 1928, the *Exeter & Plymouth Gazette* reported that 'the Star Inn at Hemyock became ignited in the thatched roof near the chimney yesterday morning, and was gutted, only the main walls standing.' The report added that the inn was the oldest in the village. The car park of the Catherine Wheel Inn now occupies the site.

Hexworthy

In 1905, William Crossing wrote that 'the whole picture commanded ... from the door of the Forest Inn at Hexworthy ... is far and away the finest view within the forest of

Dartmoor.' Many people seem to have agreed with him, for the Forest Inn has long been one of the most popular hostelries on the moor. Its first landlord was Richard Cleave. In 1878, he was listed as a farmer and shoemaker, but shortly afterwards he opened the Forest Inn, and on 4 May 1880 Mr Netherton's Harriers met there for the first time. It was the first of many such meets; the inn became so popular with the hunting fraternity that it featured in a poem by Wyndham Disney-Roebuck which appeared in the *Western Morning News* on 19 March 1926:

> Oh, the Dartmoor hounds are meeting at the Forest Inn today,
> By the Swincombe there's a very certain find,
> And you'll have to ride your hardest when the Squire's pack's away,
> Unless you're keen on getting left behind ...

... and so on for another eleven verses.

The original inn was a two-storey, thatched, whitewashed building. In the early twentieth century, a large modern extension was built beside it, and when this was extended in turn, the original building was demolished. Despite its continued popularity, it closed suddenly in early 2014, and was subsequently put on the market, the agents advising that the building 'is in need of substantial investment and refurbishment'. It can only be hoped that someone prepared to rescue one of Dartmoor's best-loved inns can soon be found.

Highampton

The Golden Inn at Highampton was probably built as a farmhouse in the sixteenth or seventeenth centuries. When it became an inn is not recorded, but it was already well established when the *Morning Post* announced that 'Mr Cohan's hounds' would be meeting there on 16 January 1835. As with many country inns, such meets provided a lucrative source of business, and in January 1851, when the *Western Times* got the inn's name wrong in its weekly list of hunting appointments, it was quick to offer a fulsome, if humorously worded, apology:

Highampton: Probably many readers of the *Western Times* last week were puzzled to know the whereabouts of the Golden Tun, mentioned in the Hunting Appointments as the meet for a pack of harriers on Tuesday last. Suffice that the Golden Inn in this town was evidently referred to, for there, on that day, the quaint anticipations of your humorous correspondent were realised. The day was unpropitious for sport in the field, but the sport at the table was very good. Mine Host was very proud of the goodly company assembled, and expressed enthusiastically the honour he felt in entertaining guests so distinguished as 'Kernal' Wiseman and 'Butcher' Blaze. By the by, the Cardinal for the occasion was in high spirits, and appeared quite a Bacchanalian god. The song, the toast, and joke went round, and the fragrant wood was in great demand.

Mine Host at this time was George Blatchford. He was succeeded by William Sampson, who died a bankrupt in St Thomas's Asylum in Exeter in December 1860. The next landlord, William Garland, was similarly unfortunate, dying in June 1864 at the age of only 32. When an auction of his effects was advertised in the *Exeter & Plymouth Gazette* on 23 September 1864, they included four cows, nine pigs, two horses, a variety of carts, ploughs and farm implements, two ricks of hay, an acre of potatoes, a rick of wood, six guns, as well as the furniture from the inn.

He was succeeded by a Mr Tucker, who served up a 'sumptuous dinner' for 'the Conservative electors of the parish (including nearly all the voters)' on 14 December 1858. The following year, the Golden Inn was taken over by a Mr Wilson, and on 3 December 1869 the *Western Times* reported that

Host Wilson who has lately taken the Golden Inn, had a hunting meeting a few days since, when a goodly number of friends met to join in the chase with Captain Arnold at their head. Some capital sport was shown by the pack of which he is the owner. The dinner was nothing lacking to show how well Mine Host understood the various wants of an Englishman after a good days run.

On 27 January 1871, the *Western Times* reported that the vicar of Highampton, the Rev G Woollcombe, 'with the landowners and farmers, have kindly given a good dinner to the aged poor and the labourers, provided by Host Wilson of the Golden Inn. It need not be said that all enjoyed the feed.'

The inn also had two long-standing friendly societies, one for men and one for women. The women's friendly society was founded in 1844, and, when it celebrated its 65th anniversary in 1909, much was made of the fact that the post of secretary had been been in the hands of the Sanders family from the start.

In October 1899, when the Golden Inn was put up for sale, it was described as

a well-built stone and thatched house, occupying a good position on the main road from Hatherleigh to Holsworthy, containing 4 bedrooms, box room, sitting room, tap room, bar, kitchen, dairy and WC. The hotel yard contains coach house, 6-stall stable, brew house, corn store, harness room, and kitchen garden. The farmyard in the rear comprises cow houses with lofts over, 3 pig sties, cart shed with corrugated iron roof, barn, together with 8 meadows, in all about 15 acres of very productive land in a high state of cultivation, the whole having been for many years in the occupation of Mr Tapson.

Despite a century of change, which has seen the Golden Inn refurbished and extended, it occupies pride of place at the heart of the community, as it has done for centuries.

High Bickington

The Golden Lion at High Bickington looks much as it did when this photograph was taken in the 1920s. Still very much a traditional community pub, serving local ales and home cooked food, numerous trophies bear witness to the success of its sports teams while old agricultural implements on the walls recall a bygone age.

West of High Bickington, at a remote crossroads, lies the old Ebberly Arms, seen here around 1910. In the nineteenth century, the inn was the venue for race meetings. The *North Devon Journal* for 21 August 1870 reported that 'the annual Ebberly Arms' Races took place on the High Down course on Monday last. The weather, though cloudy, was dry and favourable, and there was a good attendance of rural pleasure seekers.' The inn closed in 1928, when its licence was allowed to lapse. The building, now covered in white stucco and graced with a classical porch, has been renamed Ebberly Hill Barton.

Holbeton

A social gathering at the Union Inn at Holbeton in the South Hams in the 1920s. When advertised for sale in 1887, the Union was described as a 'free and fully-licensed house with stabling, poundhouse, outbuildings, orchard and kitchen garden'. Now known as the Dartmoor Union, it has had several changes of ownership in recent years, with spells as a gastropub. It also had a microbrewery for a time. New owners, who took over in April 2014, however, have concentrated on making it a popular community pub.

Holcombe

Apart from new rails around the seating area and the loss of the flagpole, the Castle Inn at Holcombe has changed remarkably little since this postcard was published a century ago. The Castle remains a traditional village inn, with a candlelit restaurant and bar.

These two photographs show the Country House Inn in Holcombe before and after it was renamed and rebranded as the Smugglers Inn – an appropriate enough name given the sort of clientele it would once have attracted. A nearby track called Smuggler's Lane still leads down to a cove whose seclusion – and suitability for landing contraband – was rudely shattered when the railway was built. Since the photograph below was taken in the mid-twentieth century, the busy road that runs past it has been realigned and widened, taking it further away from the inn. Inside, despite being refurbished to reflect changing tastes, it remains a family-run free house, with a renowned carvery, locally-brewed ales and magnificent views out to sea.

Holne

Above we see the Church House Inn at Holne in Edwardian times, shortly after the roof was raised and half-timbering applied to the porch. It is believed to have been built as a church house around 1329. It later became the Tavistock Inn before being renamed the Church House Inn around 1800. In the late 1880s, Sabine Baring-Gould stayed here for a week while gathering folk songs. 'We got together a number of singers,' he recalled, 'and gave them a supper. Then they sang each a song in turn; most of these were rubbish, many modern, published songs, and just as one old fellow began a strain in the Dorian mode, in came the village constable to order all out, because the public-house must be closed.' Well over a century later, the Church House remains a convivial local, offering a traditional welcome along with good food, real ale and roaring log fires.

The bar of the Church House Inn as it looked around 1910

Holsworthy

Above we see Holsworthy market in full swing in the mid-twentieth century, with the King's Arms on the left. Rebuilt after a fire in the early 1900s, the King's Arms has been a market inn for centuries. Until it was moved to the edge of town in 1905, the livestock market was also held in the square and many deals were struck over a few pints in the inn. The King's Arms has recently been refurbished as a bar bistro.

Across the square from the King's Arms was the New Inn. On the left, we see crowds jostling around its signboard to hear St Peter's Fair proclaimed open on 9 July 1908. With so many thirsty punters around, set on enjoying themselves, the New Inn would have had one of its busiest days of the year. We can, alas, no longer experience its delights, as a convenience store now occupies the site.

Just around the corner from the King's Arms is the White Hart, dating back to 1591 although much altered in the interim. It remains a friendly, family-run free house, with a bar and restaurant downstairs and a club-style bar upstairs.

The photograph on the left shows the White Hart in the mid-nineteenth century, surrounded by two-storey cottages.

Below we see the same view in the 1920s, with the cottages replaced by three-storey commercial premises and the White Hart refronted. Only the church remains unchanged.

The London & South Western Railway opened a branch from Okehampton to Holsworthy in 1879, and it was extended to Bude 21 years later. Just up from the station was the South Western Hotel, seen here in the 1940s, which provided refreshment for travellers. The railway closed in 1966 and a supermarket now covers much of the station site, but the South Western has experienced an astonishing renaissance as the Old Market Inn, one of the top real ale pubs in Devon. Not only has it been voted Pub of the Year by local CAMRA enthusiasts three years in a row, but it also has a well-appointed restaurant, a splendid beer garden, its own comedy club and a dedicated cocktail bar.

Honiton

Honiton was one of the most important coaching towns in Devon, with inns lining its long main street. The principal inn was the Dolphin, seen here on the left in the 1920s. According to Sabine Baring-Gould, it is 'supposed to still possess some portion of the ancient building once belonging to the Courtenays, whose cognisance is the inn sign'. In the Civil War, it was used as a military hospital, and the ghost of a soldier is said to haunt one of the upper rooms. In 1777, tragedy very nearly struck, as a report in the *Oxford Journal* for 8 February that year records:

> Monday morning about four o'clock a fire was discovered in the stables of the Dolphin Inn in Honiton, Devon, which happened by the carelessness of the driver of the Exeter post coach, who about two hours before had left a candle stuck on the side of a stable lanthorn, which falling among the litter set fire to the stable and burnt three horses, all the harness, a large quantity of corn, a great deal of leather and household goods, together with the back wing of the dwelling house, and did very considerable damage to other buildings adjoining. It was with the utmost difficulty and exertion that the inhabitants could conquer it before eight o'clock.

Like many once grand coaching inns, the Dolphin has seen many changes in recent years. The ground floor to the right of the main entrance is now occupied by a health food store, but, until recently, the rest of the building was known as the Dolphin Hotel, with Liberty's Nightclub at the back. After it closed, this part of the building lay empty for a while but has now reopened as Montgomery's Hotel. One miraculous survival in the archway leading through to the coachyard is a set of three bells once used to summon the ostler, post boy and marker.

The Globe Inn, built on the site of Honiton's bridewell, was originally known as the Carpenter's Arms, then the Baker's Arms, before becoming the Globe. This postcard view of it dates from around the time of the First World War, when William Wolland was the landlord. Since closing in 1971, it has had a varied career – Jehovah's Witness hall, antique centre, amusement arcade, and currently tattoo studio. The building to the left of the Globe – once Scott's Temperance Hotel – still survives, but the one next to that has been demolished, as has the two-storey shop on the far corner.

Above we see Edwardian children waiting outside the King's Arms for hot pennies to be thrown from the balcony at the start of Honiton Fair. This custom, dating from the thirteenth century, still survives, although the King's Arms closed in 1975 to become an antiques centre. It is now a clothes shop.

The Three Tuns, seen on the left with flags out to mark some auspicious occasion – possibly George V's Silver Jubilee in 1935. After a recent refurbishment, this old coaching inn has reopened as a traditional town-centre local, complete with skittle alley.

Horn's Cross

The dusty lane running past the Coach & Horses at Horn's Cross on this 1920s post-card is now the main road from Bideford to Bude, known as the Atlantic Highway. The cottage on the right – which once housed the police station – has been demolished, and the old entrance to the inn has been converted to a window, with a new entrance opened up at the side, but the Coach & Horses is still a traditional village pub, with a barrel of locally-brewed beer on the bar and a warm welcome.

Less than a mile west of the Coach & Horses is the Hoops Inn. Part of the building is believed to date from the thirteenth century, but much of it had to be rebuilt after a fire in 1941. The inn stayed open despite the fire, with the landlord setting up a bar in his back parlour. In March 2009 another fire destroyed part of the roof, although the inn reopened

three months later. Beers brewed for the inn are available on draught, but the emphasis is very much on food. And in case you are under any illusion as to the origin of the inn's name, it has nothing to do with crinolines or even with the iron hoops that hold barrels together. Bullfinches were once known as 'hoops' in these parts. They were in the habit of feasting on the blossom in nearby cider-apple orchards, and clubs organised to cull the birds used the inn as a meeting place.

The view of the Hoops Inn on the previous page dates from around 1910. Above is another view from around 20 years later, when cars had ousted horse-drawn carriages as the preferred mode of transport. Below is a postcard of the bar as it looked a century ago – what a treasure it would be today had it survived.

The Bar, Hoops Inn, Devon.

Horrabridge

MANOR HOTEL, HORRABRIDGE. 519.

The Roborough Inn at Horrabridge had been renamed the Roborough Manor Hotel by the time this postcard was published around 1910. It closed around 1950 and became a garage. Apart from the removal of its porch, the main building has changed remarkably little. Beyond it, a canopy extends over the forecourt, and the building in the distance, with a cart standing outside, has been demolished. The small building on the right, occupied by a saddler called Charles Harding when this postcard was published, is now an antique shop.

Hunter's Inn

The Hunter's Inn. Heddonsmouth. 18105

Hunter's Inn nestles in a deep wooded combe, less than a mile inland from one of the most dramatic coastlines in Devon. It is hardly surprising, given its location, that it is one of the best known and most visited inns in Devon. What may come as a surprise is that, unlike inns at many tourist honeypots, it is well worth seeking out. A review in the *Daily Telegraph* on 23 October 2009 summed up the secret of its success as a 'lack of pristine modernism and the sense of ramshackle rusticity and unpolished honesty'. Despite its popularity, it is still very much a locals' pub, and its annual beer and music festival is billed as 'Exmoor's friendliest festival'.

The current building replaced an earlier inn which was destroyed by fire in 1895, shortly after being acquired, along with vast tracts of the surrounding countryside, by Colonel Benjamin Green Lake, a London solicitor. He had added a new dining room to the inn, which was the only part of the building to survive. The *North Devon Journal* for 28 November 1895 left its readers in no doubt as to the magnitude of the loss:

> The news that the quaint, picturesque Hunter's Inn was on Saturday afternoon entirely destroyed by fire will be read with widespread regret. How the fire originated is not quite certain, but it is supposed to have been due to some defect in a chimney ... The new dining room, erected on the north side about three years ago, being, as it were, behind the line of fire, was fortunately saved. The rest of the hotel is in ruins ... The Hunter's Inn has none of the stereotyped hotel about it, every room being full of pretty nick-nacks, that made it home-like and conducive to personal comforts; and the fact of collegians returning year after year in student days, often later on bringing a wife to spend a honeymoon in the district, shows how the place was appreciated ... The premises were the property of Col Green Lake, the Lord of Martinhoe and Trentishoe Manors. The utmost sympathy is felt for Mr Berry and his family. Mrs Berry has received a severe shock to the nervous system. For over a quarter of a century Mr and Mrs Berry have lived there, and have seen its gradual rise. At first visitors were few and far between; last summer, it was no infrequent occurrence for 200 persons to have refreshment in the dining room during an afternoon.

Lake wasted no time rebuilding the inn, but less than five years later his business empire collapsed and he was imprisoned for misappropriation of his clients' money. In October 1900, his estate was put up for auction and Mr Berry bought the Hunter's Inn for £4,800.

The inn destroyed by fire in 1895

As can be seen from this 1920s postcard, traffic congestion at the Hunter's Inn is nothing new.

The saloon bar at the Hunter's Inn in the 1920s

51468. The Side Bar, Hunters' Inn, North Devon.

Two more views inside the Hunter's Inn in the 1920s

The Hunters Inn Parracombe. N Devon.

Iddesleigh

Few country inns can have such auspicious literary associations as the Duke of York at Iddesleigh. It was poet laureate Ted Hughes's local when he lived nearby. More recently, Jez Butterworth rented a cottage in the village, and how many of the stories he heard in the Duke of York ended up in his play *Jerusalem* is anyone's guess. Another local resident, Michael Morpurgo, turned a tale he was told in the Duke of York into his novel *War Horse*, later made into a film by Steven Spielberg. As if that wasn't enough, for over 20 years, until his retirement in 1975, the landlord was the Scottish poet Sean Rafferty. As you might expect for an inn with such a clientele and such a landlord, it is a bit special. Built in the fourteenth or fifteenth century as a church house, it was later converted to a row of cottages. One of the cottages became an alehouse, which gradually expanded to become the inn you see today. The postcard above dates from around 1905, but the scene is still immediately recognisable. Iddesleigh is perhaps one of the most inaccessible villages in Devon, and, while there is a real sense that this is a place where the modern world has been kept at bay, the Duke of York, with its roaring log fires, barrels behind the bar and convivial long tables, is one of the most vibrant and popular inns in Devon.

Ide

The sixteenth-century Huntsman nearly came to grief in February 1849 when sparks from its brewhouse chimney set the thatch on fire. Three fire engines from Exeter attended the blaze, which, thanks to plentiful supplies of water from the adjoining brook, was brought under control. The damage was soon repaired, and on 5 August 1852 the *Exeter Flying Post* reported that 'a wrestling match took place at the village of Ide, commencing on Wednesday last and ending on Saturday, under the able management of Mr Tozer of the Huntsman Inn.' In 1872,

when the Huntsman was put up for auction, it was described as a 'commodious and well-appointed inn ... with cider and spirit cellars, skittle alleys, brewhouse, hoproom, stables and piggery, and also two excellent gardens, orchard and courtyard'. This photograph shows it in the 1930s, but it has hardly changed, and remains as popular as ever.

Up at the top of the village is an inn whose name has changed several times. Opened sometime before 1795 as the Exeter Inn, it was renamed the New Inn in the mid-nineteenth century. When a station opened at Ide in 1903, it became the Railway Inn, but when the station closed in 1958, it was renamed the Poacher's Inn. Apart from the change of name, it has hardly altered since this postcard was published around 1920, and remains a popular village local with a reputation for food and ale.

Ideford

An Edwardian view of a private carriage standing outside the Royal George at Ideford, five miles north of Newton Abbot. A century ago, only the wealthy could afford their own transport. Today, personal mobility is the norm, and, as if to emphasise the point, a large hole has been knocked in the wall behind the carriage to provide access to Ideford Garage. The George closed in the 1930s, and the right-hand side of the building became a shop. In the view below, looking in the opposite direction and dating from the 1940s, the shop can be seen on the left, with Ideford's other inn, the Royal Oak, on the right. The shop has since closed, the Royal George is now a pair of cottages, and the large oak tree beside the Royal Oak was felled in 1974, but the Royal Oak itself, a traditional, friendly village inn, is still very much in business.

Ilfracombe

The Admiral Rodney stood in an alley called Rodney Lane leading from the bottom of Fore Street to the harbour. It was named after Admiral Sir George Rodney, who scored a notable victory over the French at the Battle of the Saintes in 1782. By the end of the nineteenth century, local worthies were calling for it to be closed. An idea of the sort of objections raised can be gleaned from this report of a licensing session from the *North Devon Journal* of 3 September 1891:

Mr Alfred Wrighton, analytical chemist, one of the overseers of Ilfracombe, appeared to object to the renewal of the licence of the Admiral Rodney to James Buck. Mr Wrighton said he objected to the renewal because there were several fully-licensed houses within easy distance; because the licence was not required for the neighbourhood; because a multiplicity of licensed houses tended to increase poverty and crime; because the premises were not suitable to the purpose of an inn; because there was no stabling accommodation; and because the house was situated at the end of a dark passage. Mr Wrighton said the inn was not required by the people of the district. He produced a memorial against the granting of a licence, the signatures including those of the medical officer and several ministers. Mr Ffinch explained that the Admiral Rodney was much used by the pilots, and was the house to which telegrams and instructions to pilots were addressed. He produced a

petition signed by 165 seafaring men who made use of the inn for purposes of business. The police had not the slightest objection to the house, which was conducted in a proper manner. The bench granted the renewal.

The Admiral Rodney lasted for another 22 years before being closed in 1913. It was later demolished, but its signboard survives in Ilfracombe Museum.

Just along from the Admiral Rodney, near the bottom of Fore Street, was this building, identified on this early twentieth-century postcard as the Old Gander Inn. By the time the photograph was taken, however, it was a Marine Store run by Matthew and Annie Morris. In the mid-twentieth century, fish freshly landed in the harbour was sold in the shop on the right, and the building – albeit much altered – survives today. Unlike the rest of the buildings in the street, its entrance is a couple of steps below the level of the pavement, a clear sign of great age. It looks across to two of Ilfracombe's best-known pubs, the Prince of Wales and the George & Dragon, yet there seems to be no record, apart from this postcard, of it ever having been an inn known as the Gander.

An Edwardian postcard of the Posada Wine & Spirit Vaults in the High Street, which, like many wine and spirit vaults, held a licence to sell drinks on the

premises. In this case, customers could also enjoy a game of billiards. John Gaydon, who founded the business, came from Barnstaple, where he owned a wine merchant's. He also established the Lee Bay Hotel.

The railway arrived in Ilfracombe in 1874, but a coach service from Ilfracombe to Lynton & Lynmouth continued to operate until well into the twentieth century. The photograph above dates from the 1870s and shows a coach about to set off from Ilfracombe's Royal Clarence Hotel, built in the 1820s and named after the Duchess of Clarence, wife of the future King William IV, who visited Ilfracombe on 22 July 1827. For many years this was Ilfracombe's top hotel. It was the building of the chateau-like Ilfracombe Hotel on the sea front in 1871 that prompted the owners to revamp it in the latest style. The *North Devon Journal* for 19 May 1881 reported that 'the old Royal Clarence Hotel ... now presents by recent improvements a new face as well as increased accommodation'. The result was that a well-proportioned late Georgian building gave way to the ornate and over-fussy building seen on the right, which still towers over the narrow High Street. In the mid-twentieth century, its upper floors were converted to apartments, while the ground floor became a large bar, decorated like the saloon of an ocean liner. So convincing was the makeover that locals christened it the Ship; despite the reluctance of the owner, Charles Disney, official renaming soon followed and the Ship it remained until closure in the 1990s. After a period of dereliction, the building was refurbished in 2001 and now houses apartments and retail units.

GREAT · WESTERN · HOTEL,
HIGH STREET,
ILFRACOMBE.

The Great Western Hotel in Ilfracombe High Street was originally known as the London Inn and lay about 20 feet further back, at a slightly higher level. When the Great Western Railway opened a line from Taunton to Barnstaple in 1873, it also opened a booking office next to the London Inn, from where a coach service ran to their station in Barnstaple. The inn was renamed shortly afterwards. It seems to have been a lively place, if this report of a breakdown in Anglo-German relations, from the *North Devon Journal* of 6 November 1884, is anything to go by:

Wm Lewis, a young fellow, was charged with being drunk and disorderly at Ilfracombe on October 25th. PC Shepherd said about eleven pm he was called to the Great Western Hotel, where he saw defendant, who was very drunk. A scuffle took place between defendant and a member of the Season band. Witness cautioned them to desist, but Lewis afterwards ran towards the bandsman and struck him. A friend then took Lewis away. Both the men were drunk, but the bandsman had since left the town. Defendant now alleged that his assailant commenced the quarrel, and contended that he also ought to have been summoned. PC Stentiford gave corroborative evidence, and said Lewis was thrice cautioned before he left. He wanted to fight the German, but the latter walked away. Defendant was fined 5s.

Shortly after this, the inn was rebuilt. On 12 July 1888, the *Western Times* carried an advertisement announcing that 'this old-established hotel has been recently thoroughly renovated and rearranged, and placed under entirely new management.'

When it came up for auction in September 1908, it was described as having an 'entrance hall paved with tessellated tiles, saloon bar, smoking room, parlour, kitchen, scullery and offices, store and lavatory, wine and beer cellars, all on the ground floor. Large dining or club room with separate side entrance, coffee room, smoking room, sitting room, bathroom, 3 WCs and lavatory, 14 good bedrooms, large sale room and two very large ware rooms, lock-up coach house and stables, with separate side entrance from the High

Street'. By this time, however, it was already something of a white elephant, losing trade to better-equipped hotels with that all-important sea view, and in the 1930s, it was bought by the Free Church of England, whose church in Portland Street had been acquired by the council for road widening. They demolished the hotel and built a new church, designed in art-deco style by Bruce Oliver, on the site. It opened in May 1939, but closed less than ten years later and was converted to a cinema, which opened in October 1948. The cinema – now called the Embassy – is still there today, with Meridian Place heading steeply uphill through the archway beside it, as it did when the Great Western Hotel occupied the site.

The late-Victorian photograph above shows one of Ilfracombe's long-lost hostelries, the Crown, from the balcony of the Royal Britannia Hotel. The Crown was not only one of Ilfracombe's oldest buildings; it was, as can be seen, connected with the ramshackle collection of buildings behind it. When its licence came up for renewal in September 1884, it was opposed on the grounds that 'internal communications existed between the house and a private dwelling'. After a doorway was closed off with wire netting and a window made secure, so that drinks could no longer be passed through to the house next door, the licence was granted. The Crown faced a more insuperable problem, however. The street running between it and the Britannia was only 13 feet wide – no problem when the only people using it were fishermen and a handful of visitors, but, now that a pier had been constructed so that thousands of daytrippers could be brought in by paddle steamer, totally unacceptable. In March 1894, after several petitions had been presented to the council, a local government enquiry was set up to address the issue. Some people suggested demolishing the Britannia, some suggested demolishing the Crown – some even suggested demolishing them both – but in the end it was the Crown that went. A new Crown, built in line with the other buildings on the Quay, survives today as the Sandpiper Inn.

A view of Ilfracombe from Hillsborough before the pier was built in 1873, with the Britannia in the distance. Two more old inns can be seen at the end of the quay – the Steam Packet (later renamed the Pier) and the Golden Lion. Both were demolished in 1893 to widen the road and a new Pier Hotel was built, several yards further back.

The new Pier Hotel, built of the yellow Marland brick that characterises so much of Victorian Ilfracombe, is seen here in the 1920s. Today, with the brick painted over, it is known as the Pier Brewery Tap and Grill, having been taken over and refurbished in March 2014 by Bruce Hutton of Ilfracombe's Wizard Brewery.

Three doors along from the Pier Hotel was the White Hart, seen on the left in the 1920s. It still looked much the same over half a century later when the Barbeary family ran it, and was one of the most traditional pubs in town. Since then, change has come with a vengeance in the shape of Damien Hirst, who, since taking over in 1999, has transformed it into a restaurant called the Quay.

Below, a coach and four is seen heading east out of Ilfracombe in July 1907. In the background is the Cliffe Hydro Hotel, which overlooked the harbour and for many years had a popular non-residents' bar. After lying derelict and suffering several arson attacks, the Cliffe Hydro was demolished in 2007 to be replaced by retirement flats with a grandstand view of Damien Hirst's Verity sculpture.

As it continued eastwards out of Ilfracombe, the coach would have passed this thatched cottage at Chambercombe, built in the early nineteenth century as a cottage orné in the grounds of Laston House.In the mid-twentieth century it was acquired by Charles Disney (who also owned the Clarence) and became the Thatched Inn. Its most striking feature is an overhanging roof supported on gnarled tree trunks. Inside it is surprisingly spacious, with a central fire, intricate and ancient wood-panelling and olde-world atmosphere.

After climbing past the Thatched House, the coach would have dropped down to Hele, where in 1898 the Hele Bay Hotel opened. This picture shows it on a sunlit summer's day around 1910. Although the upper floors have been converted to flats, the popular Hele Bay Pub, complete with skittle alley, is still very much open.

Instow

Just off Instow's Marine Parade, up an old lane, is the Wayfarer Inn, seen here in the 1920s when it was known as the New Inn. Surprisingly little changed, except for an extension to the glazed veranda, it remains a genuine village inn, with a friendly mix of locals and visitors, beer straight from the barrel and home-cooked food.

Ipplepen

After the demise of the Plough in 2009, the Wellington is now the only pub in the populous village of Ipplepen. Fortunately it is big enough to cope, with two large bars sharing a roaring fire between them in winter, a dining and function area, and a large garden. This postcard dates from a century ago, but, although the road past the Wellington is now much busier, the only significant change to the outside of the building has been the addition of shutters to the first-floor windows.

Kennford

The Anchor at Kennford is seen above on an Edwardian postcard. It had already had one close call in March 1891, when sparks from its chimney set fire to the thatch. Thanks to villagers who clambered onto the roof to pull off the burning thatch, serious damage was averted. On 25 June 1926, however, the thatch caught fire again, after sparks from a passing steam lorry landed on it. This time the roof was totally destroyed and the building rendered uninhabitable. Although it was rebuilt and reopened, five years later the opening of a by-pass took its passing trade away. In 1935, Simonds' brewery, which owned it, applied to transfer the licence to a newly-built inn on the by-pass. When this opened in 1936, it was described as 'an up-to-date catering house, on road-house lines'. The photograph of the new Anchor below was taken in December 1938. But times move on; the by-pass has itself been by-passed by the A38 Devon Expressway and the new Anchor, like the one it replaced, is no more.

This view of Kennford's other pub, the Seven Stars, dates from around 1905. On 26 October 1875, the *Western Times* reported that the village had been hit by flooding:

> John Casely, of the Seven Stars, had his garden wall washed down, and his broccoli washed out of the ground, the water also being in his house to the depth of three or four feet, his beer and cider casks washed about the place, and his furniture washed and smashed. A great many of the poor people took their pigs up in their bedrooms to save them from drowning.

In June 2013, it was sold by Enterprise Inns. A few weeks later, it closed and an application was made to convert it to two dwellings. This was refused, but in April 2014 permission was granted for part of it to be converted to two cottages, as long as part of it reopened as a pub 'to ensure the local community facility is retained'. It reopened as a free house in April 2015, and by all accounts has quickly re-established itself as a proper local's pub.

Kenton

The Devon Arms, seen at the bottom of the opposite page, has, since 2007, been the Chi oriental restaurant. Kenton's other pub, however, the Dolphin – seen below – is still very much a traditional village local. The Dolphin originally stood on a different site, nearer the church, and was the most important inn in the village, until it fell victim to one of the worst fires in Devon's history. On 16 April 1856, 27 buildings – almost a third of the village – were completely destroyed, with over 100 people left destitute. The Dolphin, whose landlord, Richard Anning, had recently installed a new skittle alley, was 'entirely destroyed', along with '25 hogsheads of cider, 40 hogsheads of beer, a quantity of gin and rum, some 20 bushels of barley, three pockets of hops and a malt crusher'. It reopened on its present site shortly afterwards.

ALL THE FUN OF KENTON FAIR

'Whatever have been the mutations and transformations through which Kenton has passed, and scarcely a village in England has experienced more, the fair has not been swept away but remains the same as for many decades ... It was formerly located under the wall of the churchyard, opposite the village inn, which stood ... in close proximity to the church. The great fire which destroyed 27 houses in 1856, having 'removed' the Dolphin Inn, the fair had its venue changed to the principal street in the Exeter road, where flourished, and still continues to flourish, the Devon Arms, its booths extending from the principal entrance to that commodious and ornamental hostelry for a considerable distance alongside the ample street. The fair of Tuesday last was of average dimensions, and commanded a good attendance notwithstanding the unfavourable weather. It was fairly lively, and its principal feature was the trading by the young of both sexes in toothsome and other interesting commodities at the booths. The swinging boat with its juvenile freight ... was this year conspicuous by its absence, and the 'fun of the fair' comprised the refined sports of donkey racing and dancing in the assembly room of the Devon Arms to the melodious strains of the violin. There were no shows, as in days of yore, when the rustics 'gaped to catch Jack Pudding's jokes' [or] grinned through collars ... but there was much enjoyment and hilarity, and good order, which prevailed up to the close when jovial host Lingwell politely bowed his guests down the assembly-room staircase punctually at eleven o'clock, and the fair of 1884 was virtually over.'

From the *Western Times*, 29 February 1884

Kilmington

If ever there was a place to give the lie to those cynical pubco spokesmen who, after running down yet another village pub, declare such institutions unviable, it is Kilmington. This delightful village, with a population of around 750, boasts no less than two resoundingly traditional and resoundingly successful pubs – the Old Inn and the New Inn. The Old Inn, seen above, dates from the sixteenth or seventeenth century, while the New Inn, first licensed in 1805, occupies a fourteenth-century longhouse. The New Inn, seen below, was rebuilt after a major fire on 27 February 2004. It had another close shave in March 1933, when the licensing magistrates, declaring that 'the premises were in a bad state of repair and the sanitary arrangements totally inadequate', threatened to revoke its licence. They relented when the owners promised to spend £50 'without delay on the sanitation of the house and the necessary structural arrangements'.

King's Nympton

Another splendidly traditional thatched pub, with an enviable reputation for beer and food, is the Grove at King's Nympton, seen here over a century ago when it was the New Inn. Once owned by Barnstaple's Taw Vale Brewery, it was acquired in 1889 by Arnold, Perrett & Co of Wickwar in Gloucestershire, before being sold to Starkey, Knight & Ford seven years later. This award-winning free house looks little different today, apart from a large nameboard on the wall and three owls atop the thatch.

South Molton Road station opened in 1854, and the Fortescue Arms opened across the road soon afterwards. The station was the railhead for a large area, and the Fortescue was a busy place, holding auctions and hosting hunt meets. Although the station, renamed King's Nympton in 1950, is still open, the Fortescue, with its verandah gone and a modern extension taking the place of the buildings on the left, has been converted to a house.

Kingsteignton

BERRY FARM AND DEW DROP INN, KINGSTEIGNTON.

The Dew Drop Inn in Kingsteignton was originally a thatched cottage like Berry Farm next door, but in 1903 it was rebuilt in brick, and this postcard was published shortly afterwards. Although neither farm nor inn has changed much in the intervening century, the red brick of the inn is now covered in white render.

Kingston

Kingston once had two inns – the Britannia, at the east end of the village, and the Dolphin, whose position in the lee of the church suggests it may originally have been the church house. The Britannia closed years ago, but the Dolphin, with its low beams, open fire, real ales, home-cooked food and friendly welcome is still very much in business.

Kingswear

The Royal Dart, adjacent to Kingswear station, has seen many changes – and changes of name – over the years. In the early nineteenth century it was known as the Plume of Feathers. When the railway opened in 1864 it was renamed the Railway Hotel, but only two years later it was rebuilt as the Yacht Club Hotel. The following notice appeared in the *Western Daily Press* on 10 August 1866:

> The proprietors of the Castle Hotel, Dartmouth, beg to announce that their new hotel at Kingswear is now open, and will be found replete with every convenience for the reception of families visiting this charming neighbourhood. The hotel is contiguous to the railway station and the pier for the departure of the Channel Islands Steam Packet. Excursionists on the Dart will find, both here and at the Castle Hotel, Dartmouth (which has been lately renovated), admirable accommodation for dinners and refreshment at the shortest notice.

The new hotel included club rooms for the newly-formed Dart Yacht Club. When this became the Royal Dart Yacht Club six years later, the hotel changed its name to the Royal Yacht Club Hotel. In 1881, the club moved to a new clubhouse, prompting the owners of the hotel to rename it yet again, as the Royal Dart Hotel.

In October 1886, a travel writer called Maria Susannah Gibbons recorded her impressions of the hotel:

> At Dartmouth we took the steam ferry belonging to the railway company and crossed over to Kingswear. The crossing in the night, and seeing the little boats, or rather only their lanterns, moving swiftly along the surface of the water, had a weird effect ... We put up at the Royal Dart Hotel, a hostelry the perfect situation of which makes it perhaps worthwhile to pay its rather high charges – charges which would not be at all exorbitant in the season, when it is to be supposed that they have a cook and a proper staff of servants; but a mutton chop dished in perfectly cold gravy gives an idea that the cook is a thing of the past, or of the future – certainly not of the present – and the bill should be in accordance with the cooking. However, no one who really wishes to enjoy the beauty of

Dartmouth in all its picturesqueness should stay on the Dartmouth side of the river, but should follow our example and stay at Kingswear. Notwithstanding the cold gravy, we never regretted our plan.

A proper staff of servants was doubtless in attendance in November 1902, when Princess Beatrice and Princess Ena of Battenberg, along with their retinue, took over the hotel for five nights, while visiting Prince Alexander of Battenberg, a cadet on board HMS Britannia. In the Second World War, the hotel was requisitioned by the navy. Renamed HMS Cicala, it was the HQ of the British 15th Destroyer Flotilla, much of whose work involved smuggling resistance fighters and equipment into France and picking up allied servicemen who had escaped or evaded capture and been hidden by the resistance. In recent years, the Royal Dart has had several changes of ownership, and was closed at time of writing.

Knowle

In August 1885, the Anchor Brewery of Barnstaple offered the Ebrington Arms at Knowle near Braunton to let, with 'good trade, low rent, and easy coming in'. In 1918, when the Anchor Brewery closed, the pub was bought for £525 by Starkey, Knight & Ford. The auction particulars described it as a fully licensed house 'comprising tap room, bar, kitchens, parlours, four bedrooms, stabling, gardens, etc'. This photograph shows it in the 1930s with some striking shutters and the forecourt given over to cars. In 2009, the Ebrington was bought by Lee Slade from Barnstaple and is now one of the most popular free houses in North Devon. It actually looks much better today than it did when this photograph was taken. Not only are the shutters a good deal less striking; cars have been banished to the back and the front wall has been extended to enclose a tree-shaded beer garden kitted out with decking. Inside it remains a traditional community pub, with a commitment to real ale and a growing reputation for good food.

Knowstone

Apart from the cars habitually parked where the grass across the road once grew, the Masons Arms at Knowstone, high in the southern foothills of Exmoor, has hardly changed since the postcard above was published a century ago. Dating from the thirteenth century and believed to have been built by the masons who built the church, it may have started life as a church house, although how long it has been an inn is lost in obscurity. Obscurity is not something it suffers from these days, however. In 2005, it was taken over by Mark Dodson, former head chef at Michael Roux's Waterside Inn at Bray. The Masons Arms was awarded a Michelin star in 2006, and in 2010 was Michelin Pub of the Year. With all that going on, you might think that drinkers are no longer welcome. You'd be wrong. The restaurant – all minimalist chic with a ceiling boasting an Italianate mural – is at the back, but you enter through a bar that is as traditional, down-to-earth and welcoming as you'll find anywhere. Beerwise, it has another distinction. When Cotleigh Brewery started up in 1979, the Masons Arms was one of the first pubs to take their Tawny Owl bitter. It is still served today, and the pub is now Cotleigh's oldest customer.

Landkey

The Ring of Bells in Landkey may originally have been a church house. By 1613, however, it was a row of cottages which a local benefactor left in trust for the village to help support the poor. In 1792, the feoffees opened an inn in one of the cottages, naming it, not unreasonably given its proximity to the church, the Ring of Bells. Although they let it out by tender, they remained closely involved in its management. It remained, until recently, a traditional village inn, with skittle alley, local beer and home-cooked food. In 2013, however, permission was granted for its conversion to three dwellings.

Langtree

As can be seen by the windswept tree on this early twentieth-century postcard, the Green Dragon at Langtree stands high on a windy ridge. First licensed some time before 1714, it must have been a welcome sight to generations of travellers on the lonely road from Torrington to Holsworthy. Sadly, the splendid old building seen here is no more, having been burnt to the ground in March 1924 after sparks from the chimney landed on the thatch. It was soon rebuilt, however, and remains open as a traditional inn today.

Lapford

Three West Highland Terriers are led past the Yeo Vale Hotel near Lapford station in the 1920s. The station opened in 1854, and on 19 June 1862 the *North Devon Journal* advertised the auction of 'that newly-erected house, called the Yeo Vale Hotel':

> The house is very substantially built, and contains Parlour (with Cellar under), Tap-room, Bar, Kitchen, Store-room, 6 Bed-rooms, Closet, and large Attic. Detached is a Four-Stalled Stable, Loft, Sheds, &c. The Hotel is situate at the entrance to the Station, adjoining the Turnpike Road, near the Village and the intersection of Four other Roads. The above offers an opportunity rarely to be met with, for since the House was Licensed, a lucrative trade has been done, which can be greatly extended, and also Agencies for the Sale of Manure and Coal obtained.

For well over a century, the hotel remained busy and a well-known landmark on the Barnstaple-Exeter road. Today, though, it is a sorry sight. An application to convert it to a private house was dismissed on appeal in 2007. Eight years on, closed and forlorn, its future remains uncertain.

DONKEY RACING & SKITTLES AT THE YEO VALE INN

'On Monday the annual fair was held. The fair has recently lost its charter, on account of the absence of cattle on several occasions. However, Mr Cann came with his usual tempting display of confectionery, which was liberally patronised by the juveniles. A dance at the Old Malt Scoop terminated the proceedings of the day. On Tuesday, Lapford was all astir with the unusual picnic, which was held in Mr Hern's field, adjoining the village. Tea and a variety of amusements were heartily enjoyed by the villagers. A donkey race and skittle match followed at the Yeo Vale Inn. The Morchard Tradesmen's Band gave much satisfaction.'

From the *Exeter & Plymouth Gazette*, 17 July 1868

Lee

The Grampus at Lee is one of North Devon's most popular pubs, yet it has been open for less than 40 years. Before that, this 600-year-old building was known as the Old Farm (or Ye Olde Farme House) and had tea gardens in its grounds. Despite being a relative newcomer, the Grampus not only looks like a traditional pub, it feels like one, with a range of local ales, home-cooked food, skittles, darts and pool leagues, folk, jazz, blues and poetry sessions, and even a village shop. Recently it also opened its own microbrewery. And its location, deep in a fuchsia-filled valley, is one of the most idyllic in the county.

Lewdown

The Blue Lion at Lewdown is something of an enigma. English Heritage, who have given it a Grade II listing, declare it to be 'circa 1900, probably designed by Sabine Baring-Gould'. Which is puzzling. Baring-Gould, best remembered today for collecting folk songs, was a clergyman who in 1872 inherited a 3,000-acre estate at Lewtrenchard from his father. Nine years later, when the living fell vacant, he appointed himself vicar. He remained there until his death in 1924 and during that time was responsible for restoring the church and carrying out other building work in the village. The Blue Lion, however – originally called the Lewdown Inn – was there long before he was born. Documents in Devon Record Office show that in 1823 it was owned by Edward Searle, and in 1854, when it was known as Perkin's Lewdown Inn, a sale of '424 superior oak trees' was held there. On 16 June 1899, a notice appeared in the *Western Times*:

> To be let by tender all that fully-licensed house and premises, known as the Lewdown Inn, in the parish of Lewtrenchard, Devon, together with about 63 acres of land, late in the possession of Mr Thomas Hutchings, deceased. The house is situated on the main road from Launceston to Okehampton, and is the only fully-licensed house between Lifton and Bridestowe.

It was still known as the Lewdown Inn on Whit Monday 1904, when the Lewdown Friendly Society held its annual dinner there, 'attended by the Launceston Band', but it had been renamed by November 1906, when 'the half-yearly rent audit of the tenants of the Rev S Baring-Gould was held at the Blue Lion.' Baring-Gould, as lord of the manor, was undoubtedly behind the renaming, and, with his interest in restoring and designing buildings, may well have made alterations to the inn, but the core of the building appears to date from the eighteenth century if not earlier. Evidence provided by old OS maps confirms not only that the Lewdown Inn and the Blue Lion were the same building, but that its footprint hardly altered from the mid-nineteenth to the mid-twentieth century. The postcard above shows it around 1930. The only major change since then has been the continuation of the ground-floor extension along the whitewashed side wall of the building. In 2014, it was sold to a local man who aims to make it once again the social hub of the village.

Lifton

On 1 December 1842, the *Exeter Flying Post* advertised the sale by auction of

> that commodious and desirable property, called the Arundell Arms Inn in the town of Lifton ... now and for many years past in the occupation of Mr William Newberry ... consisting of kitchens, bar, cellars, and three parlours on the ground floor; one large room for public occasions, and seven bedrooms on the first floor, besides other rooms and conveniences; courtyards, outhouses, pump, dairies, three stables (having an extensive frontage towards the street containing accommodation for 50 horses), coach house, old malt house, pigs' houses and other outbuildings, together with an orchard and excellent garden, with a large summer house.

One thing the advertisement failed to mention was the cockpit, a reminder of less refined times, but now, converted to a fishing-tackle store, one of the inn's most treasured features. Today, behind its unassuming façade, stripped of the creeper that covered it when the photograph above was taken in the early twentieth century, lies one of Devon's best loved hotels, which has been run by the Fox-Edwards family since 1961.

Littlehempston

The Bolton Arms at Littlehempston near Totnes almost certainly started life as a church house. It is not known when it became an inn, although it must have opened some time before 1840, when the *Exeter & Plymouth Gazette* announced the death on 1 December of 'Mr J Evans of the Bolton Arms, sincerely regretted by his numerous friends and acquaintances'. Apart from an extension to the gable end, it still looks much as it did when the postcard at the top of the opposite page was published in the 1930s. In 1952, it was renamed the Tally Ho, after a farmhouse half a mile north of the village. After closing in November 2011, the villagers campaigned against an application by the owners to convert it to a house, negotiating with them to explore ways of reopening or buying it and holding regular meetings to drum up support. In December 2012, it was listed as an asset of community value, and in March 2014, after raising the money to buy

it and carrying out the necessary work, it reopened as South Devon's first community pub. At a time when so many pubs are going to the wall, the crowning of the efforts of Littlehempston's villagers with success is not only fantastic for them but serves as a splendid inspiration to those whose local pubs are similarly under threat.

Liverton

The Welcome Stranger, like the Toby Jug at Bickington, the Anchor at Kenton and the Woodpecker at South Brent, stood on the old A38, long since superseded by the Devon Expressway. Unlike them, however, it has survived the loss of its passing trade. Originally known as the New Inn, this postcard was published after Simonds renamed it the Welcome Stranger in the 1940s. In June 2014, it was taken over by new owners who brought with them a reputation for food from their previous pub, the Claycutters at Chudleigh Knighton.

Longdown

The Lamb at Longdown, just west of Exeter, has changed little since this postcard was published in the early twentieth century, but it is now surrounded by modern houses rather than thatched cottages. It remains a traditional two-roomed free house, divided into restaurant and bar, with a growing reputation for well-kept ale and home-cooked food

Lower Ashton

A small two-storey extension has been added to the Manor Inn at Lower Ashton in the Teign valley, but otherwise it still looks much as it did when this postcard was published in the early twentieth century. Although it has an enviable reputation for food, it still remains a welcoming village pub with a selection of local real ales.

Lundy Island

For centuries, Lundy Island, home to only a handful of families, managed without an inn. All that changed in 1863 when a company won the rights to quarry granite on the island and shipped around 300 quarrymen in. They erected several buildings, including a store, part of which was used as a tavern. Despite massive capital investment, the quarries closed in 1868, but the store and the tavern remained open. The photograph of the tavern above, with an advert for Allsopp's India Pale Ale prominently displayed, appeared in the *Wide World Magazine* in 1906.

It isn't clear when it became known as the Marisco Tavern, but by 5 February 1940, when the *Western Morning News* featured the story of a 19-year-old land-army girl called Margaret Burfitt who had been sent to the island, they could write that 'the centre of social life on Lundy is the Marisco Tavern, built who knows how long ago, with granite walls two feet thick, and a granite floor polished by the iron-shod feet of generations of fishermen and farm men, captains of pilot cutters, and the crews of windbound vessels sheltering in Lundy's roads. The tavern is more of a club to the inhabitants of Lundy than a pub. They all forgather there most nights of the week, and play games of darts, shove ha'penny and table skittles, listen to the radio and talk.' On 22 August 1946, the *North Devon Journal* reported that 'no taxes are levied on the islanders and its only public house is ready to serve the twelve inhabitants at any hour of the day.'

In 1959, the American writer John Sack, in a book called *Report from Practically Nowhere*, included an account of a typical night at the tavern:

I returned to the Marisco Tavern; the tourists had left, and Mr Gade, Audrey, and two or three islanders were sitting quietly in the darkness, desperately trying to recover their poise. Now the Marisco Tavern was a friendly, easygoing place, and these people made it so. Mr Gade, using all the slow deliberation of a bartender pouring a pousse-cafe, had filled his pipe, and he was leaning against the gray stone wall, cheerily smoking it; the others were sitting with beer mugs in their laps and talking idly of the unimportant, important things of life. They were dressed in plaid shirts and disintegrating pin-stripe suits; their faces were stubbled, weather-beaten. The Captain and Charlie, who ran the boats at the waterfront, came from there in black turtleneck sweaters, nodded for a beer apiece, and started throwing darts at a raggedy bull's-eye, beginning each of their games with an esoteric cry of 'Middle for diddle!' or 'Muggs away!' A few others drifted in, and every now and then the gathering raised its glasses, toasting itself with enthusiasm: 'All the very best!'

The postcard below shows the tavern as it appeared around this time. In 1982, the Landmark Trust, who had taken over responsibility for Lundy in 1969, embarked on a programme of modernisation. The island's increasing popularity meant that the old bar was far too small, but many regular visitors were unhappy with the changes, which extended the tavern into the building to the left, and substituted a serving hatch for the old bar counter. In 1984, a brewery was set up at the tavern, but, after brewing had to be suspended for a couple of years due to an acute shortage of water, it closed in 1995. Today, memories of the old Marisco Tavern have faded, and, despite the reservations expressed at the time, it remains a place which should feature on every pub-lover's must-visit list. The food – featuring Lundy lamb, Lundy venison and Lundy goat – is terrific, the bar, ably run by Grant Sherman, serves beers from St Austell Brewery, and the conviviality is second to none.

Lydford

The Castle Inn dates from around 1550 and may originally have been built for the keeper of the nearby castle. It later became a farmhouse, with a sideline in selling beer and cider, before opening as the White Horse Inn in 1807. By 1868, it had been renamed the Castle. With its slate floors, high-backed settles and a twelfth-century fireplace from the castle, it is a popular and welcoming hostelry, despite having one of the most forbidding buildings in Devon for a neighbour.

On the main road a mile west of Lydford, with the moor at its back, is the Dartmoor Inn, which from the outside looks much the same today as when this car pulled up outside in the 1920s. In January 1867, Horace Waddington recorded his impressions of this ancient hostelry after a 15-mile tramp over the moor:

With this we had reached the Lyd, here dividing the granite from the adjoining metamorphic slates. A water wheel, some 30 feet in diameter, ruinous buildings and perilous old shafts, here mark another shaft abandoned by miners. We crossed the stream, and traversing Highdown, entered once more by a gate upon the civilised world, sitting down somewhat weary in the clean little parlour of the Dartmoor Inn ... The Dartmoor Inn is a mile from Lydford, but is a better hostelry than will be found in the village itself. We had two large jugs of freshest milk; for this, with bread and cheese, and a bottle of lemonade, the large sum of one shilling was demanded, a charge which we recommend to the imitation of landlords, the envy and astonishment of travellers in general.

Waddington was privileged, for most visitors got no further than the small bar at the front of the building. In 1966, though, the parlour was turned into the back bar. Since then, the inn has been transformed into one of Devon's top dining pubs, with five subtly-lit dining areas and a menu influenced by Scandinavia and New England. Real ale is still available in the bar, however, and a log fire still burns in the grate.

Lympstone

YE OLD SADDLERS ARMS LYMPSTONE 22285

The Saddler's Arms in Lympstone has sprouted single-storey extensions to the front and side since this postcard was published early last century, transforming a small village inn into a large dining pub. Events such as steam rallies and furry dances are still held at the Saddler's, although the annual Lympstone Fair seems to have fallen into abeyance. Judging by a report in the *Western Times* on 24 July 1866, that may not be such a bad thing:

> Lympstone Annual Fair – This annual affair came off in the field behind the Saddler's Arms on Thursday. For a wonder there was only one accident. Mr W Payne, late of the Saddler's Arms, in wrestling 'for fun' with an athletic young man-of-war's-man, got thrown so violently that his collar bone was fractured and he was obliged to be taken to the hospital.

Lynmouth

When the Rising Sun at Lynmouth was put up for auction in 1895, it was advertised as having 'a most lucrative business, being the nearest licensed house to the terminus of the cliff railway, the esplanade and the proposed pier and to the present landing place. It is calculated that the visitors to Lynmouth will more than double when the railway from Barnstaple is opened, and every visitor to the well-known Lynmouth beach and tower passes these premises, which, in fact, form one of the picturesque objects of this charming spot.'

Almost 120 years on, the railway from Barnstaple has come and gone, the proposed pier was never built, and much of the historic fabric of this most romantic of all Devon's resorts was swept away by the devastating flood of 1952. The Rising Sun, however – seen above around 1910 – has not only survived (along with the cliff railway) but has expanded into several adjoining cottages. Despite being at the epicentre of one of North Devon's tourist honeypots, the Rising Sun not only looks much the same as it did a century ago, it still offers a traditional welcome and a selection of local ales.

A charabanc heading down into Lynmouth in the 1920s

Malborough

The Royal Oak in Malborough, seen here in 1934, looks much the same today, and is still a popular local, with regular acoustic jam sessions and live music. When it was advertised for sale in the *Exeter & Plymouth Gazette* on 1 April 1887, it came with a 'stable, piggery, shed, and premises thereto belonging'. When it came on the market again 38 years later, the *Western Daily Press* of 11 September 1925 advertised the freehold, fixtures and utensils for a 'quick sale' at £775.

Marldon

When this photograph of the Old Smokey House in Marldon was taken a century ago, the sign above the door bore its official name of the Ship Inn, although the sign above that proclaimed it to be the Old Original Smokey House. A correspondent in the *Western Morning News* on 28 July 1927 revealed that 'behind this queer title

there is a lost story of the thrills and tragedies of smuggling days, for a "smokey house" was a secluded and conveniently-placed rendezvous, from the chimneys of which volumes of smoke, caused by piling the wide fireplace with peat and brushwood, could be viewed from a ship at sea when danger was abroad.' Since this photograph was taken, the building of an enormous extension has transformed the old alehouse into one of the most popular dining pubs in the Paignton area

Meavy

The Royal Oak Inn at Meavy was built as a church house in the fifteenth century, and is still owned by the parish council today. It takes its name from the oak tree on the green, estimates of whose age range from 800 to 1000 years. This postcard shows it a century ago and it has hardly changed. Remarkably unspoilt and unashamedly traditional, the Royal Oak, despite its reputation for fine food and local ales, is still very much a community pub, with a programme of live music and other events throughout the year. With its flagstone floor, beamed ceilings and superb setting, the Royal Oak comes about as close to the ideal of a traditional village pub as you are likely to get.

A VISIT TO MEAVY IN 1834

'The secluded hamlet of Meavy is situated in a broad valley, on the very edge of the great Devonshire moor. It consists of a few neat cottages and an antique church, surrounded by the 'last home' of many a moorland peasant. Immediately in front of the churchyard wall is the gigantic Meavy Oak. This venerable tree, though it has suffered from the touch of age, still continues proudly magnificent. It is of an extraordinary circumference, and is completely hollowed out by the slow but never-failing operations of time. The cavity, as is affirmed by mine hostess of the Royal Oak, a little inn standing hard by, once accommodated nine persons at a dinner party: it is now used as a turf house ... The only 'hostel' in the village is the Royal Oak which, though of humble exterior, affords comfortable accommodation to the way-worn traveller. In summer this is a halting place for amateur fishermen who stroll from the neighbouring towns to try their piscatorial skill in the waters of the Plym. He who is fond of studying character in the kitchen of a country inn cannot do better than spend a winter's evening by the blazing peat fire of the Royal Oak, for it will afford him a fine opportunity of remarking the peculiarities of the untutored children of the moor; and perchance he may be treated with a tale of the pixies which are said to haunt the rugged brow of Sheepstor.'

From the *South Devon Monthly Museum*, No 19, July 1834

Meeth

The New Inn at Meeth – now renamed the Bull & Dragon – is a popular fifteenth-century hostelry in west Devon. Although it looks much the same today as when this postcard was published a century ago, the buildings to the left of it have gone. Inside, it retains the ambience of a traditional village pub, with a strong community following and a reputation for an adventurous range of home-cooked food

Merrivale

The Dartmoor Inn at Merrivale in the 1920s, with spoil from Tor Quarry looming over it.

Originally built as a row of cottages, it stands near the old bridge which carried the packhorse road from Princetown to Tavistock across the River Walkham. Tor quarry closed in 1997, the road has been diverted across a new bridge, and it is walkers rather than quarrymen who now frequent the Dartmoor Inn, set amid some of the finest scenery on Dartmoor, with four local ales lined up to quench their thirst.

Milton Abbot

There were once two inns in Milton Abbot: the King's Arms and the New Inn. The New Inn closed before the First World War, and in the late 1920s it was announced that the King's Arms would be demolished for road widening. As this would have left the village with no pub nearer than Lamerton or Launceston, a petition with 230 signatures was handed to the magistrates asking for the licence to be transferred to another building. They agreed, and a new pub, the Edgcumbe Arms, opened in 1930. It is seen here on a postcard from the 1940s, but looks much the same today.

Milton Combe

On 28 March 1906, a correspondent in the *Exeter & Plymouth Gazette* wrote that, 'in the hamlet of Milton Combe, there are two public houses. One is called the First and

Last ... but the other bears the extraordinary title of the Who Would Have Thought It Inn. The explanation given is that the former was the first inn established, and that when the second was opened it was called by its extraordinary title as a sarcastic reference to the opinion of the first landlord that his would be the First and Last.'

Both were originally beerhouses, run by Abraham Beer and John Spear. By 1893, although John Spear was still a beerhouse keeper, Abraham Beer was landlord of the fully-licensed Who Would Have Thought It. An alternative explanation as to how it got its name is that, when Abraham Beer applied for a full licence, his surprise at it being granted caused him to utter the words immortalised on the signboard. Be that as it may, in 1908, as part of their campaign to reduce the number of public houses, the magistrates refused to renew the licence of the First and Last. The postcard on the previous page shows Abraham Beer standing at the door of the Who'd Have Thought It at around the time it became the only pub in the village. A century on, it remains a cosy, traditional pub with a wood-panelled bar and an excellent choice of ales, while its commitment to locally-sourced food includes chicken and black pigs at the bottom of the garden. Proof once again that, however small the village, it is never too small to support a well-run pub.

Milton Damerel

WOODFORD BRIDGE HOTEL, MILTON DAMEREL, N. DEVON.

This postcard of the Woodford Bridge Hotel at Milton Damerel was sent to Worthing in Sussex on 15 August 1939, and included the information that 'this hotel is converted from an old inn on the Holsworthy to Bideford road.' Although originally known as the Woodford Bridge Inn, by 1846, when the landlord was a Mr Blake, it was also known as Blake's Hotel. On 20 March 1914, the *Exeter & Plymouth Gazette* advertised for sale that well-known freehold hostelry, with a full seven days license, called and known as the Bridge Inn, situate at Woodford Bridge in the parish of Milton Damerell, Devon. The house contains bar, bar parlour, large kitchen, large dining room, dairy, scullery, and other offices with 6 large bedrooms above. There are a capital stable, loose boxes, carriage house, cow houses, a nice grass paddock, orchard, garden and skittle alley, the whole extending over an area of about one acre. Woodford Bridge ... abuts on the River Torridge, well known for its fishing, and is one of the best wayside inns in the country, being a well-known resort for fishermen and tourists, and is in the centre of a country regularly hunted by a pack of foxhounds.

In 1926, it suffered a fate that has since befallen so many once famous inns; its owner, Frederick Mills, closed it and converted it to a private house. Thirteen years later, however, he reapplied for a licence, only to face concerted opposition from local residents, as this report from the *Exeter & Plymouth Gazette* for 3 February 1939 reveals:

Opposition which he described as incredible and fantastic faced Mr T Oerton of Bideford, when applying on behalf of Mr Frederick William Mills, of the Woodford Bridge Hotel, Milton Damerel, for a conditional licence, authorising the sale of liquor only to persons resident in the hotel or bona fide dining, lunching, or partaking of food, at Holsworthy Brewster Sessions yesterday.

Mr WM Mitchell of Launceston opposed the application on behalf of residents in the parish and submitted a petition bearing 143 names.

Mr Oerton said the premises were always fully licensed up to 1926, when Mr Mills surrendered the licence and converted the hotel into a private house. Since then the applicant had suffered financial loss and now wished to reopen the premises as a private hotel. Improvements effected had cost nearly £8,000.

The question of what constituted a meal was asked, and Mr Mitchell submitted that nothing prevented a visitor or parishioner calling for a small sandwich and being served with drink, but Mr Oerton said the difficulty could be overcome by serving only persons with substantial meals at a cost of about two shillings.

Evidence was given in opposition that the granting of a licence would exercise a disastrous effect on young people, while the Rev Merritt (superintendent of the circuit) contended that the application was simply 'a multiplication of noughts', and that the motive behind it was wrong, morally and socially.

After hearing evidence lasting nearly two hours, the Bench decided to grant the licence subject to the following conditions: liquor to be supplied as suggested by Mr Oerton, only to persons residing in the hotel and bona fide lunching or dining there; the monopoly value to be paid as agreed by the Customs and Excise, and that fire extinguishers should be provided as required by the police.

Since then the hotel has gone from strength to strength. Although the thatched building seen here, which housed the original inn, looks much the same, not only has it been greatly extended, but it is surrounded by a complex of suites and lodges, with 103 guest rooms, a heated indoor pool and spa facilities, all of which goes by the name of the Woodford Bridge Country Club.

Modbury

Despite being some distance from the church, the Bell Inn was originally the Church House Inn. It was renamed the Bell when the bell from the yarn market was moved there after the market was demolished. On this postcard from around 1905, the housing for the bell can be seen to the left of the signboard. In 1881, when the Bell was put up for sale, 'with the consent and approval of the charity commissioners', it was bought by the tenant, James Beard, for £515. Less than 30 years later, in 1909, the magistrates withdrew its licence. Although it has long been a shop, the bell is still there, and the opening ceremony of the annual glove fair still takes place outside the building.

The half-timbering on its façade may be a twentieth-century pastiche, but the Exeter Inn is the oldest surviving inn in Modbury, dating back to the sixteenth century or earlier and boasting a splendid plasterwork ceiling on the first floor. It is believed to have been first licensed in 1563, and Royalists are said to have met here during the Civil War. When offered for sale in December 1823, it was described as 'that well-known and much frequented inn and tavern', with 'a new and substantially built malthouse, with suitable storerooms, stables and other appendages, contiguous to the inn yard, but having a distinct communication, capable of working 160 bushels weekly'. On this early twentieth century postcard, the inn can be seen with its newly applied half timbering on the right. Today, the Exeter Inn remains a popular and welcoming meeting place, with a reputation for food and entertainment.

MODBURY NAPPY ALE

Although now little more than a village Modbury once returned members to Parliament, and rejoiced in a portreeve, two constables, and an ale-taster, the latter being a most important functionary in Modbury at a time when the little town was famous for its nappy ale, described by the historian Westcote as being the best in the county. He attributes the longevity of the inhabitants of the town to the free use of the home-brew, being, as he avers, meat, drink, and almost clothes.

From *Picturesque South Devonshire* by WHK Wright, 1905

Monkokehampton

An early twentieth-century postcard of Monkokehampton, with the Old Swan Inn in the distance. When advertised to let in 1886 it was described as an 'old established and fully licensed public house' with 'good fishing in the neighbourhood'. A report in the *Exeter Flying Post* for 14 December 1854 gives an idea how central the inn was to village life:

> The two adjoining parishes of Monkokehampton and Broadwoodkelly are being united in an endeavour to give encouragement, in the immediate districts, to those employed in agricultural pursuits by offering prizes for the best ploughing; and to labourers and servants, prizes for long servitude. The result of their first united efforts came off on Wednesday, the 29th ult. The ploughing took place on Barnstown estate, Monkokehampton, occupied by Mr William Snell (Upcott); and a dinner was provided at the Swan Inn, Monkokehampton, to which a goodly and respectable number sat down, under the presidency of the Rev Henry Mowbray Northcott, assisted by Mr William Snell as vice ... The usual loyal toasts and attendant sentiments were duly gone through; but the crowning toast was 'Success to the Monkokehampton and Broadwoodkelly Ploughing Match'.

In 1983, the inn was bought by Peter and Midge Andrews, who ran it successfully for a time, although by the early 1990s it was clear that trade was declining. After Mr Andrews died in 1997, his widow continued to run it for a year before calling last orders, claiming that there were only two regulars and on some nights she was on her own in the bar. She applied to convert it to a house, but in 1999, following a campaign by villagers, West Devon Council refused permission. Sixteen years on, it is still stalemate, with the bar just as it was on the night the Old Swan closed.

Moretonhampstead

The Plymouth Inn in Court Street was opened by John Bellamy in the 1830s and remained in his family until the early twentieth century. The postcard above, looking west, shows it as it looked around 1910; the postcard below, looking east, shows it after the ground floor was altered and the dormer windows removed around 1930. It closed in 2003, and has since been converted to holiday lets.

The White Hart was Moretonhampstead's principal coaching inn. Believed to have been built on the site of a group of cottages destroyed by fire in the eighteenth century (although one source suggests it dates back to 1693), it was not only a posting house, but also the venue for balls and assemblies, and for the meeting of the last great stannary parliament in 1793. Seen here on a postcard from around 1905, it has hardly changed, although its portico has been moved closer to the wall to make more room for passing traffic, and the White Hart Tap, which can be seen at the back with its own entrance, has been incorporated into the inn. The White Hart is one of the best appointed and most popular inns on Dartmoor, having reopened under new management after a major refurbishment in mid-2012.

Next door but one was the White Hart's great rival, the White Horse, seen on the opposite page. First recorded as an inn in the late eighteenth century, for over a hundred years – from the 1820s to the 1930s – it was run by the Gray family. On 11 September 1838 the White Horse, along with the White Hart, was nearly destroyed by fire. According to a report in the *Western Times*, the fire

is supposed to have originated in the house of a person named Langridge, adjoining the White Horse Inn, kept by Mr S Gray ... In the out premises of this inn there was lodged a small barrel of gunpowder, to get at which, in the then state of the building, would have been a work of the greatest hazard; and for a time it rendered persons very cautious how they approached this part. The explosion, however, at length gave notice that no further danger was to be apprehended from this source, and the exertions of the inhabitants were redoubled. To the eastward, the fire communicated to the house and premises of Mrs Stevens, which immediately adjoin the White Hart Inn. To save the former was evidently impossible, the town engine therefore, the only one they had, was brought to play with great effort on the latter, and by these means, and the extraordinary exertions of the inhabitants, this inn was saved from destruction, although not without injury to some part of the premises, but not so as to interrupt the business of the house. Westward, the

flames made terrible havoc, clearing the houses between and extending from the White Horse Inn into Pound Street, until checked in that street by a house covered with slate, the intervening buildings having been covered with thatch ... Great fears were entertained for the houses on the opposite side of the way from Mrs Stevens, and the White Hart, and also for the houses between Pound Street and Court Street, being all covered with thatch, but by men stationed on these, and supplied with water, they were preserved ... We are informed that Mr Samuel Gray is removing to a house at a short distance westward in the same street, where he intends to accommodate his numerous customers pro tem; and which from Mrs Gray's and his well-known civility and attention, many respectable and influential individuals are endeavouring to secure for them their favours, now that his loss has been so severe in this calamitous conflagration. The loss of Mr Gray is very great, and among other property of his, eleven fine pigs were burnt to death. The barrel of gunpowder that was on his premises was 56lb of rock powder, which was lodged there but a day or two before, for a farmer in the country. Mr Gray had a great objection to it being left at his house, and when he at length consented, ordered it to be taken to the back part of his premises, and lodged in his slaughter house; and but for this precaution, the consequences might have been much worse. As it is, to this it was most probably owing that the pigs were burnt, for immediately on the alarm, Mr Gray made it publicly known that gunpowder was there, and the place in which it was lodged, but the fire spread with such rapidity in that direction that forbad anyone from going near it. When the explosion took place, the concussion was sensibly felt, and the glass in many windows at a distance from the fire was shattered.

By 2006, the White Horse, though still a popular drinking venue, was very much in need of refurbishment. Since then, new owners have transformed its fortunes, renaming it the Horse and turning it into one of the most popular dining spots in the area, while keeping it as a community pub, with regular live music.

The White Hart and White Horse may have escaped the flames, but Moretonhampstead's New Inn has not been so lucky. It was built in the late fifteenth or early sixteenth century and extended in the seventeenth. By the mid-eighteenth century it had closed as an inn – presumably because its centuries-old charm was no match for the attractions of the White Hart or White Horse. It was divided into four properties, one of which became the Punch Bowl Inn. On 15 January 1839, when the whole building was put up for auction, it was divided into two lots. Lot 1 was 'all that old established inn or public house called the Punch Bowl ... consisting of a large underground cellar, tap room, bar and parlour, and lodging room over, divided by sliding partitions, together with a garden skittle alley, stabling, piggery, brew house, and other offices, all adjoining, with an abundant supply of water'. Lot 2 comprised 'three dwelling houses, now in the occupation of ... yearly tenants, and formerly occupied by a tallow chandler, to which purpose it can again be converted at a trifling expense. This lot also has the advantage of an extensive yard, garden, and suitable offices immediately behind the dwelling houses; in front a never-failing spring of water, on which account it would be advantageous for carrying on the malting trade.' When it was sold by auction again on 21 September 1869, this time as one lot, a shoemaker's shop had opened in one of the adjoining houses. The auction particulars included the information that the building had 'a frontage of nearly 60 feet and [extended] over 200 feet in depth'. The renewal of the Punch Bowl's licence was refused by the magistrates in 1908, as part of a campaign to reduce the number of licensed premises. The first of the two postcards opposite was published before the Punch Bowl closed; its sign can be seen above the cart parked outside the shoemaker's shop. The second was published some years later, when a variety of businesses, including tea rooms and a petrol station, occupied the building. It survived until 11 September 2007, when a devastating fire ripped through it, virtually destroying it and leaving an empty space where one of Moretonhampstead's best-known landmarks had stood for over five centuries.

Another of Moretonhampstead's oldest hostelries – despite appearances to the contrary – is the Bell. It was first recorded in 1740, when it belonged to Thomas Brock and was described as 'a public inn known by the sign of the Bell formerly in the possession of William Ashford deceased and now of James Hillman'. An ancient oak beam in the bar is said to have borne images of the king's head, before it was defaced by parliamentary soldiers in the Civil War. Upstairs, recently uncovered and restored wall paintings are believed to have been executed by Napoleonic prisoners of war. In the eighteenth and nineteenth centuries, it was the venue for assemblies, balls, wrestling matches and other social and sporting occasions. The Bell does not look that old, however, because in the late nineteenth century it was acquired by St Anne's Well Brewery, who were clearly unhappy with the state of it. On 28 May 1919, the following report appeared in the *Exeter & Plymouth Gazette*:

Before the justices at Moretonhampstead Petty Sessions yesterday Mr LD Thomas, on behalf of the St Anne's Well Brewery Company, Exeter, submitted plans for proposed alterations at the Bell Inn, Moreton, and asked for the approval of the bench ... The owners felt that the house at present was badly lighted and inadequately ventilated. The absence of sufficient light, he submitted, made supervision, both by the police and the landlord, difficult, and the absence of proper means of ventilation was, of course, undesirable, and a matter they wished to remedy. The only way his clients had seen it possible to defeat these two defects was by acquiring the adjoining cottage. Consequently, they had taken this, and were prepared to commence reconstruction at an early date if the bench approved. By the acquirement of the cottage, the accommodation of the house would be greater. There would be more bar space, but, as far as the tap room was concerned, that would be reduced in size. A new feature was proposed in the nature of a tea or commercial room which would, in the opinion of the owners, supply a want in the town. The rooms would be well lighted and of good ventilation, and would be easy of supervision by the licensee from the centre of a circle and by the police.

The proposals were accepted, and the Bell Inn was transformed from the modest building seen above, on the left-hand corner of Cross Street, to the half-timbered edifice seen below, whose etched-glass windows still bear the name of St Anne's Well Brewery.

Mortehoe

View from Top Hill, Mortehoe.

Copyright L.L.Mho.32.

The Chichester Arms, seen in the postcard above on the right, was built in the eighteenth century as a vicarage and became an inn in 1820. Slate-hung, like many buildings on this wild stretch of coast, today it has been painted white and its windows adorned with blue shutters. Although popular with the holidaymakers who flock to this area in the summer, it is still very much a village pub with an excellent selection of real ales.

Muddiford

A postcard published by Grattan Phillipse, an Ilfracombe photographer, of a coach outside the New Inn at Muddiford in 1906. Mr Pugsley, the landlord, stands by with

arms proudly folded. The New Inn was on the scenic road from Barnstaple to Ilfracombe, built by a turnpike trust in 1830 to avoid the steep gradients on other routes between the two towns. By 1906, however, travellers between Barnstaple and Ilfracombe went by train and the New Inn was forced to rely on local trade and excursions such as the one seen on the previous page, with a group of men out from Berrynarbor for the day. With the advent of mass motoring, the New Inn's fortunes rose once again: the postcard above shows the inn around 1930, newly extended and refurbished, with a car standing by a petrol pump on the forecourt. Today, renamed the Muddiford Inn, this wayside hostelry is more popular than ever, with a large car park across the road and an award-winning restaurant serving locally-sourced food.

Newton Abbot

The Wolborough Inn on Wolborough Street as it looked in the 1920s. While many much grander inns have fallen by the wayside, the Wolborough has survived to become one of Newton Abbot's top real-ale pubs, with a growng reputation. Still recognisable today, the windows on the right have been fitted with glass to match those on the left.

Fred Tozer, whose name appears on the sign-board of the Devon Arms in East Street in this Edwardian photograph, was a noted greyhound trainer. After a spell as the Greene Man, the pub is now known as the Teign Cellars, and stocks one of the widest ranges of craft and cask beer in the county. Its cellar once formed part of the Newton Abbot poorhouse, whose inmates were forced to pick oakum where barrels of beer are now stored.

The Cork Club sets off on an outing from the Cider Bar on East Street in Newton Abbot in 1911. Over a century on, the Cork Club is still going strong, as is the Cider Bar. With over 20 local ciders and country wines, a visit to this time-warped tavern is essential not just for cider aficionados but for anyone who wants to soak up the atmosphere of one of Devon's most iconic and idiosyncratic gems. It opened some time before 1878, when William Vening was the landlord. Eleven years later, he was listed as a 'cider and milk dealer' – an interesting combination, and one not continued by his successor, Frank Hambly, nor indeed by Richard Knibbs, who has now been running the Cider Bar for over 40 years.

IN PRAISE OF CIDER

Traditional farmhouse cider is more popular than ever, but Devon, the home of so much good cider and so many good cider makers, has had 90% of its cider orchards grubbed up or abandoned since 1945. That does not just mean that far less cider is being produced; it also means that many local varieties have disappeared for ever. Cider makers are fighting back, however, and new orchards are being planted, some of them the result of council-backed schemes to create community orchards. For the first time in over a century, the number of cider apple trees in Devon is actually increasing, as the demand for traditional, locally-grown produce grows.

The list of the cider apples grown in Devon is a long and distinguished one, redolent of a vanished world. The names are as rich and heady as the aroma of the ciders once made from them: names such as All Doer, Beech Bearer, Bewley Down Pippin, Bickington Grey, Blue Sweet, Butterbox, Buttery D'Or, Coleman's Seedling, Court Royal, Crimson King, Dufflin, Fair Maid of Devon, French Long Stem, Golden Ball, Great Britain, Green Bittersweet, Hangdown, Horner's

YER, 'AVE A HUNK 'O BRAID'N CHAISE, AN' A GLASS 'O DEVENZHUR ZIDER.

Handydown, John Toucher's, Killerton Sharp, Killerton Sweet, Kingston Bitter, Langworthy, Longstem, Major, Paignton Marigold, Payhembury, Pear Pine, Pocket Apple, Ponsford, Pound, Rawlings, Slack Ma Girdle, Sops in Wine, Sour Bay, Sour Natural, Spicey Pippin, Spotted Dick, Stone Pippin, Sugar Loaf, Sugar Sweet, Sweet Alford, Sweet Bay, Sweet Bramley, Sweet Cluster, Sweet Coppin, Tale Sweet, Tan Harvey, Town Farm No 59, Wellington, Whimple Queen, Whimple Wonder, White Sheep's Nose, Winter Stubbard, Wyatt's Seedling.

Some of the names indicate the towns or villages where the varieties were first developed. Other varieties are forever associated with a particular location: Billy Down Pippin with Membury, Brown's with Staverton, Cornish Pine with Exminster, Crimson Victoria with Shute, Ellos Bitter with Newton St Cyres, Golden Bittersweet with Netherton, Halstow Natural and Johnny Andrews with Tedburn St Mary, Jackson's with Chardstock, Listener with Landkey and East Buckland, Northwood and Woodbine with Crediton, Royal Wilding and White Close Pippin with Exeter, Sercombe's Natural with Dunsford, Sugar Bush with Lapford, Sweet Cleave with Barnstaple, and Tremlett's Bitter with the Exe Valley.

Cider, as any seasoned drinker knows, needs to be treated with respect. It seems unfair that something which tastes so innocuous can have a kick like a bad-tempered donkey on steroids. The effect of a few pints of scrumpy on unsuspecting tourists has been a staple theme of comic postcards for decades. It is good to be able to report that respect is now also being paid to the orchards where the cider comes from, and to the long and noble tradition of cider-making.

The invitation to a traditional Devon repast on the opposite page appears on a postcard from around 1906, while below we see a wagon loaded with barrels of cider opposite Eliott's Farm in Galmpton, just east of Hope Cove, around 1906. This view has changed almost beyond recognition. The barn still survives, albeit drastically reduced in height, but Eliott's Farm is now a private house set in two acres of gardens, while Eliott's Cottage and a barn across the road have been converted to holiday lets.

Newton Poppleford

The road past the Cannon is a lot busier than when these two postcards were published in the early twentieth century, but, apart from being painted white, the inn has hardly changed. There has been a Cannon Inn on this site for well over 200 years, but the present building dates from 1901, when Vallance's Brewery of Sidmouth decided to rebuild it. George Vallance's initials can be still be seen on the datestone on the chimney stack. The Cannon is a quirky, little-known gem, full of character (and characters), with beer served from barrels and an annual beer festival. Vallance's Brewery was taken over in 1946 by Woodhead's of London, which was subsequently absorbed by Devenish's. In 2013, however, the Mighty Hop Brewery in Lyme Regis starting resurrecting some of Vallance's long-lost brews, using original recipes, and supplying them to pubs in East Devon.

Newton Tracey

The Hunter's Inn at Newton Tracey is another little-known gem, hardly changed since this photograph was taken in the 1920s. On 19 November 1857, after the inaugural ploughing match of the Mid-Barnstaple and Torrington Ploughing Society was held at Prestacott Farm, Tawstock, 'the patrons and supporters of the ploughing match repaired to the Hunter's Inn in the village of Newton Tracey, where Mr Clarke, "mine host", served up in good style a substantial dinner to which a large and respectable society sat down.' Those stalwart Victorians would doubtless find as warm a welcome today. The orchard at the side may have been turned into a car park since their day, but the Hunter's Inn remains a friendly, traditional country pub, with excellent home-cooked food.

North Bovey

The Ring of Bells in North Bovey was built as a farmhouse, with an open hall, in the late fifteenth or early sixteenth century. It was later extended before becoming an inn. For many years it was run by the Colridge family: John Colridge, who was there by 1844, was succeeded by Susan Colridge and Ann Colridge. Eliza Colridge, whose name appears above the entrance in this photograph, had taken over by 1889 and was still there in 1923.

These three photographs of the Ring of Bells show parts of this rambling old building as they looked in the 1940s. The Ring of Bells remains one of Devon's most atmospheric inns, with its historic features – such as that grandfather clock set into the wall – largely intact.

North Tawton

A busy scene outside the Fountain in Exeter Street, North Tawton around 1910. Some years earlier, when the Fountain came up for sale, a local resident tried to start a campaign to delicence it, writing a letter which appeared in the *Western Times* on 21 September 1883:

> Now that this well-known inn is for sale, a capital opportunity is offered for starting a coffee tavern or refreshment house, which is very much wanted for the accommodation of those people who come into the town to market, or on other business, and who do not care about going to public houses. The premises are centrally situated, are very commodious, and the large room could be utilised as a public hall, or for religious meetings. There are already sufficient public houses in the place to supply the wants of the population in that direction, while, on the other hand, there are also temperance people enough here to support a coffee tavern if one could be started.

The idea didn't catch on – perhaps he was wrong about the number of coffee lovers in North Tawton – and the Fountain is still open today. It's a lively old place as well, with cider festivals, a real ale club and live bands, but from the outside it looks much as it did a century ago.

Northam

A brake stands outside the King's Head – otherwise known as Penhorwood's Family & Commercial Hotel – en route from Westward Ho! to Bideford around 1905. The King's Head is no longer a hotel and the render has been stripped from its ground and first floors to reveal the stone and brick beneath. Its central doorway has survived, but shopfronts have replaced the windows on either side.

To the left of the King's Head was the Kingsley Hotel, which was originally a beerhouse before receiving a full licence in 1868. The partly-thatched building, a corner of which can be seen above, was destroyed by fire on the afternoon of 27 February 1914. The photograph on the right shows the rebuilt inn in the 1920s. Now renamed the Kingsley Inn, it looks much the same today, and remains a popular, friendly and lively meeting place.

Okehampton

Okehampton's principal coaching inn, the White Hart, is seen here around 1910, with the omnibus to the station standing outside. Although still recognisable, the inn has seen many changes, with the parapet removed, dormer windows inserted in the roof, a white hart installed over the entrance and the side railings above the portico replaced by walls. In 2014, it was acquired by JD Wetherspoon.

West Street, Okehampton around 1910, with the London Inn on the corner and the Plymouth Inn at the far end of the row. Both are still open. The London Inn – also known as Bar 22 – is a sports venue par excellence, with wide screen TVs and pool tables. The Plymouth Inn, by contrast, is a traditional establishment, famous for real ale, popular for home-cooked food, and known as 'the country pub in town'.

Oreston

The King's Arms has long been the only inn in Oreston, but there were once at least three others. The Old Inn, at the north end of Marine Road, and the Ferry Boat Inn both closed in the nineteenth century; the Foresters Arms, at the far end of Marine Road, closed around 1900. When the photograph above was taken in the 1920s, the King's Arms had recently been refronted and extended. The original building, with a canopy over its entrance, can be seen on the right, with the new extension on the left. The photograph below, taken from the other direction a few years earlier, shows the King's Arms beside the ancient cottage demolished to build the extension. It also shows that it stood on the quayside of a small harbour. In the 1960s, however, after concerns had been expressed over damage to the quay wall at high tide and the unsightliness of the muddy beach exposed at low tide, rubble from the construction of a nearby gasworks was used to fill the harbour in, and today the King's Arms looks across wide lawns to a broad promenade along the seafront.

Ottery St Mary

The Five Bells on Mill Street was probably built in the early nineteenth century by a builder called John Perriman, whose son, John Perriman the Younger, became its landlord. Despite a report of his bankruptcy – in the *Exeter Flying Post* of 14 February 1811 – he continued to hold the licence of the Five Bells and was still there in 1830. He was succeeded by John Webb, whose tenure came to an untimely end, as this report from the *Exeter & Plymouth Gazette* for 7 September 1839 records:

> On Tuesday week, as Mr John Webb of the Five Bells Inn, Ottery St Mary, was returning from the Justice Meeting at Woodbury, where he had been to obtain his licence, his horse fell and threw him, whereby he received a violent blow in the head which occasioned a concussion of the brain. The poor sufferer lingered in a state of apparent insensibility till Saturday last, when he expired.

Under the next landlord, James Harris, the Five Bells seems to have gone steadily downhill, for on 6 September 1856 the *Western Times* reported that the renewal of his licence had been refused 'on the ground that he kept his house in a noisy and disorderly manner'. Eighteen months later, when it was sold, the *Exeter Flying Post* of 1 April 1858 reported that the auctioneer 'dwelt on the many advantages that must necessarily accrue to the town from the railway now under construction in the neighbourhood [and] sold the property, after a very spirited competition, at the extraordinary price of £700.'

The postcard above dates from around 1910, when it was known as Matthews' Five Bells Inn – the landlord being Fred Matthews. It survived until the 1970s when it was demolished to make way for a new road – Canaan Way – between Mill Street and Hind Street.

Paignton

The 1906 Ordnance Survey map shows the Manor Inn at Preston, near Paignton, amid orchards, with only a few cottages and the manor house across the road for company. By the time of the 1933 OS map, the manor house had gone, and, instead of orchards, rows of villas and terraced houses lined newly-built roads. The inn, along with a few cottages, survived the redevelopment, a reminder that what is now seaside suburbia was once the heart of the country. This postcard shows the Old Manor Inn shortly after its rural seclusion was shattered forever. It still looks much the same today, and, although its multi-room layout – with snug and jug & bottle – went in the 1960s, and Bass is no longer served from oak barrels, it remains a friendly and traditional pub, as befits its rural origins.

Parkham

Bell Inn, Parkham

The Bell Inn at Parkham was once a forge and a couple of farm cottages. Today the left-hand side of the building houses the village store. This postcard shows it around 1905, and, apart from a new extension at the right and the conversion of the stables at the back, it looks much the same today. Despite being one of the most popular dining and real-ale pubs in this part of Devon, it remains a traditional community pub, whose beer festivals feature ceilidhs, dog shows, hog roasts and gurning.

Parracombe

In 1892, the Fox & Goose at Parracombe was acquired by Henry Blackmore, the younger brother of a local landowner. Despite being a well-appointed establishment, with stables, yards and a club room, it was somewhat old-fashioned, having started life as a pair of cottages, and Mr Blackmore wasted no time in drawing up plans to rebuild it. Work started the following year, and, to accommodate customers while it

The Fox & Goose in the aftermath of the devatatsing floods of August 1952

was going on, he opened a bar in the stables across the road. The new inn opened earlier than anticipated, on 3 June 1894, when the Wesleyan Sunday School, meeting to celebrate its anniversary, found that the town hall was not available. Accordingly, 'Mr Blackmore placed his new building ... at their disposal. Although still in its rough state, a vigorous use of brush and duster made it presentable, and when the tables were placed and decorated with flowers, plum cake, etc, the unfinished parts were not noticed. It certainly was a rather singular opening of a public house.' The postcard above shows it around 1910, when coaches were still the principal means of transport in this remote corner of Devon. Over a century on, the Fox & Goose, with Henry Blackmore's initials still chiselled into the wall, is a remarkably unspoilt village inn, with local ales, locally-sourced food and a relaxed, unhurried atmosphere.

Plymouth

The Barbican a century ago. The Admiral MacBride pub, on the left, is still open today, but the Seamen's Bethel now houses the Cattewater Harbour Commission. The Mayflower Hotel – originally the Brunswick, but renamed when war broke out in 1914 – was lost in the Blitz and the Mayflower Visitor Centre now stands in its place.

A few streets back from the Barbican was Old Town Street, home to some of the city's most historic buildings, including at least twelve inns. Although it was the Luftwaffe who finished off Old Town Street, many of its oldest buildings disappeared years earlier. The Rose & Crown, seen here on the right, was rebuilt shortly after this photograph was taken in 1894, but closed just 30 years later.

The Old Four Castles, taking its name from the four castles on Plymouth's coat of arms, was ten doors along from the Rose & Crown. Dating back at least as far as 1657, it closed in 1895 and was demolished the following year. Old Town Street still exists, albeit on a slightly different alignment. The east side of the street, where both the Rose & Crown and Three Castles once stood, is now lined with banks and building societies.

Treville Street ran eastward from Old Town Street. Its junction with Old Town Street, once the busiest in Plymouth, was the site of Plymouth's first traffic lights, installed in 1929. At the east end of Treville Street was the Mail Inn, seen on the left in the 1920s. This area was devastated in the Blitz and Treville Street no longer exists. The approximate site of the Mail Inn is where Breton Side runs between two car parks near the Staples superstore.

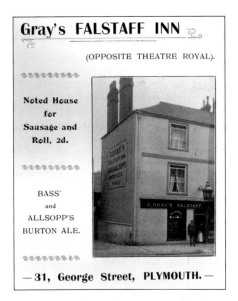

An Edwardian advertisement for the Falstaff on George Street, destroyed by an air raid in March 1941. A Travelodge now stands on the site.

The Star Inn on Union Street in the 1920s, with Starkey, Knight & Ford's brewery depot to the left. Inn and depot now form part of a large nightclub.

Further along Union Street, on the corner of Battery Street, was the Royal Sovereign, seen here around 1910. Originally a beerhouse called the King William IV, by 1878 it had received a full licence and, in its rebuilt form, was renamed the Royal Sovereign. It is still open today, as the Firkin Doghouse, and its ornate frontage, now vibrant in yellow, green and red, is remarkably intact.

Plymouth's first station, the terminus of the South Devon Railway, opened at Millbay in 1849. Passengers leaving the station were confronted with five pubs in a row on the other side of Millbay Road – the Brunel, the Bosphorus, the Terminus, the Greyhound and the South Devon, the last of which is seen here around 1920. Its licence, along with that of the Terminus, was revoked by the magistrates in 1922. Millbay station closed to passengers in 1941, and the Pavilions Leisure Complex now occupies the site. The site of the South Devon Inn, on the corner of Bounds Place, is now a car lot. Next to it, however, the Greyhound, the only building in the row to have survived, was until recently a bar-bistro called Sippers, which closed in 2013 but is reported to be reopening as a restaurant.

Fore Street, Devonport

Devonport's Fore Street was one of the busiest – and grandest – streets in Devon, with over 15 inns. The Luftwaffe put paid to all that. The only inn to survive, the Western Hotel (formerly the London & South Western Railway Tavern), now stands in near isolation on a street that gives no hint of its former importance. So comprehensive was the damage to the eastern end of the street – the busiest stretch – that the Admiralty built a wall around it, topped with barbed wire, to extend the dockyard. It was soon christened Devonport's Berlin Wall; what had been one of the liveliest streets in the west was now a no-go area.

In the photograph on the left, crowds watch a band march past the Prince George on Fore Street around 1910. A stable block at the back of the Prince George Inn housed the first post-Reformation Roman Catholic church in Plymouth until a purpose-built church opened in St Mary's Street in 1807.

At the top of Fore Street was the Military Arms, seen above around 1910. The tram in the distance marks the approximate point at which the Berlin Wall would later close off the street.

The New London Hotel, seen on the right in the 1920s, stood at the bottom end of the street. When advertised for sale in 1924, it was described as

> a valuable fully-licensed property, situated in the principal thoroughfare ... and being the nearest licensed house to the main entrance to the dockyard. The premises were practically rebuilt two years ago in a most substantial manner and the accommodation afforded is ample for

doing a large trade, viz: bar 33ft by 17ft with alcove at end 12ft by 8ft, conveniently divided by cathedral glass screens; excellent dry and lofty cellars, billiard room with overhead light, two large sitting rooms with folding doors, capital kitchen, bathroom and five bedrooms. The property is a free house and is being offered with vacant possession.

The New London Inn, like the Prince George, the Military Arms and most of Fore Street, was destroyed by bombing in the spring of 1941. Today, after standing for more than 50 years, the wall that turned much of what had once been Fore Street into an exclusion zone is finally coming down. In January 2007, after the Admiralty released the site, the first section was demolished. The area behind it is now being redeveloped with homes, shops and offices. There are, however, no plans to replace the 15 inns that lined the street in its glory days.

DARK DEEDS IN STOKE DAMEREL

On Easter Monday, according to annual custom, the lower order of holiday folks numerously assembled at Stoke Fair, to enjoy the revels. In the evening, a dancing party of the town's people were interrupted by some Marines, who wished to introduce a fifer into the room; a quarrel ensued in consequence, and the soldiers were turned out. On the following evening, a large party of the latter, to the number of 80, obtained leave, and armed with sticks, staffs and drawn bayonets, again proceeded to the fair, for the purpose of having a row: accordingly, about eight o'clock, they entered the dancing room of the Pear Tree public house, which they immediately cleared by bruising and knocking down all who opposed them: they then departed until between nine and ten o'clock, when they made a second and more determined attack on the people who had reassembled, by entering the room with drawn bayonets, and sweeping all before them. We are sorry to state that a young man called William Northey (in the breakwater employ), interposing, lost his life, having been stabbed through the head: his brother, John, had nearly shared the same fate, having received a dreadful wound near the umbilicus, and many others received considerable injury, in endeavouring to escape by the door and windows. A piquet from the Marine barracks, and another from the 19th regiment arrived about ten o'clock (soon after the murder) and took most of the ringleaders into custody.

The same night a party, connected, it is said, with the above, committed the most wanton depredations in the neighbourhood, particularly at the Church House Inn, near Stoke church, which they entered with naked bayonets, and after destroying the furniture broke nearly all the windows in the house.

An inquest was held on the body of the person killed on Thursday, by Joseph Whitford, Esq, coroner, and a respectable jury, who, after the strictest investigation, during nine hours, not being able to affix the murder to any individual persons, returned a verdict of wilful murder against some person or persons unknown.

Exeter Flying Post, 17 April 1817

Named after Admiral Hood, who distinguished himself in action against the Americans and the French, the Lord Hood stood on King Street, which ran north from the bottom end of Fore Street. In the 1840s, a Masonic lodge – the Lodge of Friendship – met at the inn. The photograph on the left shows it around 1920. In 1938, the renewal of the Lord Hood's licence was objected to by the chief constable 'on the grounds of redundancy'. It not only survived, but came through the Blitz relatively unscathed, although many nearby buildings were either destroyed or demolished after being declared unsafe. In February 1945, after the death of the landlord, Jeremiah Shanahan, the licence was transferred to his widow, Mary Shanahan. Although the pub still appeared on the 1966 OS map, it was demolished when the area was redeveloped as a housing estate.

Despite its imposing appearance, the Prince Arthur in Morice Town, seen below after being refronted in 1902, was a beerhouse. It was known by a succession of names. In 1857 it was the Royal Oak, by 1878 it was the Wellington Inn & Refreshment House, but by 1890 it had become the Prince Arthur. It stood on the corner of William Street and Tamar Road, just south of the Keyham Gates. It was destroyed by bombing in 1941 and the dockyard was later extended to cover the site.

A more recent casualty was the Friendship Inn on Albert Road. It stood on the corner of Ross Street, about 400 metres from the Prince Arthur, and survived until 2008, when it finally closed. It is seen here around 1910, when James Frederick Feabes was the landlord.

North of Moricetown, along Saltash Road in Keyham, is the Royal Naval Arms, still open and still boasting one of the finest frontages in Plymouth – a columned façade of deep green and brown ceramic tiles dating from a rebuilding of 1898. It is seen here in the early twentieth century with – appropriately enough – a naval rating making his way towards it.

To the east of the city was the George Hotel on the Tavistock Road, seen here around 1900. Today, flanked by large extensions, it is the Toby Carvery.

Plympton

The Devonshire Inn on Ridgeway in Plympton opened some time before 1771. In 1899 it was acquired by the Octagon Brewery of Plymouth, and appears to have been rebuilt or refronted shortly thereafter. It is seen here around 1905, when Stephen Sandover was the landlord. In 1935, the magistrates revoked its licence, and it became a library. It is now a computer access centre linked to nearby Ridgeway School.

Postbridge

In 1789, the Greyhound Inn – later renamed the Post Bridge Inn – was built near a bridge over the River Dart on the turnpike road from Moretonhampstead to Tavistock. On 27 July 1882, the *North Devon Journal* reported a mysterious death nearby:

> The wild moorland spot known as Post Bridge has been the scene of a fatal occurrence, which at present is enveloped in mystery. The solitary inn at Post Bridge was visited by two men who arrived in a vehicle. It was evident that both were the worse for drink. Apparently they were strangers, and on being directed to Ashburton they drove off. The next morning the dead body of one of them was found on the highway and the horse and conveyance were found close by. The body was conveyed to the Post Bridge Inn, where it awaits an inquest ... It appears that at a late hour on Saturday men resembling the two already described drove up to the Duchy Hotel at Princetown, and after staying there the night drove off in the direction of Ashburton. They were seen on different parts of the moor on Sunday, and ... amongst their adventures, they being the while in a state of intoxication, it would appear that they drove into a large pool by the roadside outside the enclosure of the Powder Mills, which are between Two Bridges and Post Bridge, and the consequence was that both men and the horse were well bespattered with mud. They reached Post Bridge about six o'clock, but the landlord thought their condition such as to warrant him in refusing to supply the drink they demanded; and they then drove on the road towards Ashburton. It is thought probable that they called at an inn about two miles further on; but after that – judging from the place where the body was found – they must have somewhat retracted their way. No trace of the other man has yet been found.

Judging from the absence of subsequent reports, the mystery was never solved, and it may have been the shock of this untoward occurrence that prompted the landlord to turn the inn into a temperance hotel. It was still a temperance hotel when the postcard above was published around 1910. In 1930, the landlord, Solomon Warne, after changing its name to the East Dart Hotel, tried to get the licence back, but ran into stiff opposition, and had to settle for a residential licence. The East Dart was eventually granted a full licence, and is still open today, as popular as ever and noted for well-kept local ale and home-cooked food, with a splendid frieze of hunting scenes running round the bar.

Two miles up the road from the East Dart Hotel is the Warren House Inn, whose fire, according to legend, has not gone out since the inn opened in 1845. It replaced an earlier inn across the road, built in the 1760s for men working in the nearby tin mines. On 9 September 1843, the *Exeter & Plymouth Gazette* published an account of a walk westward from Moretonhampstead, which included a stop at the original inn:

> It has by many been thought that there is nothing interesting or worthy of admiration in so sterile a district, and that the view of so much barrenness would rather tend to chill than to cheer the spirits. It is true that there is not the rich woody luxuriance of the vales of Devon ... but there was the majesty of space, the tors whose heads touched heaven, their summits crowned with myriads of blocks of granite, thousands of tons of massive stone ... A short distance from the road might be seen giant circles formed of irregularly shaped pieces of stone, apparently the remains of temples once consecrated to the mysteries of the ancient druids; on the left is the remains of a tin mine, which we left till our return, and then repassed in haste. A little further on is the first sign of human habitation, a stone cot surrounded by a low wall and a peat stack; a board suspended nearest the roadside proclaims to the way-worn traveller that Jonas Coaker is a licensed victualler; his wife is the mother of four really fine and truly clean children, whom she assured us she was bringing up on the moor, and they certainly did credit to her pasture.

Some years earlier, on 27 July 1831, the Rev EA Bray called at the inn, and recorded the inscription on the sign:

> Here is cider and beer,
> Your hearts for to cheer.
> And if you want meat
> To make up a treat,
> There be rabbits to eat.

The rabbits came from a nearby warren, established by the mine owners to provide meat for the miners, with a full-time warrener in charge. The Rev Bray also noted that 'the house was then very much out of repair; so much so that the mistress said that she had

The rebuilt Warren House Inn around 1900

been advised by a pedlar to pull it down and rebuild it on the other side of the road.' And in 1845 that is what happened. The new building, like the old inn, was originally known as the New House; it only became the Warren House Inn several years later. On 10 June 1903, the *Western Times* carried an account of a journey by four-horse charabanc across the moor from Moretonhampstead to Princetown, which included a stop at the Warren House Inn:

> The peat fire in the large open grate looked homely and comfortable, and to some who had not seen peat burnt before, excited a little curiosity. Connected with the Warren House is the legend of a former landlord who died during the winter. The snowstorms prevented his being taken to the cemetery, so his wife salted him down for a more convenient time for his removal. The salted body was placed in a box in one of the bedrooms, and gave a great shock to a traveller who had engaged a bed for the night. Next morning, after a (naturally) very sleepless night, he questioned the good lady of the house on the matter. 'It's only feyther,' was the reply, and then she explained that owing to it being impossible to have his funeral, she had 'salted 'un down'.

The same writer also published an account of his journey in the *Exeter & Plymouth Gazette*, omitting the story about the salting, but describing the inn's 'highly impressionist signboard picture of three rabbits (presumably) and a warren (presumably), its rustic interior, its sweet-smelling peat fires, its delightful old master and mistress, and its very good beer'. Seven years later, however, a survey of the inn concluded that it was in a poor state of repair; renovations were put in hand and finished just before the outbreak of war in 1914. A century on, the miners have long gone, but this extraordinary inn, the highest in the south of England, with more than its store of legends, is still serving good beer, together with a menu that doesn't just feature rabbit.

The Warren House Inn in the 1930s

An early twentieth-century postcard of its famous fire

Poundsgate

When it comes to legends, there are few more dramatic than that associated with the Tavistock Inn at Poundsgate. Until 1864, Poundsgate was in the parish of Widecombe, and every Sunday, church dodgers from Widecombe would head over to the Tavistock Inn, because it was too far away for the vicar to catch them. Among them was a young tin miner called Jan Reynolds who, to fund a lifestyle based around drinking, gambling and womanising, sold his soul to the devil. When the time came for the pledge to be redeemed, the devil turned up at the Tavistock Inn one Sunday, only to find that Jan had decided to go to church instead, possibly in the belief that he would be safe there. Sadly, he was wrong, and, amid thunder and lightning, with masonry crashing into the church, the devil scooped him up and galloped off. It seems likely that the latter part of the legend recalls an incident in 1638, when lightning struck Widecombe church during a service, causing part of the building to collapse, killing six people and injuring 62 others. How the Tavistock Inn came to form part of the story is anyone's guess, although a poem hanging in the bar commemorates what happened when the devil came to call:

> He was served with a drink by the innkeeper's wife,
> Who sniffing the brimstone went in fear of her life.
> The pure golden ale hissed in his throat
> As sparks from his beard lit him up like the tote.
> The glass when returned was almost red hot;
> It burned the counter – you can still see the spot.
> But thanks to the beer that the devil partook
> It was too good for evil, so he slung his hook.

Estimates as to the date of the Tavistock Inn range from the fourteenth to the seventeenth century. The postcard above shows it around 1905, before its thatch had been replaced by slate. It remains one of Dartmoor's friendliest and most traditional inns, and one the devil would still find himself decidedly uncomfortable in.

Princetown

In 1785, Sir Thomas Tyrwhitt, secretary to the Prince of Wales, leased part of Dartmoor from the Duchy of Cornwall, and drew up plans to develop it. He built himself a grand house called Tor Royal and an inn called the Prince's Arms, which stood at the heart of a village which he called Princetown. In 1806, at Tyrwhitt's instigation, Princetown was chosen as the site of a gaol for French prisoners of war, thus beginning its association with England's most notorious prison. By the 1850s, the inn had been renamed the Plume of Feathers, and in due course became popular not just with quarrymen and miners but also with tourists. This postcard shows it in the early twentieth century. It remains slate-hung today, but, with the single-storey extension between the protruding wings replaced by a glass-fronted lobby, it looks altogether more cheerful. Inside are log fires, oil lamps, slate floors and exposed beams, as well as the excellent Jail Ale brewed just around the corner at Dartmoor Brewery – the highest in England.

Prixford

The New Ring of Bells at Prixford – so called to distinguish it from the Old Ring of Bells in the nearby village of Guineaford – was first recorded in May 1833, when an auction was held there. On 21 December 1856, its landlord fell foul of a vicar not over-imbued with Christmas cheer. The following week's *North Devon Journal* reported that

> William Hancock, the landlord of the New Ring of Bells Inn at Prixford in the parish of Marwood, appeared at the instance of the Rev Mr Collinson, the rector of that parish, for keeping open his house for the sale of beer during the prohibited hours of Sunday the 21st instant. Mr T Carder, the constable, deposed that at the request of the complainant, he went to the defendant's house about four o'clock in the afternoon of the day named, and there found six or seven people drinking, two of whom were inhabitants of the parish. Complainant stated that he felt it his duty to bring the case before the bench, first, as the conservator of the morals of the parish, and, secondly, as a heavy ratepayer, for he felt quite sure that drunken habits brought many to the Board of Guardians. There was no defence and defendant was convicted in the penalty of £1, with 10s expenses.

Its name was later shortened to the Ring of Bells, and, when the lease was advertised in August 1888, it was described as a 'fully-licensed inn ... doing a good trade. Baking and grocery has been carried on in connection and butching [sic] may also be carried on, premises being well adapted for same.' It was owned by John Hancock Richards, listed in Kelly's 1889 *Directory* as a 'maltster, auctioneer, manure, corn and hop merchant and farmer'. On January 1881 he had hosted a dinner which was reported in the *North Devon Journal*:

> On Saturday last, Mr JH Richards, maltster, of Middle Marwood, agent for Messrs Stevens, Son & Co, 33 Mark Lane, London, held his first audit at the Ring of Bells, Prixford ... when a goodly number sat down to an excellent dinner of roast beef and plum pudding, served up in good old English style by Mrs Smith, the landlady. After dinner the usual toasts were given and responded to, the chairman, Mr WS Down of Middle Marwood, spoke of the good qualities of manures supplied by Messrs Stevens, Son & Co, and said if they continued to supply the same genuine article as last year he believed through the energies of their agent Mr JH Richards they would do a much larger trade this year.

John Richards was declared bankrupt in 1889, and the Ring of Bells was taken over by the Anchor Brewery of Barnstaple. It later passed to Starkey, Knight & Ford, and then to Whitbread, before being bought by Martin and Janet Squire in December 2007. Just over four years later, on 8 April 2012, they called last orders and shut up shop. With the real-estate value of 'character cottages' in rural boltholes like Prixford far outstripping the value of pubs, closures such as this have become all too common. The one thing that prevents wholesale conversion is a legal requirement for local councils to protect community facilities, and the hurdle that any would-be developer has to jump is getting approval for change of use. This is one case where the locals are determined to fight any move to deprive them of their pub. They have set up a campaign group and a website (saveourpub.org), which acknowledges the problems facing landlords in the present climate, but points out that, 'whilst there is a business to run first and foremost, there is also an implied moral responsibility on landlords to preserve such an important social venue for the community – and if the business doesn't work for them, an equal implied responsibility to pass on the baton to the next landlord to preserve the legacy. A community has grown around the Ring O' Bells for almost two centuries and it would be a desperate shame if it ceases to provide that connection for future generations.' Stirring words, and it is to be hoped that their battle to save their pub is successful.

The New Ring of Bells in the 1920s. Now known as the Ring O'Bells, locals have launched a campaign to save it after the owners closed it in April 2012.

Rackenford

It has been suggested that the Stag Inn in Rackenford (seen on the left in the early twentieth-century postcard above) may have been built as a church house, although its layout, with an entry through a cobbled horse passage, suggests it may originally have been a longhouse. Despite a recent refurbishment, tradition reigns: no pool, juke box or games machines, just good ale, good food, and a settle by an open fire, where you can sit and raise a glass to the Rev E Pole, who, when the magistrates threatened to revoke the Stag's licence in 1883, told them 'it was indispensable as a hostelry for horses and vehicles of old and respectable farmers going to church on Sundays from the moor'.

Ringmore

The New Inn at Ringmore is said to have been built around 1190 to house the masons building the church, which suggests it was originally a church house. By 1685 it had become an inn, with part of the building used as a council chamber. In the 1920s, RC Sherriff wrote a play while staying at the inn. Taking its title from the poem 'Journey's End' by Cicely Fox Smith, it was based on his experiences in the First World War and was the hit of the 1929 season. Two years later, the New Inn was renamed the Journey's End. The postcard on the previous page shows the New Inn around 1910; the view below dates from shortly after its renaming. Today, this gloriously traditional hostelry is as good and as popular as ever.

Rockbeare

The Bidgood Arms started life as a small wayside inn, but eventually grew into something much bigger. Although it was advertised to let as a fully-licensed house in 1836, it was later downgraded to a beerhouse. By the time this postcard was published in the mid-twentieth century, however, its full licence had been restored. The A30, which once ran past it, was rerouted in 2000 and the Bidgood Arms is now a Chinese restaurant.

The Crown & Sceptre Hotel, Rockbeare, Nr. Exeter.

A quarter of a mile east of the Bidgood Arms along the old Fosse Way was the Crown & Sceptre. In October 1883, when the landlord was a butcher called Mr Gibbings, the outbuildings were destroyed in an arson attack. The postcard above shows the inn around 1906, when horse-drawn transport was the order of the day, while the one below shows it in the 1920s, when a petrol pump and garage had been provided for the convenience of motorists. In the 1930s, fake timbering was applied to the first-floor to give it the appearance of a roadhouse, but thankfully this has now been removed. Since being renamed the Jack in the Green – the traditional name for this part of Rockbeare – and gaining a large single-storey extension where the garage once stood, the old Crown & Sceptre has gained a reputation as one of the top gastropubs in the Exeter area.

Rockbeare.

Salcombe

The Shipwright's Arms was known as the Plymouth Inn until around 1850. When advertised for sale in 1921, it had a 'tap room, three parlours, sitting room and four bedrooms, together with three large cellars ... and a productive garden, etc at the rear'. It closed in April 2001, and now houses a gift shop.

Sampford Courtenay

Sampford Courtenay station, originally known as Okehampton Road, opened on 15 January 1867. The following April, John Snell opened 'an hotel and refreshment room ... called the Courtenay Railway Hotel' there, with 'a range of stabling attached'. Facilities at the hotel – later renamed the Railway Inn – must have been limited, for in 1888 Arnold, Perrett & Co of Wickwar commissioned Arnold Thorne, a Barnstaple architect, to design a new inn, which opened the following year. This photograph shows it in the 1920s. Although the station closed in 1972, it has since been used for summer Sunday and heritage services, but the inn, long a private house, remains firmly shut.

Sampford Peverell

Lower Town, Sampford Peverell.

Since this postcard was published in the 1920s, the Globe at Sampford Peverell has changed almost beyond recognition. Half timbering has been applied to the first floor and render stripped from the ground floor, while the two large buildings beyond the pub and the cottages further along have all gone. Despite the changes, the Globe remains a popular and traditional local, well known in the area for good food, local beer and cider.

NO FOOD AT THE INN

'At the Brewster Sessions for the Cullompton Petty Sessional Division, Supt WJ Joslin stated that ... the licence holders at Sampford Peverell had been cautioned for not supplying food to a traveller when requested. He received a complaint in writing from a gentleman saying there were three houses in the village and that none of them could supply him with anything whatever ...

Mr TJW Templeman ... wished to say, on behalf of the licensees of the Hare & Hounds and the New Inns, that the gentleman had never been refused. One of them said the man called and asked if he had any food, and while the licensee went to ask his wife the man departed. At the other house, the licensee told him he could not get anything then as his wife was ill, but if the caller would wait he would send out and get something. The man would not wait, however. The licensee of the Globe Inn came forward and said the man called at his house and asked for food. Witness told him things were not ready, but he could supply him later ... There was a shortage of food at the time, and ... the fire was not sufficient to boil water. They were for some weeks without coal and now were only allowed one cwt a week.

Mr WJA Grant, another justice, advised publicans to get oil stoves.

Mr Templeman submitted that the man was in a hurry and had not the time to wait ...

The chairman said ... they wished to make a special point of the complaint from Sampford Peverell that meals and non-alcoholic refreshments of a reasonable character must be supplied during the hours houses were open. If any complaint of such a character came before them again, serious notice would be taken of it.'

From the *Exeter & Plymouth Gazette*, 13 February 1920

Sandford

The Lamb Inn has hardly changed since this postcard was published a century ago, although the square in front of it, once the venue for fairs and markets, is now cluttered with cars. The Lamb – all open fires and low beams – is a community pub par excellence, with a reputation for local ales and food. It also has a cinema in the skittle alley, and hosts regular social events and live music. On St George's Day 2006, after playing a fundraising gig to help keep the village post office open, Phil Beer and Steve Knightley of Show of Hands were awarded the accolade of Greatest Ever Devonians in a ceremony at the Lamb after topping a Radio Devon poll.

The Lamb always seems to have had a lively events programme. On 2 July 1881, the *Western Times* reported that

> Mr Tucker of the Lamb Inn has for some years past been much interested in the grand old sport, Devon wrestling. He is now making active preparations to get up a grand meeting of the best men of the day, and in order to induce good players to come forward he has given orders for a very valuable silver cup. This is to be open to any man in Devon or Cornwall (bar Pike), and will be contested for on Sandford fair day.

William Tucker was succeeded by Lewis Snow, who, when a fire broke out in the village in 1891, opened the inn as a refuge and command post, and was dragged before the magistrates for his pains. The *Western Times* of 29 January 1891 described what happened:

> Lewis Snow, landlord of the Lamb Inn, Sandford, was summoned at the Crediton Petty Sessions ... for keeping his house open during prohibited hours on the 20th inst ... PS Fursdon stated that about 1am on the 20th instant he was on duty at Sandford when he visited defendant's house ... where he found a large crowd of people ... Defendant was standing in the bar in the act of drawing some spirit from a cask. Witness asked him what was the meaning of all those persons being there, but defendant seemed to take no notice of him. Witness then asked him what authority he had for keeping his

house open, and he retorted, 'I have no authority but I'll close my house if you wish' ... Mr Friend, in his defence, said during the whole of his practice as a solicitor he had never seen anything to resemble the present prosecution. He contended that the case ought never to have been brought before their worships ... It seemed that defendant was extremely generous and active on the occasion of the fire. The night was very cold, and the roads were in a bad state for travelling, but, notwithstanding that, defendant rode to Crediton on horseback, and summoned the fire brigade. When he returned home he found that someone was about to force open the door of his house with a crowbar in order to obtain some brandy for a woman who had been removed from the fire, and who was said to be dying. Defendant immediately opened his premises, and supplied the spirit asked for, but he did not take any money for it. Subsequently other persons came for spirit, and the vicar of the parish sent for three gallons of beer for the firemen, and the defendant supplied it ... Mr Friend was about to call another witness when the chairmen said that the bench, considering the special circumstances of the case, would dismiss it.

Seaton

The Golden Lion in Seaton, seen here in the 1930s, had a most imposing sign over its door. Today, although a lion still guards the entrance, the building has been converted to shops and flats.

Shaldon

The Crown in Shaldon, first recorded in 1828, was known as the Crown & Anchor until 1881. Today renamed the Ferry Boat Inn, it remains a traditional pub, with a beer garden overlooking the beach and a good selection of local ales.

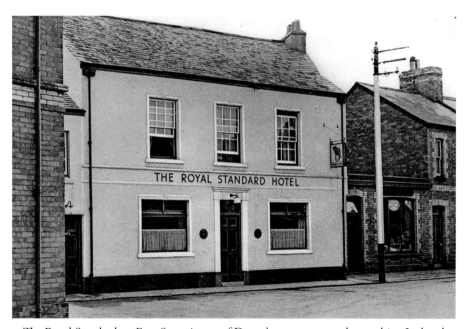

The Royal Standard on Fore Street is one of Devon's most recent pub casualties. It closed in 2009, and in 2010 permission was granted to convert it to a house, which has since gone on the market for £545,000.

Shebbear

The New Inn at Shebbear, seen above in the 1920s, has long had a reputation as one of the most haunted inns in the country. This may have something to do with a large stone on the other side of the square, dropped, according to legend, by the devil, and turned over in a ceremony every Guy Fawkes Night to preserve the village from harm. There are rumours of a tunnel running from the inn to the church, and it has been suggested that the building was originally a church house. In the mid-nineteenth century, the landlord was James Bowman, during whose tenure it was downgraded to a beerhouse. He had first come to the attention of the police in Torrington some years earlier. According to the *North Devon Journal* of 13 October 1853, 'James Bowman of Shebbear was placed before the bench on the grave charge of resisting the constable in the execution of his duty, at the Black Horse Inn on fair night. He was "making night hideous" by fighting with one John Colliford of Bideford, and, when the peace officer interfered, was equally disposed to fight him. To teach him better manners, he was fined £2.' He took out a 99-year lease on the New Inn the following year and put in a tenant to run it. In September 1857, however, he applied for a licence to run it himself. This was opposed by GL Coham of Upcott Avenel, a magistrate and deputy lieutenant of the county, 'on the ground that neither the applicant nor his wife were proper persons to conduct a house of this description'. Although the licence was granted, just over two months later, on 15 November, Bowman was summonsed for allowing gambling on the premises. The New Inn rapidly gained the reputation of an unruly house, and, at two o'clock on the morning of 30 May 1859, things spiralled so far out of control that Bowman had no option but to call the police. On the previous day, the annual meeting of a local friendly society had been held at the inn. It was followed by a prolonged drinking session which degenerated into a brawl. The two police officers who tried to quell the disorder were beaten and savagely kicked whilst lying on the ground by seven of the troublemakers, six of whom were later fined £5, the maximum penalty for common assault. Eighteen months later, on 27 December

1861, Bowman himself was charged with assaulting a police officer and fined £5. The following September, when Bowman's wife applied for a renewal of the licence, it was refused, and she was forced to take out a beerhouse licence instead.

The New Inn remained a beerhouse for the next three years. The *North Devon Journal* for 21 September 1865 describes how its full licence came to be reinstated:

> Mr L Bencraft applied, on behalf of Mr WH Hearn of Shebbear, for a victualler's licence for the New Inn in that parish. Some years since, the house was occupied and kept by Mr Bowman, the owner; owing, however, to various irregularities and complaints respecting the manner in which it had been kept, the licence was withheld. Bowman afterwards got into trouble and went to America. Several applications have since been made for a renewal of the licence, but the bench have refused to grant it unless a respectable tenant could be procured. A short time since, Mr Hearn (who is the son of a respectable farmer of Shebbear) married the daughter of Mr Bowman, and he has been keeping the premises as a beerhouse. The applicant had obtained the lease of it for a term of seven years. The house was built a few years since on church land, and was said to be in every way adapted for an inn. The parish business is done there, and two clubs hold their meetings in it. Several respectable farmers attended to support the application, and stated that it would be a great convenience to have the licence granted. The bench, having listened to a long address from Mr Bencraft, granted the licence.

The statement that the New Inn 'was built a few years since on church land' seems to discount claims for its great longevity. However, there is a tradition that it burnt down in the eighteenth century and was rebuilt, so perhaps there was an inn occupying an old church house on the site in the seventeenth century or even earlier.

The New Inn's mid nineteenth-century career as a place where even the police feared to tread is, thankfully, long behind it. Now renamed the Devil's Stone Inn, this beamed, flagstoned building is not only popular with the hunting and shooting set, but also with those in search of good food, good wine, well-kept beer and the atmosphere of a friendly, traditional village local. In October 2014, however, it was put up for sale. A month later, to pre-empt hasty conversion to a private house, it was listed as an asset of community value.

Sheepwash

Until a fire destroyed most of Sheepwash in 1743, it hosted one of the largest weekly markets in north Devon, with numerous inns for those who came to buy and sell. Sheepwash never recovered its former importance, and by the beginning of the nineteenth century only two inns remained – the White Hart on the south side of the square and the Half Moon on the north. When the White Hart closed in the 1880s, the Half Moon was left as the only inn in the village.

For some reason, Sheepwash always seems to have been a musical place. On 18 November 1837, the *Western Times* reported that

> on Monday last, a grand concert of ancient and modern music took place, spontaneously, at the Half Moon Inn, Sheepwash. The performers were of the most efficient class, collected from various adjoining parishes to do honour to the worthy host. The club room over the post-office apartment was filled to excess, there to listen to the 'concord of sweet sound' to be elicited from the first performers of this part of the country. Mr Wonnacote of Zeal presided. Among the number most prominent stood Mr John Crotch

of the White Hart Inn, Oakhampton; Wannell, organist, of Oakhampton; Drew of Zeal; Cornish of Zeal; Honey of Holdsworthy; Risdon of Hean; Heard of Awsland; Tucker of Park; and Snell of Newcourt, with others. Everything was well conducted, and the evening was spent with the utmost good feeling, God Save the Queen with a few hearty cheers crowning the whole.

Twenty-nine years later, on 5 June 1866, the *North Devon Journal* reported that

the members of the male and female friendly societies held their anniversary on Tuesday, the males at the Half Moon and the females at the White Hart. A capital dinner was served up at each of the above hostelries by Messrs Finnamore and Ward ... Church, dinner and business over, dancing and other amusements were commenced, and kept up with great spirit, until the Hatherleigh band was compelled to cry 'quarter'. The evening was enlivened by the arrival of a troupe of nigger melodists, who, in the expressive language of a bystander, had 'zeed a girt deal more of Hatherleigh than old Varginny'.

No event, it seems, was complete without a musical accompaniment. On 6 December 1895, for instance, the *Exeter & Plymouth Gazette* informed its readers that

the annual Manure Audit was held at the Half Moon Inn, and the gathering was a large one. The financial business being disposed of, the company sat down to a capital dinner ... The proceedings were enlivened with many capital songs by Messrs R Finnamore, R Crocker, Tapson, S Pope and F Harris.

When the postcard above was published, Mary Finnamore was the licensee of the Half Moon. She was the widow of Richard Finnamore, who was landlord until his death in 1905. As well as running the inn, he farmed 100 acres and was a churchwarden. The thatch, which here looks in urgent need of attention, has been replaced by slate, and the building generally presents a much smarter face to the world. It remains, however, the archetypal village inn, with a roaring fire, exposed beams and old settles, along with good food, wines and beer. It has long been a Mecca for fishermen as well. In the nineteenth century, Richard Finnamore rented fishing rights from Lord Clinton, and exclusive fishing rights on ten miles of the Torridge are still available to guests today.

Shillingford

The turnpike road from Taunton to Bampton was built through Shillingford in the late 1820s and the Barleycorn Inn opened soon afterwards. First recorded in 1850, with Mary White as licensee, this postcard shows it in the early twentieth century. It closed in 1999 and is now a bed & breakfast establishment called Barleycorn House.

Shute

The Shute Arms at Seaton Junction opened in 1898 and is seen here around ten years later. It remained open after the station closed in 1966 and was rebuilt following a serious fire in 1987. In 2007, however, it was converted to flats.

Sidbury

Sidbury's two pubs, the Red Lion and the Royal Oak, are seen here on mid twentieth-century postcards. The Royal Oak has long been converted to a private house with self-catering accommodation, leaving the Red Lion as the village's only pub. In April 2013, however, Punch Taverns put it up for sale. Locals, concerned that it could be converted to a private house, campaigned for it to be listed as an asset of community value, before setting about raising the money to buy it through a share offer. Although they failed to raise the necessary amount, their campaign was successful, as a local businessman came forward to buy the Red Lion. It reopened – as a traditional local pub – in September 2014.

HOT COINS AT SIDBURY

The tradition of hot coins being thrown down to children from the windows of Sidbury's two inns to mark the start of the annual fair dates back centuries. Even though the Royal Oak has long been closed, coins are still thrown from its windows, along with those of the Red Lion, every September. Today they are pennies, but in former times other coins were thrown as well. On 16 September 1938, the *Western Times* reported that 'Sidbury's ancient fair, a relic of bygone days, was heralded in on Tuesday, midday, by the putting out the glove, gaily bedecked with flowers, from the Royal Oak window. At the same time, excited children scrambled in the village street for hot farthings, halfpennies and pennies. A few fortunate obtained a sixpenny bit, and even a shilling.'

Sidford

The Rising Sun in Sidford opened on 15 January 1856, when the landlord, John Cawley, held a celebratory dinner for 'about 50 of the tradesmen of Sidmouth, and those friends who supported him in obtaining the magistrate's licence'. The following year, when the freehold was put up for sale, it was described as 'a newly brick-built inn' with 'brewhouse, covered skittle alley, and summer tea garden, together with a dwelling house adjoining ... in the yearly tenancy of Mr John Cawley'. This postcard shows it around 70 years ago. It remains very much a community pub, with a varied programme of events and live music (as well as an annual beer festival), and a reputation for home-cooked food and real ale.

Slapton

When the Queen's Arms was offered for sale in August 1923, it was described as 'an old-established free, fully-licensed inn ... containing bar, bar parlour, tap room, sitting room, kitchen, etc, on ground floor, four bedrooms above, yard, store, etc, at rear, together with a stable, with loft over, on the opposite side of the road.' Seen here in the 1940s, with the ruined tower of a medieval chantry in the distance, it is still a traditional and very popular local at the heart of the village, with a fascinating collection of memorabilia on its walls.

Nearby, in the shadow of the ruined tower, is the Tower Inn. Its first landlord was Robert Pepperell, who was granted a licence in 1847. Twenty-seven years later, when he put it up for sale, the *Western Times* carried a comprehensive description of the property:

The premises comprise bar, bar parlour, kitchens, cellars, brew-house and necessary offices on the ground floor, and five good bedrooms, and a large room adapted for clubs and public meetings, over. There are good stables, with loft over; lock-up coach-house, piggeries, and court-yard adjoining the property; and at the rear is a most productive walled garden, in a high state of cultivation, well stocked with choice fruit trees, and a greenhouse producing about 2 cwt of grapes annually.

The premises are well and substantially built, and in good repair; most of the buildings and all the roofs have been erected at a considerable cost by the present owner. A respectable and snug business has been conducted on the property, since the granting of the license in 1847, and the present offers a good opportunity to persons seeking a public business or as an investment.

In 1904, it came on the market again. It was bought for £660 by John Steere, a farmer whose wife held the licence of the Church House Inn in Churchstow. She became the licensee of the Tower, and for a time all seemed well. Five years later, however, in December 1909, the neighbourhood was shocked to discover that Steere, while drunk, had dragged his wife from her bedroom, attempted to drown her in a water cistern in the back yard, and, when that failed, tried to strangle her with a stocking. He was given a three-year prison sentence; she went to Bristol to run a refreshment room, and the inn was sold to Bartlett's Brewery of Dartmouth.

Happily, the Tower Inn's reputation as 'respectable and snug', which Robert Pepperell had worked so hard to build up, was soon restored, and is exemplified by the sun-drenched drowsiness of the 1920s postcard opposite. The Tower remains a superbly atmospheric and traditional inn, with the crumbling, lichen-covered tower next door lending it just the right amount of mystery.

Smeatharpe

Smeatharpe, on the border with Somerset, is one of the most evocative and little-known places in the county. When this photograph of the King's Arms was taken in the 1920s, it stood at the end of a lane west of the village. Beyond it, fields stretched to the horizon. Its rural seclusion came to an abrupt end in 1943, when those fields were requisitioned for RAF Upottery, used by American transport and reconnaissance units in the run-up to D Day. The King's Arms had never been busier, but its glory days were short-lived. The RAF took the airfield over in July 1945 for storing surplus material. It closed three years later and much of the land reverted to agricultural use. All three runways survive, however, and parts of the site are home to a flying club, a stock-car racing track and a highway maintenance depot. The King's Arms, long converted to a private house, has changed relatively little, although the single-storey extension on the right has acquired another storey and a porch.

Sourton

The New Inn at Sourton – a classic country pub, hardly distinguishable from dozens of others, offering refreshment and accommodation to travellers, its origins lost in the mists of time. Or at least it was when this postcard was published in the 1930s. In 1959, however, it acquired new owners – and a new identity. When locals heard that Buster and Rita Jones from South Wales had taken it on, little could they have suspected that their quiet one-roomed pub was about to be transformed into one of the most extraordinary hostelries in the country. Warning bells must have rung when the New Inn was renamed the Highwayman; by the time the old Launceston to Tavistock stagecoach was installed as the front porch, it was clear that it was to be a far cry from the wayside local they had been accustomed to for so long. Over 50 years later, the refurbishment has never really stopped, with new features being added and old ones tweaked. Superlatives and similes cannot begin to do justice to what has been achieved; this is one inn to which the word 'unique' can, without hesitation, deviation or repetition, be aptly applied.

THE SONG MAN OF SOURTON

In the West of England, and it was probably the same elsewhere, every village inn retained its song-man who amused the company by his ballads and lyrics, and was repaid by the topers with free drinks. Their repertoire was extensive. James Parsons, who went by the name of the 'Singing Machine', was one evening at the tavern at Sourton with three other men, one of whom, named Voysey, worked for me. Parsons by profession was a hedger and thatcher. He told me that upon the occasion mentioned, a bet had been laid that he could not go on singing fresh songs all the night from sunset to daybreak. He did so, and won the bet. I found it difficult to credit the story, so I asked Voysey whether it was as Parsons had related. 'Ay! It's true enough,' said the man, shaking his head. 'I reckon I shan't forget that in a hurry, as I had to empty my purse to pay the bet.'

Sabine Baring-Gould, *Further Reminiscences, 1864-1894*

South Brent

The nineteenth century façade of the Pack Horse Inn in South Brent hides a much older interior. As its name indicates, it was originally a resting place for the drovers in charge of the packhorse trains that carried goods from the farms and mines on Dartmoor to the coast. Its stables and outbuildings were destroyed by vandals in 1975, but the inn – apart from having its black and white colour scheme replaced by a gentler shade of cream – looks much the same as it does on this postcard. Inside, tradition reigns, with open fires, real ales, folk sessions, and food prepared in what was once the forge.

Opened in the mid-nineteenth century to replace an inn of the same name next door which had fallen victim to temperance campaigners, the Royal Oak – now known as the Oak – is South Brent's other surviving inn, with a reputation for food and a commitment to real ale.

South Brent once had two other inns – the London Inn on the Exeter Road, which closed in 2010 for conversion to housing, and the Anchor, seen here on the left (with the Royal Oak in the distance) around 1910. A particularly attractive feature was the room projecting over the entrance and supported on granite pillars. The inn has an important place in working-class history, as a report in the *Western Times* for 4 March 1837 records:

> A numerous meeting of agricultural labourers was held at the Anchor Inn, South Brent, on Friday, the 24th instant, to form an association for the purpose of establishing a mutual good understanding amongst each other, in order more effectively to protect their common interests, and improve their condition. Upwards of 150 individuals were present, and enrolled themselves in this association, which has taken for its model a previously existing union, styled 'the society of masons' labourers and quarrymen', which last it seems renders support to all who are in any way connected with those callings, whenever a 'legal strike' is declared.
>
> The immediate cause of the present meeting was stated to be the existing low rate of wages, and the principle and avowed object of the association was to obtain an advance of those wages, which were stated not to average more, at present, than eight shillings weekly to able-bodied labourers within the district – this amount is deemed wholly inadequate to the maintenance of a family, especially at the present market prices of the necessaries of life, and ten shillings per week was mentioned as the sum deemed fair and reasonable. The business of the meeting was conducted with perfect propriety and good order, and the open and constitutional mode of managing the proceedings, at least, claims respect for intelligence and right feeling.

The Tolpuddle Martys had been sentenced to transportation for forming a similar association less than three years earlier, and, although they had been pardoned in March 1836, meetings like this were still vigorously opposed by landowners. Those attending them risked losing their jobs or being blacklisted, so this demonstration of solidarity was not something to be entered into lightly. As for the Anchor, it suffered a serious fire in 1990, and, although subsequently restored, it is now a convenience store.

Just over the border in Ugborough, but generally assumed to be in South Brent, was the Carew Arms, which, like the Anchor, had a room over its entrance supported on granite pillars. The photograph above dates from around 1900. In the photograph below, taken in 1938, the inn presents a much smarter image, in keeping with its new-found role as a roadhouse. As with other inns along the old A38, it was the rerouting of the road that sealed its fate. Although it was renamed the Woodpecker, the change of name could not revive its fortunes. After it closed in 2007, it was acquired by property developers, but, although the building has long been reduced to a pile of rubble, work to redevelop the site has yet to start. In March 2014, an application to build 20 'low-cost live/work units, office hub and associated parking' on the site' was rejected. An appeal has since been lodged.

South Molton

UNICORN HOTEL.
SOUTH MOLTON.
N. DEVON.

ESTABLISHED OVER 300 YEARS.

When the lease of the Unicorn Hotel in South Molton was advertised in February 1892, the accommodation included 'dining, commercial, smoking and sitting rooms, bar, lobby, hall, front and back kitchens, brew house, skittle alley, with stabling for 50 horses', plus 'six lofty bedrooms, sitting room, spacious dining or ball room, servants' rooms, etc' on the first floor. In 1917, when Samuel Cole gave up the lease of the inn, it was taken over by the government, and for the next two years was used as a camp for German prisoners of war, before being refurbished and reopened in 1920. This postcard shows the Unicorn in the 1930s, after half timbering had been added to the first floor. In 1965, it was renamed the Goose & Gander. It later became the Old Coaching Inn, since shortened to the Coaching Inn. The half timbering has been extended not only to the ground floor, but also to the building next door, formerly the stables and later a garage, but now part of the hotel. This popular town-centre venue has a large open-plan bar with a carvery, pool table and choice of seating areas, as well as a large function room.

AN UPROARIOUS FOLK SINGER

Mr Bussell and I went to South Zeal, a quaint old village, which was once on the high road from Exeter to Okehampton and Launceston. When the new road was made, it was left very much to itself. We put up at the Oxenham Arms ... A number of singers were collected in the evening, and the villagers crowded the entrance and peered in at the windows to see and hear what went on. But we had no success that evening, as one of the men present got drunk and was uproarious. However, we had the singers in one by one the next day, and obtained from them some very rugged and peculiar tunes. One of the best singers went by the name of 'Lucky Fewins.'

Sabine Baring-Gould, *Further Reminiscences, 1864-1894*

South Zeal

The Oxenham Arms at South Zeal is one of the oldest and most remarkable inns in the county. Built as a monastic grange or hostel in the twelfth century, it later became the dower house of the Burgoyne family, before opening as an inn. Needless to say, the legends surrounding it are legion – ghostly visitations naturally, but also real-life visitors such as Lord Nelson and Charles Dickens, who is said to have written part of *The Pickwick Papers* while snowed in here. One legend – of the white-breasted bird whose appearance heralded the death of one of the Oxenhams,

who were lords of the manor – found its way into Charles Kingsley's *Westward Ho!* In August 1894, while staying at the inn, Sabine Baring Gould collected some of his finest folk songs – although not without difficulties, as the story on page 250 indicates. The postcards reproduced here, including the one below showing the prehistoric menhir or standing stone around which the inn is said to have been built, date from around 1930. Eighty years on, the Oxenham Arms remains one of Devon's most enigmatic and evocative inns. In June 2012, after being closed for a year, it reopened under new management, and reports suggest it has now regained its place as one of the most popular as well.

Spreyton

From one of Devon's most historic inns to one of its most celebrated, yet for most of its life the White Hart at Spreyton – seen above around 1910 – was a village local like hundreds of others, tucked away well off any tourist trail in a village most Devonians had never heard of (its story is told on pages 256-9). All that changed in 2002 when Roger Cudlip, a butcher from North Tawton, and his wife Carol, took over what by then had been renamed the Tom Cobley Tavern. Roger's ambition was not just to continue to run a welcoming community pub and serve top-notch home-cooked local food; he wanted it to be the best in the country. Four years later, the Campaign for Real Ale declared it National Pub of the Year, largely due to what must surely be the most impressive line-up of local beers in the county. There have been other awards – including one from *Devon Life* for Best Community Pub – which prove, if proof is needed, that the Tom Cobley is about a good deal more than beer. It is, quite simply,

The bar of the Tom Cobley in the 1960s

one of the finest, friendliest family-run pubs you are likely to find anywhere, and one that people from miles away just cannot help coming back to.

TOM COBLEY & WIDECOMBE FAIR

"Choriss, gen'lmen—'Old Uncle Tom Cobleigh and All.'" "JAN STEWER" SERIES.

'Widecombe Fair' is Devon's best-known folk song, yet its origins are shrouded in mystery. When Sabine Baring-Gould began collecting folk songs in Devon in 1887, it was one of only two songs (the other was 'Arscott of Tetcott') still in general currency. Yet the characters involved, the events it celebrates and the date they took place have long been the subject of conjecture. Its echoes of songs and folk traditions from elsewhere suggest it was an old song or tale updated to commemorate a particular event, and, while that event may be difficult to pin down, there can be little doubt as to the identity of the central character in 'this shocking affair'.

In the churchyard at Spreyton there is a grave to 'Thomas Cobley, Gent, late of Butsford in the Parish of Colebrooke, who departed this life Jan 4th 1844, aged 82 years'. He was something of a local celebrity, riding to hounds almost until the day he died. On 14 February 1842, the *Sherborne Mercury* reported that,

> on Wednesday last, there was a good and most gratifying [hunt] meeting at Colebrooke, when the hounds, now in charge of Samuel Norris, Esq, were turned out, and had two splendid runs, killing their hare in each instance. The venerable and highly respected father of the field in that district – and former master of these hounds – Mr Thomas Cobley, was present, and although 80 years of age, rode as boldly as the youngest throughout the day, nor was this thorough sportsman found in the rear at the close of either run. The business of the field being concluded, a party of about 30 sat down to an excellent dinner at Dawe's New Inn, Colebrook ... and the evening was spent in the utmost conviviality and harmony.

The inclusion of this item in a Dorset newspaper suggests that Thomas Cobley's fame was widespread. And, although this report referred to him as Mr Thomas Cobley, the *Western Times*, covering a similar day's hunting on 17 December 1842, gave him the appellation by which he is better known today:

> The morning of Wednesday being an auspicious one for the true lovers of the chase, the gallant pack of S Norris Esq, formerly in the possession of Uncle Tom Cobley, were unkennelled for their legitimate sport, 'hare hunting'.

He seems to have been known as Uncle Tom for some time. This report comes from the *Exeter Flying Post* for 3 January 1828, when he was still very much master of the hounds:

> On Saturday last, Mr Cobley's harriers had a most excellent day's sport. After running a hare for two hours across the country and killing, they returned to try on Coffins [a farm in Spreyton]; after beating about some time, Jem Roberts sung out that he had pricked a hare at the bottom of a very thick brake, and ... was soon heard crying out, with 'at him Old Mad Cap – now on him my old boy – push him up old fellow', and cheering up the rest of his pack in a very different strain from what he generally does when on a hare. Uncle Tom swore 'twas a Varment, and so it turned out, for the brake was soon in a blaze, and in a few minutes Jem was heard Tallyhoing the Fox; and laying the dogs close on his brush – but 'twas no go – they were too close on him – and he was obliged to return to the cover in view – but here he could not rest – they worried him up and down at such a rate, that he again broke cover – and Tallyho was heard sweeping up the vale from Uncle Tom's melodious voice – away they went like wildfire, and Jem along with them on his old Gray, with Turner, Cann of Fuidge, Shute and Uncle Tom close on his heels. The fox first made for Nymph Woods, down the wind, when turning short and facing the wind, he made for Spreyton Woods, slap through those thick covers, and away to Fursdon, thence to Fuidge, up the bottoms, and away to South Zeal, West-week, and then got on Dartmoor, over Cawson Hill, crossed the Taw, to Belstone Woods, and again got on the Moor; crossed East Okement river, to Bowtor Miltov [sic], when he made a turn, and came back again across Okement-river, Taw river, and away to Superton Tor, Wild Tor, and Watern Tor, where he got the Rocks almost in view, after a most slashing run of nearly three hours, without a single check; some idea may be formed as to the pace we went at when the old Gray could not make a gallop of it, just as he got on the Moor, so sharp had been the run; in fact, all hands were dead beat, and had not the fox made a turn, the game would have been all up, for no horse can live with the hounds on the Moor, the bogs are so extensive; fortunately the Gray and another horse got in with them just as the Fox went to rocks, and not having any terriers they were compelled to leave him as night was fast closing.

Thomas Cobley's grave in Spreyton churchyard raises two questions. The first concerns his age. In the 1841 Census, he was recorded as a farmer at Butsford in Colebrooke, aged 75. This would have made him 78 when he died in January 1844, but the age recorded on the gravestone is 82. Then there is the matter of why he chose to be buried at Spreyton, around six miles from his home. The *Exeter Flying Post* for 18 January 1844 reported that 'his remains were followed to the family vault at Spreyton by a numerous circle of relatives and friends, who were all anxious to pay the last tribute of respect to so worthy a man', which seems to settle the question. However, is it not possible that his choice of last resting place was because of an ill-fated journey that started there long years before, a journey that had been celebrated in a song that would keep his memory green for centuries to come? Sadly, local newspapers were not geared up to chronicling the exploits of local worthies in the far-flung reaches of Devon in the early years of the nineteenth century, but, just along the road from the churchyard, a sign outside the Tom Cobley Tavern – known as the White Hart in Uncle Tom's day – records the local tradition that it was from here in 1802 that 'Uncle Tom Cobley and all' set off for Widecombe Fair.

THE ANNALS OF THE WHITE HART AT SPREYTON

The earliest reference found in a newspaper to the White Hart at Spreyton comes from the *Exeter Flying Post* on 31 January 1805:

> To be let for a term of years, as shall be agreed on, from Lady-day next, all those Griest [sic] Mills, called SPREYTON MILLS, with about thirteen acres of good arable and pasture land ... For which purpose a survey will be held at the White Hart public house, in Spreyton aforesaid, on Wednesday the 13th of February next.

By the time of the 1841 Census, the White Hart was in the hands of Simon Martin, a farmer, and his wife Deborah. They had two sons – one of whom, William, was a butcher – and two daughters. Four agricultural labourers also lived at the inn. Shortly afterwards, Simon Martin handed the inn over to his son William, took over nearby Coombe Farm and acquired 19 acres in the parish of Bow where he established a new farm called Huddishill. The 1840s were not a good time for business ventures of this sort, and, in the *Exeter Flying Post* for 9 November 1848, Huddishill was advertised for sale. A few months later, on 24 February 1849, the *Western Times* announced the sale, at Coombe Farm, of 'the whole of the live and dead farming stock, household furniture, etc, the property of Mr Simon Martin'. By the time of the 1851 Census, Simon and Deborah Martin were living at Milk Street in Exeter, where Simon was working as a butcher. He was then 57 years old, and by the time of the 1861 Census had retired with his wife to Spreyton to live with his widowed daughter Mary.

William Martin only stayed at the White Hart for a few years, before moving to North Tawton, where he kept a butcher's shop in the square. The White Hart's next landlord was Josias Middlewick or Middleweek, originally from Hittisleigh, who had settled in Spreyton after marrying a woman from the village. She had died, age 35, in 1852, leaving him with two young daughters. He was a shoemaker, a trade he kept up after taking the inn. After leaving the White Hart in 1864, he remarried and settled at Whiddon Down, where he continued to work as a shoemaker.

The White Hart was taken over by William Isaac, a butcher from Sampford Courtenay who had also married a local woman and settled in the village. The 1871 Census, which listed him as a butcher and farmer with 100 acres, also recorded three farm servants and one female domestic servant living at the inn. On 11 August 1871, the *Western Times* carried news of an event for which he provided outside catering:

> On Saturday a grand pic-nic came off on the beautiful grounds of Jestment [Justment] Green, the residence of Mr John Bolt, yeoman, who kindly granted their use. The Green is about three miles from [North Tawton] and ditto from South Tawton and Bow, and about a mile and a half from Spreyton. To the Green people from all those places moved off, and about four the North Tawton band burst on the scene with a storm of music setting them all agog. The arrangements were those known as 'rural sports', beyond which our civilization has not yet travelled. Host Isaac of Spreyton opened a booth for the sale of drinks, there was also a fine tea feast. It was supported by the gentry and farmers of the district. The Green is a splendid place for the purpose, the scenery charming. The band played capitally, and it was not until after dark that the people began to leave. One party it is said was led by the Pixies into a field, and that these roguish sprites so bewildered them there that it was upwards of half an hour before they could find

the way out. A vote of thanks was given to Mr and Mrs Bolt for their kindness in granting the grounds – but this was done before the arrival of the Pixies.

William Isaac's wife, Mary, died on 3 May 1879, and by the time of the 1881 Census he was married again, to another Mary, the daughter of William Martin, butcher and former landlord of the White Hart.

The White Hart not only went from strength to strength under William Isaac's stewardship; the farm attached to it also gained an enviable reputation. On 3 October 1890, the *Western Times* reported that

> Mr Wm Isaac, of the White Hart, has a very small but prolific head of cows. Two of them were served by Mr Wm Snell's (Broadnymett) bull last Christmas, and have brought forth four calves within the last month, this making the third twin birth our genial landlord has been favoured with during the year.

A report published a couple of weeks later, on 17 October, indicated that the sporting tradition established by Uncle Tom Cobley was being upheld:

> The Chagford Harriers met [at Spreyton] for the first time this season on Monday last. The weather being so dry was considered unfavourable to hunting, so a large party did not assemble at the meet. After a refresher at the White Hart, Huntsman Baker took the pack, in the pink of condition, to Coombe Farm, generally a favourite spot for hares, and which now proved no exception to the rule. A hare was quickly on the move, but got in about the farm yard where the hounds were unable to pick up the trail. On going back to the original starting place another hare was soon found, and made away to Heath Farm, from thence to the left to North Beer, and Downhayes, the hounds following her in rattling style to Justment, Yendacott, and Cessland Farm, South Tawton, back over Coombe and over the same ground three times almost in a circle until, at last, the hounds effected a kill in the open grounds in a meadow just under Coombe House.

William Isaac died, aged 69, in 1902, after running the White Hart for almost 39 years; his widow, eight years his junior, continued to run the White Hart until her death in 1908. On 20 November 1908, the *Western Times* announced the sale of that 'well-known Freehold and Fully-licensed House ... the White Hart, with ample accommodation, Outbuildings and Garden Dwelling House, Bakehouse, Stable, Traphouse adjoining, 2 well-built Cottages, with every convenience and gardens'. It was bought by John Sampson, one of the best-known men in the village.

John Sampson was born at Blackstreet in South Tawton in 1870, one of nine sons of a farmer with 100 acres. By 1891, he was working as a journeyman miller at Yeo Mill in Chagford. His uncle owned Cessland or Sessland Farm in Spreyton and by 1902 he was living there and working as a manure representative. Although this may sound faintly risible, manure was one of the lynchpins of the rural economy, and his role gave him considerable standing in the local community. On 10 November 1902, for example, as local representative of Messrs C Norrington & Co, manure manufacturers of Plymouth, he held an annual audit and dinner at the Seven Stars in South Tawton, attended by around 60 local worthies. Then, on 18 November, he presided over a similar event, this time as the representative of Burnard & Alger Ltd of Plymouth, at the Gostwyck Arms in North Tawton. On 14 April 1903, he married Amy Smith, the headmistress of Spreyton school and moved to the School House in the village. To mark the occasion, South Tawton Parish Council presented him with a 'handsome barometer'. His first son, christened Kenneth, was born, prematurely, less than seven months later. In September 1903, John Sampson was elected clerk to the school board and in April 1906 was appointed assistant overseer of the Okehampton Union, a post which involved administering poor relief. In 1907, his wife bore him another son, who died at the age of five months; their final son, Roy, was born a year later. By this time, however, Mrs Sampson's health was failing. Despite constant medical attention, she continued to worsen, and, despite being sent to Bournemouth for a complete rest cure, she died there, aged 31, in March 1909.

John Sampson had bought the White Hart just over a month earlier. One of his first changes, according to the *Western Times* for 11 February 1909, was 'to make a bar in the bar parlour, the liquor at present being drunk in the kitchen'. Although he now had an inn to run, as well as looking after two young boys, he continued to work as manure representative, assistant overseer and clerk to the school board. He also became clerk to the parish council. In 1911, he married Emily Hill of Fuidge Farm, and on 23 May 1913 placed a notice in the *Western Times*:

> Mr John Sampson, proprietor of the White Hart Hotel, Spreyton, begs to announce that he has purchased a 20-h.p. Ford Car, which will be available for hire in conjunction with the Hotel. Experienced driver engaged. Every accommodation for Visitors. High elevation; perfect sanitary arrangements. Within easy reach of the Dartmoor Hills. Fishing, Shooting, Hunting, Golf Links. Terms very moderate.

John Sampson was also instrumental in the revival of Spreyton Market at around this time, taking on the role of secretary to the market committee. When he died, at the age of 51, the *Western Times* of 8 March 1921 wrote that 'his sudden demise ... cast a deep gloom throughout the district in which for many years his figure had always been familiar and welcome ... Of the most jovial and happy disposition, he was always well hailed and ... his loss will be felt by a host of friends'.

John Sampson's widow, who had borne him a son in 1915, was 14 years younger than him, and continued to run the White Hart until the 1950s, catering for clay pigeon shoots, hunt meets, auctions, darts and skittle matches, the Spreyton Revels, and events such as this one reported by the *Western Times* on 18 August 1950:

> A happy evening was spent at the White Hart, Spreyton, by permission of Mrs Sampson, on Thursday last, the occasion being an impromptu vegetable and flower show. The results were very surprising, there being several entries of a very varied nature. One of the most interesting exhibits, and the largest, was a cabbage-cum-Brussel sprout, the diameter being 3ft 6in, and the height 4ft, grown by Mr E Butt, and the smallest exhibit was a perfectly shaped broad bean, three-quarters of an inch long, containing one bean, grown by the organiser and judge, Mr V Gilbert. Some very fine carnations grown by Mrs Sampson in the Victory Garden of the White Hart were greatly admired and won first prize in their class ... The happy affair finished on Saturday evening with a darts match, the proceeds of which, together with those of the 'mock auction', etc, amounting to £3 2s, are being sent to the Royal National Institute for the Blind. The prizes, given by Mrs Sampson, were distributed by Mrs FM Rooney, former headmistress of Spreyton Council School.

Starcross

Murray's 1851 *Handbook to Devon* described Starcross as 'a town rising, through the influence of the rail, to the remunerative dignity of a watering place'. The inn that catered for well-heeled visitors was the Courtenay Arms. Dating from the late eighteenth century, it had a superb riverside location, with an uninterrupted view across to Exmouth. Then, in the 1840s, Brunel drove the South Devon Railway between the inn and the river. To add insult to injury, he built a pumping station alongside it as part of his revolutionary atmospheric method of propulsion. On 15 October 1846, a few months after the line opened, the *Exeter Flying Post* announced that

> a new, elegant, and spacious inn will shortly be erected by the South Devon Railway Company at Starcross; the present site of the Courtenay Arms being required to give more space for the railway. The situation chosen for the new inn is quite as eligible, where 'mine host', the present worthy landlord, it is hoped, will entertain in his usual excellent way.

The atmospheric experiment was soon abandoned, however, leaving the company in serious financial difficulties. Among the projects cancelled was the rebuilding of the Courtenay Arms. In this early twentieth-century postcard, the Courtenay Arms, with the pumping station behind it, is seen from the down platform of Starcross station. Although superficially little changed, the Courtenay Arms has now been converted to flats as the Courtenay Arms Mews.

Across the road is the Galleon, originally known as the Ship. It has changed little since this postcard was published over 60 years ago, apart from losing the tall chimney at the front. In 2011, following the closure of the local post office, villagers petitioned the county council for help in opening a new one, and a site was eventually found in the Galleon Inn. At a time when pubs, post offices and other community facilities are closing at an

unprecedented rate, the trend towards combining them under one roof to help them survive is to be welcomed. Less welcome is the news that, on 3 November 2012, a stray firework set fire to one of the outbuildings behind the Galleon. Fortunately, although the outbuilding was gutted, the inn escaped unscathed.

The Railway Inn at Starcross seems to have predated the railway, and may originally have been known as the Half Moon. When the railway opened in May 1846, it became the Railway Inn and later the Railway Hotel. Here it is seen in the early twentieth century, when Thomas Venning was the landlord. Today, renamed the Atmospheric Railway, its walls are lined with railway memorabilia, while a family room at the back has been adapted to look like a railway carriage.

Staverton

The Sea Trout Inn in Staverton is seen here in the mid-twentieth century before it was swamped by extensions. Originally it was known as the Church House Inn, and, although information regarding its history is scanty, it is believed to have been built in the fifteenth century. Today it is a popular dining inn, with exclusive rights to fishing on a stretch of the Dart, open fires and a relaxed country ambience.

Stibb Cross

The Union Inn at Stibb Cross looked distinctly worse for wear when this photograph was taken in the 1920s. Today, it not only looks in much better shape, but is thriving, with pool, darts and euchre teams, along with race nights, folk sessions and bingo. The Union came close perilously close to extinction in February 2009, when it

was transformed from a centuries-old meeting place to a boarded-up and rapidly deteriorating ex-pub. Fortunately, a local haulier called Nigel Harris was not prepared to see it disappear, and took it on in September 2009. He set about refurbishing it to ensure that it not only remained a family-run pub at the heart of the community, but became the sort of place people would want to travel to. When he moved on three years later, it was taken over by new owners who have built on his success.

Sticklepath

Sticklepath is, for anyone who loves traditional inns, one of the finest places in Devon. Although it has a population of less than 500, the village supports two – the Devonshire Inn and the Taw River Inn – both of which are thriving. This is the Devonshire Inn as it looked a century ago, and it has hardly changed, although the wall on the right has gone. The gentleman on the right would still feel at home if he walked into this cosy, multi-roomed inn today, so lightly has the hand of the twentieth century touched it. Beer straight from the barrel and local cider, pasties warmed in the Aga, and nothing bar the clink of glasses to disturb the murmur of conversation. Sadly, the Devonshire Inn's long-serving landlord, Peter Verner-Jeffreys, died in December 2011, but his widow, Ann, continues to run this genuine classic among English inns.

Sticklepath's other inn was originally known as the Cornish Arms, presumably because the road through the village was once the main coach route from Exeter to Cornwall. When the lease was advertised in 1866, it was described as a 'desirable and well-accustomed inn ... together with walled garden, convenient coach house, stabling, yard, and about one acre of superior land'. Sometime between 1878 and 1882, with the coaching trade in decline, it was renamed the Taw River Inn, although by the time the postcards opposite were published around 1910 it was the Taw River Hotel. Larger, livelier, but no less traditional than the Devonshire Inn, the Taw River has two datestones on its front wall – one from 1660 and one from 1694 – although the core of the building may well be older. You enter through what appears to be the remains of a horse passage – a common feature of Devon longhouses – and it has been suggested that the inn may originally have been the manor house. The Taw River is a community pub par excellence, with a excellent range of ales and good home-cooked food, not only serving those fortunate enough to live in Sticklepath, but, like the Devonshire Inn, drawing in customers from miles around.

Stoke Fleming

The seventeenth-century Green Dragon at Stoke Fleming, seen here around 1940, has changed little, apart from the removal of the tall chimney to the right of the entrance. With open fires, wooden beams and rumours of a tunnel leading to the beach, this very traditional inn has a nautical theme. Popular with locals, it is noted for its real ale, and has a reputation for food

Stoke Fleming's other inn, the London Inn, has long been converted to a private house. It is seen here around 1910, with the Dartmouth to Kingsbridge coach rattling past. Incredibly, this is still the main road today, and, while the Green Dragon has the fortune to be on a side road up by the church, a steady stream of coaches, lorries and cars towing caravans continues to squeeze through the gap by the old London Inn.

Stoke Gabriel

An Edwardian view of the Church House Inn, one of Devon's most historic hostelries. Certainly there by the sixteenth century, but possibly built around 1150, part of the building once housed a courtroom. Despite its popularity, it remains a traditional and largely unspoilt village inn, with beamed ceilings, inglenook fireplaces, oak partitions – and a mummified cat.

A narrow lane opposite the Church House Inn ran down to the Victoria & Albert, seen here in the mid-twentieth century, when it was noted for its collection of pewter, brasses and other curios

hanging from low-beamed ceilings. Go down the lane today, though, and, while the building still survives, you may struggle to recognise it, so thoroughgoing has been its conversion to residential use since closing around ten years ago.

Stokenham

This early twentieth-century postcard features one of the most popular inns in the South Hams, the Tradesmen's Arms at Stokenham. It is also one of the most curious, made up of three distinct buildings, part thatched, part slate, and part dating back to the fourteenth century. Although noted for food, it has a traditional bar, popular with locals and visitors. Had the licensing authorities had their way, however, the Tradesmen's Arms would not even be a fading memory, for in March 1935 they threatened to revoke its licence on grounds of redundancy. A local policeman, asked to report on the numbers using the Tradesmen's Arms, 'said he had not seen more than six present when making his visits'. The lawyer acting for Mrs Michelmore, the owner, however, said that 'he had letters from many regretting

that this "old-world public house and village club of the best type" was to be closed. There was also a petition from 180 people of the village against the reference to the committee.' Faced with this, the magistrates relented and the Tradesmen's Arms survived.

Tamerton Foliot

The Seven Stars at Tamerton Foliot is seen here in the early twentieth century, with the Queen's Arms in the distance. Although all the other buildings on this postcard have gone, both pubs survive and remain open. When the Warleigh Estate was broken up in 1914, the Seven Stars was bought for £675 by Blundell's of Plymouth. The accommodation at the time consisted of a parlour, bar, tap room, spirit store, kitchen, store room, club room, two bedrooms, two WCs, urinal, coach house, wash house and two-stall stable. In the early 1930s, it came perilously close to disappearing. On 13 March 1934, the *Western Morning News* reported that

> an application by Mr Elliot Square for the renewal of the licence of the Seven Stars, Tamerton Foliot, was granted at Roborough Licensing Sessions yesterday. Supt Smith said the licence of the house was considered redundant in 1931, but it was renewed subject to alteration of the premises. This was carried out, and the premises were now in a fair condition. In spite of that it was still considered there were too many licensed houses in the neighbourhood. Mr Square, on behalf of the owners, Messrs Blundell & Co, Plymouth, said they had fully carried out the magistrates' instructions to renovate the house, and they were entitled to some consideration.
>
> 'What we should consider,' he said, 'is that Plymouth is extending its tentacles in every direction. Air Ministry officials have been down to Tamerton to inspect a site for a possible airport, and several building sites are being developed. There is every reason, therefore, to think that this licence may be very valuable in years to come.'

How right he was. Tamerton Foliot is now part of Plymouth, and it is reckoned that the Seven Stars is the oldest inn within the city boundary. It may have started life as a church house, it may have been built as a grange by monks from Plympton Priory, but, as you step down from the street, through a door that looks as though it was old in Drake's day, into this stone-floored, low-beamed inn, there is no doubt that you are stepping where many generations have stepped before.

Tavistock

On the corner of Madge Lane in Tavistock there were once two inns – the Globe and the Union – as well as a temperance hotel. By 1905, however, when the Union was taken over by Samuel Scown – whose name can be seen above the door in this photograph – the Globe and the temperance hotel had closed. Before taking the inn, Samuel Scown had been yard man at the Tavistock Hotel, where his wife Sarah was reception manageress. The Union, along with the former Globe and temperance hotel, were part of the Bedford Estate, and, when this was split up in 1911, the three properties were sold as a single lot. They were bought by Bass, Radcliffe & Gretton of Burton on Trent for £22,000, and, when Samuel Scown's lease ran out the following year, the new owners demolished all three properties to build a new Union Inn. Samuel Scown took on the South Western Hotel while the work was being carried out, but returned to become landlord of the new Union Inn when it opened. Today, it remains a lively community pub, with a good selection of real ales and a popular bunkhouse.

Tedburn St Mary

White's 1850 *Directory* lists two inns at Tedburn St Mary – the King's Arms, kept by William Lake, and the Red Lion, kept by Daniel Marchant. Both are still open, although the King's Arms – seen above – nearly disappeared on 28 May 1890, as this report in the *Western Times* records:

> A fire occurred on Wednesday night at the King's Arms Inn, occupied by Mr Miller, caused by the bursting of a petroleum lamp, which was suspended to the ceiling of the bar. A young man named Hucklebridge was passing the house at the time, and with the assistance of Messrs Phillips and Davey, succeeded in extinguishing the flames by means of buckets of water ... The house, which is covered with a thatch roof, is very old, and it was with difficulty that the fire was prevented from spreading.

The King's Arms is still thatched, but the Red Lion, whose thatch had been replaced with corrugated iron by the time the postcard below was published, now has a tiled roof.

Teignmouth

Teignmouth is the oldest resort in Devon, apart from Exmouth. Long before the visitors came, however, it was an important port, with shipyards and a fishing fleet which sailed to Newfoundland. It was twice sacked by the French, in 1340 and again in 1690. In the late eighteenth century, the docks were enlarged to ship out granite quarried on Dartmoor. Teignmouth remains one of the busiest ports in the south west, the main export today being ball clay from the Teign valley.

In the Second World War, the town was repeatedly hit in tip-and-run raids in which 79 people were killed, 151 were injured, and many buildings were destroyed. Shortly before the war, an unknown photographer went round Teignmouth, taking pictures of 27 of its pubs and publishing the results on a postcard. Inevitably, the pictures were very small – less than the size of a postage stamp – but they comprise a valuable record, which, with the aid of digital technology, we have remastered, enlarged and reproduced on the following pages, along with archive photographs from other sources, to indicate the richness of Teignmouth's pub culture over 70 years ago. Given the size of the originals, the quality of the photographs, most of which feature little more than the entrances to the various pubs, is not great, but we hope it is good enough to convey a sense of what a pre-war pub crawl round Teignmouth might have been like.

Of the 28 pubs featured here, only nine are still open. Five have been converted to other uses, but 14 have disappeared entirely, with those lost to bombing far outnumbered by those lost to post-war redevelopment. The most ill-conceived project was a dual carriageway pushed through the town centre in the early 1970s, which swept away five pubs. It was so underused that in 1995 most of the westbound carriageway was closed and a supermarket and car park – and later a fire station – were built on the site.

We start, though, with the Jolly Sailor – now Ye Olde Jolly Sailor. Set back from Northumberland Place, its façade belies an interior of fascinating antiquity. Believed to

date from the twelfth century, it survived when the rest of the town was sacked by marauding Frenchmen in 1690, by virtue of them making it their headquarters. In 1966, it featured in the Norman Wisdom film, *Press for Time*, in which he is sent to 'Tinmouth' as a reporter on the local paper, with predictable results. Today it is a popular and friendly local with possibly the oldest pool room in the county. Since this photograph was taken, the door on the left (through which Norman Wisdom and a host of extras ran in the film) has been blocked off, and the brickwork covered with render.

Just north of the Jolly Sailor is the Devon Arms, built in the early nineteenth century. On 16 April 1842, Richard Provo placed an advertisement in the *Western Times* to 'inform the commercial gentlemen and the public generally that he has succeeded to the business of the above hotel, and having made extensive alterations, hopes, by strict attention and keeping wines, spirits, ales and other articles of the best quality, to obtain their joint patronage, which it will be his constant study to observe'. He also added a postscript, assuring potential customers that the hotel had 'well-aired beds and good stabling'. The Devon Arms, which had its own brewery until 1900, remains one of Teignmouth's most popular free houses.

On the east side of Northumberland Place, next to the house where John Keats stayed in 1818, was the King William IV, a red-brick building dating from around 1850. It replaced a pub of the same name in Park Street, whose landlord moved here when it opened. Around ten years ago it became F&Rs, billed as 'Teignmouth's most desirable venue', with resident DJs, cocktails and karaoke.

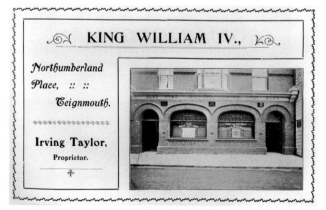

An advertisement for the King William IV from around 1910

Just west of Northumberland Place is the New Quay Inn, dating from 1785 and originally known as the Newfoundland Fishery Inn. It was renamed in the 1820s, when George Templer built a new quay to ship granite from his quarries at Haytor. It seems to have been enlarged and remodelled at the same time, acquiring embellishments such as the elegant portico which still survives today. The view below, of the inn from the quay, dates from the 1930s. It is a scene that changed little until a large concrete wall was built up against the foundations of the inn in 2012 as part of a £4M flood prevention scheme.

Just along from the New Quay Inn is the Ship, opened in the 1830s and originally known as the Pilot. Its unusual and eye-catching arrangement of bay windows, with

a doorway let into the one on the left, survives almost intact, although the windows are now uPVC. Like the New Quay Inn, the Ship has a superb location, looking westward over the beach and the estuary. There can be few better places to sit nursing a beer and watching the sun go down than the terrace in front of either of them.

Teignmouth got its first lifeboat in 1851, and a beerhouse on the Strand known as the Lifeboat Inn opened shortly afterwards. On 24 August 1887, the *Western Times* reported that James Knowles, the Lifeboat's landlord, had applied to upgrade it from a beerhouse to a fully-licensed inn. He claimed that 'it was a house near the river where persons were often taken in cases of boating accidents, and when a little liquor was called for', and produced a petition from local residents, 'including several teetotallers', in favour of granting him a spirit licence. Despite his application being refused, the Lifeboat did eventually get a full licence. Sadly, this supremely friendly street-corner local closed in 2010 and is now set to be converted to flats.

On 5 July 1845, the *Western Times* advertised the Market Inn in Brunswick Street 'to let with immediate possession ... The sum required for the incoming tenant will be very moderate, and from the thriving character of the town, and the extension of the railway, this will afford an eligible opportunity for an industrious steady man'. With the market across the road, the inn must indeed have seen busy times – but the market has long been a car park, and the Market Inn has been shut for decades. Since closing, it has been a Liberal Club, a tobacco warehouse and an auction house, and has recently been refurbished yet again.

The Royal Hotel on the Den was once the grandest in town, and it was still good enough for the Beatles when they came to Teignmouth in 1967 – to be mobbed by around 400 fans – while filming their Magical Mystery Tour. After it closed, the Grade II Regency-style building stood empty for a time, before being delisted and demolished to make way for a vapid block of post-modernist retirement flats. The wonderfully atmospheric photograph overleaf – a chance survival in an old family album – was taken in the bar of the Royal Hotel on 3 February 1947, a fascinating memento of a lost part of Teignmouth's heritage.

In the bar of Teignmouth's Royal Hotel, 3 February 1947

Further north along the Den Promenade was the Beach Hotel, now converted to apartments.

Judging by its name, the Beach House Inn also stood in this part of town, although information as to the exact location of this long-lost beerhouse has not been forthcoming.

Just back from the sea front, in Regent Gardens, is the King's Arms, a busy, friendly local, little changed since this photograph was taken.

The Dawlish Inn, opposite the King's Arms, was originally known as the Seven Stars, but renamed in the 1830s when the turnpike road to Dawlish was opened. On 24 August 1886, Frank Tucker, the landlord, placed an advertisement in the *Western Times* offering to provide 'every accommodation for excursionists, picnic and waygoose parties' in a 'large room recently added to the premises'. Today, much altered, it is a popular Irish pub called Dicey Reilly's.

The Half Moon in nearby Hollands Road has also had a change of name, and is now the Brass Monkey. This popular town-centre pub, which had its own brewery until 1910, is now owned by St Austell Brewery.

The Sebastopol (right) stood on the corner of Myrtle Hill and Brook Street East. Before being renamed to commemorate the famous siege in the Crimean War in 1854-55, it was known as the Brewery Inn. It was the tap for the Myrtle Hill Brewery, established by James Henry Martin. After his death, his executors placed an advertisement in the *Exeter & Plymouth Gazette* on 23 July 1859:

> To be let, with immediate possession, all that very desirable free public house and brewery, called the Myrtle Hill Brewery and Sebastopol Inn, situate in the fashionable watering place Teignmouth, in which a good trade has been carried on for many years. An unusual opportunity is now offered to anyone desirous of entering upon the above business, which is capable of much extension. Much attention having been bestowed by the late proprietor in fitting up the brewery, malthouse, etc, it will be found replete with every convenience for carrying on an extensive business.

It was taken by a Mr Hellier, but less than a year later, in April 1860, the lease was advertised again. The premises were described as consisting of a 'malthouse, extensive cellars, brewhouse, covered skittle alley, eight bedrooms, dining room, parlours, kitchen, bar and tap room'. Although the inn soon found a taker, the brewery did not, and seems to have closed around this time. The Sebastopol, still fondly remembered as a popular and lively local, was demolished around 1972 to make way for the dual carriageway.

Another victim of the dual carriageway was the Railway Hotel at the top of Station Road, opposite the station. It was originally known as the South Devon Railway Hotel, and its landlord, Thomas Stevens, was something of an entrepreneur. On 19 April 1851, he placed an advertisement in the *Western Times* announcing his intention of being part of the Great Exhibition festivities in Hyde Park:

> T Stevens, South Devon Railway Hotel, Teignmouth, most respectfully informs his friends, and the public of the West of England, that he intends visiting the metropolis, on the occasion of the approaching industrial exhibition, with his MONSTER SALOON, which is 500 feet long, and which has been erected at the Park Fair. He begs to assure those ladies and gentlemen who may honour him with their support, that every article on sale will be of the best quality, and the terms reasonable.

The Railway Hotel closed and was demolished in 1973.

The Bird in Hand was in Lower Brook Street, just west of Station Road. In the early twentieth century, the landlord was George Furler, who also ran the Fore Street Brewery at 22 Fore Street. The brewery closed after he was declared bankrupt in 1913. The Bird in Hand survived, but was eventually demolished to make way for the dual carriageway.

There was also a beerhouse called the Gardeners Arms on Lower Brook Street. Its licence was revoked on grounds of redundancy in 1936.

The Royal Oak stood on Commercial Road, opposite the Baptist church, and was demolished to make way for the dual carriageway in 1973 ...

... as was the Prince of Wales on the corner of Higher Brook Street and Fore Street. It adjoined the Fore Street Brewery, which closed in 1913.

The Beehive stood in Bitton Street (now part of Bitton Park Road), just west of St James's church, in an area that was heavily bombed in World War Two.

The Ring of Bells on Willey Lane, just south of the Beehive, was destroyed in an air raid on 10 January 1943.

Two pubs – the Golden Lion and the Black Horse – once stood next to each other at the junction of Coombe Vale and Bitton Park Roads. When the Golden Lion was demolished in the 1940s to widen the road, its licence – and name – was transferred to a house across the road. Long one of Teignmouth's most popular real-ale pubs, and a thriving local, it closed in 2005 and permission has since been sought to develop the site for flats. The Black Horse survived on its original site after the demolition of the original Golden Lion, but in 1977 it too was demolished for road widening.

The White Horse on the corner of Teign Street and Saxe Street was described as 'an old established inn' when it was advertised to let in 1870. It was destroyed by enemy action in January 1943. The site now forms part of Pellew Arcade.

The London Hotel in Bank Street dated from 1742. After closing in 2004, it was converted to flats. Although this portico survives, it has been smothered, like much of the building, in pebbledash.

The Custom House Inn on Old Quay Street was known until around 1890 as the Locomotive. After closing, it housed offices before being converted to flats around 2000. With the rerouting of Old Quay Street, the old inn now stands on a new street called Custom House Hill.

The Blue Anchor on Teign Street opened some time before 1827. In 1887, it was acquired by the Well Park Brewery of Exeter, which was taken over by Devenish's in 1925. Since 1985, however, the Blue Anchor has been a free house, and, with six real ales, is one of the most popular traditional pubs in Teignmouth. The photograph above shows a charabanc trip setting off from outside the pub around 1912.

The Old Quay Inn, seen here with a quay company lorry parked outside, closed and was demolished in February 1985 so that new warehouses could be built on the quay.

Thorverton

The Exeter Inn in Thorverton opened sometime before 1804, but was renamed the Duke of Wellington to commemorate Wellington's victory in 1815 at the Battle of Waterloo.

On 9 April 1831, the *Exeter & Plymouth Gazette* reported that 'the second Exeter troop of yeomanry cavalry assembled for exercise on Wednesday week and afterwards dined at the Duke of Wellington Inn, Thorverton'. Later renamed the Wellington Arms, its end was dramatic, as the *Exeter & Plymouth Gazette* reported on 27 October 1855:

> Shortly before midnight on Tuesday last an alarm was given in the village of Thorverton that the Wellington Arms public house was on fire. Messengers were immediately despatched to Exeter, and the West of England and Sun engines were sent off with all haste. The fire, however, had in the meantime extended with much rapidity, and, notwithstanding the most energetic exertions of all the parties engaged, the inn and five adjoining houses were destroyed. The stock in the inn was also consumed, but we understand that it was insured, as was likewise the building itself, which belonged to Mr Paine, of this city. During the conflagration a portion of the ruins fell upon some of the firemen, who narrowly escaped with their lives.

It was quickly rebuilt and, when finished, reverted to its original name. On 31 January 1857, an advertisement appeared in the *Exeter & Plymouth Gazette*:

> Exeter Inn, Thorverton, Devon: To be sold or let, with early possession, the above well-situated inn. The house is free, with a respectable trade, and very recently built, with every accommodation for conducting the business satisfactorily. The renter or purchaser will be required to take the furniture at a fair valuation.

Three years later, Richard Pain (presumably the same Mr Paine described as the owner of the building in the report of the fire) was declared bankrupt, and the inn was put up for sale once more. It was not the freehold which was for sale, however, but the remainder of a 21-year lease from the Dean and Chapter of Exeter Cathedral, which had commenced in 1853. The inn was taken by John Clark, who was also a coal dealer, but less than four years later, in April 1864, he went bankrupt as well.

Despite all these vicissitudes, the inn survived, to be acquired by William Hancock & Sons of Wiveliscombe in 1897. Since just after the Second World War, however, it has been a free house run by the Mann family. This very traditional, very friendly village inn is noteworthy not only for an old well – which survived the rebuilding – in the middle of the bar, but also for a fascinating collection of antique weaponry on its walls.

A mile east of Thorverton, on the main road from Exeter to Tiverton, lies the Ruffwell Inn. Since this photograph was taken in the 1920s, the building has lost its porch but gained a clock turret, along with extensions to the back and side. Until just over a couple of years ago, the Ruffwell, long boarded up and forlorn, looked set to become another of Devon's lost inns. It was saved by Peter Cairns, formerly at the Hare & Hounds in Sidbury. After a much-needed refurbishment, the Ruffwell has quickly established itself as one of the most popular dining inns in east Devon, as well as staging beer festivals and regular live music gigs. Amid all the doom and gloom, with pubs closing at an ever increasing rate, it is heartening to see one that has so decisively bucked the trend.

Tipton St John

The Golden Lion at Tipton St John in the Otter valley has seen a few changes since this postcard was published around 1905: the recessed bay in the centre of the building has been altered and the brick on the ground floor covered in render. These changes, though, pale into insignificance compared with those that took place a few years before the postcard was published. The Golden Lion originally occupied an old thatched building on the other side of the road. On 24 March 1848, the *Exeter & Plymouth Gazette* reported how it had narrowly escaped destruction:

> Ann Browne was indicted for feloniously setting fire to a house at Tipton near Ottery St Mary. Hermann Ham, blacksmith, keeper of the Golden Lion at Tipton, said that the prisoner was in his employ on the 27th of December. He smelled fire the night before Christmas, and all his family were on the alert to discover whence it proceeded ... On Christmas Day, the prisoner said that she had found some burnt mats of straw at the corner close to the millstream. He went there, and found some mats of reed, and some of the rafters of the cellar burnt. That day she went away, and returned on Sunday night. He had a talk with her, and she said, those that set fire to the place would certainly do it again. He said he hoped not, for he would certainly keep a sharp look out, and, if he caught them, they should never set fire to any house in this country any more. The next morning he was at work, when the prisoner came in and wanted some wood. He told her to go to the stable to get it herself, as he could not attend to it. She came back with some keys, and he told her which was the right one. She then went away, but soon afterwards she called his attention to some smoke that she said was coming round the corner. He went there, and found the roof of the cellar on fire. The roof was thatch. He gave the alarm, and it was put out in about ten minutes. About seven feet in length of the thatch was burnt. He informed the constable of this, and he took her into custody. Whilst in custody the aunt and sister came, and he heard the aunt say, 'What made you set the place on fire?' She said she did not know, but if her master would forgive her she wouldn't do it again ...
>
> William Davey, constable of Ottery, said he apprehended the prisoner. She said she set the house on fire. She had a very good master. He placed her in the parlour of the house, and remained there all night. Several persons saw her in the course of the afternoon.
>
> William Wood Ham, brother of the prosecutor, said that he was at his house on the 27th. He heard the prisoner crying, when he and Davey entered the room; when asked why, she said she did set the place on fire, but not the first time. She further said that she took two congreve matches, and with one lighted the candle, and with the other set fire to the thatch ...
>
> William Davey, constable, recalled, said that the prisoner said that she was very sorry for what she had done. The learned judge having summed up, the jury returned a verdict of Not Guilty.

Thirty years later, in 1874, the railway came to Tipton St John, but, although the station opened next to the inn, no plans were made to rebuild it until, after its acquisition by Heavitree Brewery, the council granted planning permission for a new inn across the road in August 1896. Three months later, on 8 November, a fire broke out in the roof of the old inn, which was completely destroyed. The new inn opened a few months later.

Shortly afterwards, the station assumed a greater importance when it became the junction for a branch to Budleigh Salterton, which was extended to Exmouth a few years later. The station closed in 1967, and the Golden Lion's beer garden now extends over the old trackbed, while inside, art deco prints and paintings by local artists provide the backdrop for 'British, Mediterranean and rustic French cooking'.

Tiverton

The Prince Regent on Lowman Green is seen here on the morning of Sunday 6 April 1930, after what the following week's *Western Times* described as

> one of the most disastrous floods at Tiverton in the past half century ... Rain fell practically continuously for about six hours, but it was not until early evening that the disquieting signs became apparent. The first indication was the sudden failure, one after the other, of the gas and electricity supplies of the town, and this was followed by residents of the low-lying parts noticing a rapid rise of the waters, and they then realised that their dwellings were in danger of becoming involved.
>
> Lowman Green was the first part to become entirely inundated, and in the darkness of the night the scenes in the streets can be more vividly imagined than described. Crowds thronged the vicinity of the Lowman and Little Silver bridges, and the roar of the surging waters was all the more fearsome because of the rain and intense darkness.
>
> The water swirled in a devastating torrent over the river banks near the clock tower, and in about three-quarters of an hour it had risen four feet. It rapidly climbed to the window sill level of the Prince Regent Hotel, and in a short time barrels of beer were floating about in five feet of water.

It was not the first time the Prince Regent had been inundated. On 26 October 1875, the *Western Times* reported that the River Lowman had risen 14 feet above its normal level, and that 'in the Prince Regent Inn ... the water was several feet in depth [and] the casks of liquor floated from the jibs'.

In December 2010, after being closed for 18 months, the newly-refurbished Prince Regent reopened as the Inn on the Green. And, while the events of 1875 and 1930 have thankfully not been repeated, the front door of the inn had to be protected by sandbags in October 2012 after the River Lowman burst its banks, with customers having to use the back door.

As can seen from this photograph, the Country House Inn on St Andrew Street also suffered in the 1930 floods. When Hanbury & Co of Taunton advertised the lease of the inn in the *Western Times* on 20 September 1890, the premises included a grocer's shop as well as a bar. When it was advertised again, in the *Exeter & Plymouth Gazette* on 1 August 1895, there was no mention of the grocer's shop, but there was 'stabling'. The Country House Inn is still there, with its brickwork covered in render, but has long been closed, permission having been granted in 1993 for conversion to housing.

The Hare & Hounds, a nineteenth-century beerhouse at 138 Chapel Street. In 1937, Starkey, Knight & Ford, who owned both the Hare & Hounds and a fully-licensed house called the Elmore Bell at 46 Chapel Street, applied to transfer the licence of the Elmore Bell to a 'commodious new building [on] a site near the Hare & Hounds'. The old Hare & Hounds was demolished to make way for a new and much larger Hare & Hounds, which closed in 2013. Enterprise Inns sold it the following year and an application to convert it to housing has since been submitted. The old Elmore Bell has also been converted to housing.

The White Horse was a major coaching inn, with coaches between Taunton and Exeter calling regularly. When the railway from Taunton to Exeter opened in 1844, bypassing Tiverton, much of its trade disappeared, although one coach operator, called George Smale, fought back, placing the following advertisement in the *Exeter & Plymouth Gazette* on 28 September 1844:

> The public are respectfully informed that the Protector coach still continues to leave the Buller's Arms, St Sidwells [Exeter] every morning at a quarter before ten, performing the journey in the same time as by the railway, and at one half the fare, over a beautiful line of country, acknowledged to be the most delightful ride in the West of England, through the villages of Stoke Canon, Rewe, and within half a mile of Thorverton and Silverton ... The Protector leaves Goodland's White Horse Inn, Tiverton, every afternoon, at a quarter past three o'clock, arriving in Exeter in time for all coaches to the South Coast.

In 1848, however, the Bristol & Exeter Railway opened a branch to Tiverton, and the coaching era, as far as the White Horse was concerned, was over. The inn continued to play an important part in the life of the town, however, hosting functions such as the annual general meetings of the Tiverton Agricultural & Labourer's Friend Society.

In the early hours of Friday 23 January 1863 a fire broke out at the inn, completely destroying it, along with an adjoining house and most of the outbuildings. When it was rebuilt, access to the coachyard was retained, but a shop was built on one side of the archway. This was clearly regarded as one of the White Horse's selling points when the lease was advertised in the *Exeter & Plymouth Gazette* on 2 November 1891:

The White Horse as rebuilt in the 1860s

> To let, that old-established fully-licensed house, the White Horse Inn, Tiverton, situated in the main thoroughfare, and having a good yard and stabling accommodation. The front being fitted as a shop, it offers every facility for doing a good retail wine and spirit business.

Still open today, and little changed externally since this photograph was taken in the 1920s, the White Horse is one of Tiverton's most popular inns, while the shop is now a baguette bar.

Topsham

The earliest deed for the Bridge Inn at Topsham, dating from 1691, mentions 'recently erected buildings', although it is not clear whether these were erected on a greenfield site or added to pre-existing buildings. The inn stands beside a bridge built in the early eighteenth century to replace a tidal ford across the River Clyst, where there had been quays for centuries. There is a legend that ships carrying stone from Beer to build Exeter cathedral docked here, and the inn may have started life as a hostel for the stone masons. As it stands today, the Bridge Inn is a fascinating medley of buildings from different periods, including a cob-walled cottage, a slate-hung building with an impressive two-storey bay, and a former malthouse.

The marshes below the Bridge were once an important source of rock salt. There is a record of a salt officer called John Britnell at Topsham Bridge in 1732, and on 16 October 1797, the *Sherborne Mercury* advertised for sale,

> the fee-simple and inheritance of all that commodious dwelling house, known by the name of the Topsham Bridge Inn, stable, orchard and garden; a small field on the other side of the road, containing about two acres; two neat dwellings, a garden, and convenient quay, with the salt refinery. For sale of which a public survey [auction] will be held at the said inn, on Monday the 30th day of October instant, at three o'clock in the afternoon ... For particulars apply to Mr Evans, salt merchant.

On 6 December 1799, Jonathan Evans was fined £100 for removing salt before it had been checked by the excise officer. The quay and salt refinery were still there in 1819, for on 13 May that year, the *Exeter Flying Post* advertised to let

> a moiety of the salt works situate at Topsham Bridge, Devon. Adjoining the salt works is an excellent quay, with every conveniency for the landing and warehousing of rock salt, coal, etc. It is well worth the attention of those who wish to engage in the salt trade, as the salt manufactured there is superior to any imported. A man who has worked at the above works for some time can again be hired. Further particulars to be had ... of Mrs Ferguson, Dyer's Court, Rock Lane, Exeter.

By this time, the salt works and quay no longer had any connection with the inn, which three years earlier had formed part of a rather unusual auction advertised in the *Exeter Flying Post* on 20 July 1815:

> To be sold in lots, to the best bidders, before Abel Moysey, Esq, Deputy Remembrancer of the Court of Exchequer, at the Valiant Soldier Inn, Holloway Street, Exeter, on Saturday the 5th day of August 1815, at twelve o'clock at noon, pursuant to an order of the said court, made in a cause – 'The King against Francis Cox and Philip Pyle'. Several freehold messuages, tenements or dwelling houses, gardens, orchards, malthouses, and appurtenances; consisting of the Topsham Bridge Inn, in the parish of Topsham, in the county of Devon, now in the occupation of Mr William Lake; a freehold house in Monmouth Street Hill, in the same parish; and a garden, stable and courtlage situate in Chapter Street in the same parish.

When we next hear of the Bridge Inn, Philip Pyle Jr is the owner. On 14 December 1839, he placed a notice in the *Western Times*, advertising the lease

> of that well-accustomed and long-established inn, known as the Topsham Bridge Inn. To any individual desirous of connecting the malting with the public business, the above inn will be found highly advantageous, inasmuch as there is an extensive malthouse immediately attached, which will carry at least 50 bushels.
>
> The house is complete with every requisite, and contains a good parlour, dining room, several bedrooms, etc, and is pleasantly situate half way between Exeter and Exmouth, and is in the immediate vicinity of the large and populous town of Topsham.
>
> There is also a garden of about ¾ of an acre, adjoining, well stocked with fruit trees, etc. The coming in, as well as the rent, will be found moderate. For further particulars, application, if by letter post paid, to Mr Philip Pyle Jr, of Topsham, the owner, will be immediately attended to.

Ten years later, when he advertised the inn to let in the *Exeter & Plymouth Gazette* on 2 June 1849, the accommodation was described as consisting of 'a bar, parlour, several bedrooms, kitchens, cellars, brewhouse, stables, garden, etc', with no mention of the malthouse. Either he had leased this separately, or it was being used as a brewhouse, for, when the inn was advertised for sale in the *Western Times* on 31 December 1853, a malthouse – but not a brewhouse – was mentioned. By this time Philip Pyle Jr had moved on. The advertisement included not only the information that a Mr Matthews was the current tenant, but also that 'the property ... is in good repair, the late owner, Mr Edwin Teed Boys, deceased, having expended considerable sums in repairing and improving the same'.

The Bridge Inn in the mid-nineteenth century had a reputation for sporting fixtures of a decidedly robust character. On 21 September 1839, a correspondent in the *Exeter & Plymouth Gazette* informed readers that 'a purse of sovereigns will be wrestled for at the Topsham Bridge Inn, on the Exmouth road, on Tuesday next. The play to begin at twelve o'clock; good sport is expected.' On 8 May 1847, the same paper reported that

> on Monday a pigeon match took place at the Topsham Bridge Inn, between Messrs Francis, at ten birds, for £2, against Messrs Stogden and Hayward, which was won by Messrs Francis, who killed all their birds, the others losing by one. Another match was then made between Messrs Francis and Pridham, at five birds each, which was won by Mr Francis. There was another match for £1 between Messrs Francis and Hayward, at

seven birds each, which could not be decided, for want of birds, each party killing ten out of eleven. On Whit Tuesday another pigeon match will take place at this inn.

By 1861, Philip Duffett was landlord of the Bridge. He was succeeded by his son, Richard John Duffett, who, according to his obituary in the *Western Times* on 6 June 1899, 'was well-known to shooting men throughout the county, and ... landlord of the Bridge Inn near the Clyst Valley Range ... He joined the battalion some years since when the Topsham detachment was formed.' By then, William Gibbings had moved from Clyst St George, where he had been head gardener at the rectory, to take over the tenancy of the Bridge. In the early twentieth century, the inn became famous for livestock auctions and shows held in the adjoining field under the auspices of John Pratt, an auctioneer from Ottery St Mary. Celebratory dinners were regularly held in

the inn after the business of the day had been concluded. A report in the *Exeter & Plymouth Gazette* on 7 August 1908 gives an idea of the camaraderie that characterised these occasions:

> An interesting incident was witnessed at the Bridge Inn, Topsham, after the conclusion of the monthly stock auction, a presentation being made to Mr EG Fisher, who has for many years carried on business as a miller in the parish, and who has now removed to Cullompton. Mr G Pyne occupied the chair, and Jessie Pyle spoke in testimony of the good feeling which had existed between Mr Fisher and his fellow townsmen during the time they had been associated. Mr Fisher had always taken great interest in all affairs for the benefit of the parish, and they did not wish him to leave Topsham without some recognition of their feelings towards him. Mr JM Pratt then handed to Mr Fisher a handsome marble timepiece, together with an illuminated list of the names of the subscribers, numbering upwards of 70. Mr Fisher suitably acknowledged the kindness of his friends, and said his interest in Topsham would ever remain.

The Bridge was also the meeting place of the Topsham & District Accidental Club, a friendly society with almost 500 members, for which William Gibbings acted as treasurer, and the Topsham Rational Club, of which he was president.

On 13 November 1908, the Bridge Inn, 'in the occupation of WJ Gibbings', was advertised for sale in the *Exeter & Plymouth Gazette*. Just over two weeks later, on 28 November, the *Western Times* reported that

> Mr Herbert A Fulford, auctioneer, conducted an auction for the sale of the Bridge Inn, with a cottage and outbuildings, Topsham, at the Half Moon Hotel, Exeter, today. The inn produces a rental of about £25 per annum, while the cottage is let at a weekly rental of 2/6. There are also a garden, orchard, and paddock. Bidding opened at £400, and rose to £565, at which price it was sold to Mr WJ Gibbons [sic], the present occupier.

The Bridge continued to be a popular venue for celebratory dinners. On 29 November 1912, the *Exeter & Plymouth Gazette* reported that

> the annual dinner of the Topsham Territorials, held in the skittle alley of the Bridge Inn, proved, as usual, a great success, and a most enjoyable time was spent by the large company. The improvised dining room was nicely decorated with flags and greenery, and the arrangements made by Sergt HL Taylor (the hon secretary) proved admirable.

Twenty-eight years later, on 3 May 1940, the *Western Times* carried a report of another celebration:

> Topsham British Legion's 'dugout' supper took place at the Bridge Inn on Friday [26 April]. Over 70 assembled in a room, the entrance to which was sandbagged and lit by candles in bottles in true 'dugout' style. The meal comprised bully beef and beer, hot dogs and pickles. Those contributing to the musical programme were Messrs H Bricknell, Towell, Lacy, Spike, Luscombe and Galt.

A toast was proposed to 'the visitors' by the local British Legion chairman, Major Gould – presumably the Lieutenant Gould who had proposed an identical toast at the Territorials' dinner 28 years earlier.

In December 1929, William Gibbings and his wife Harriet celebrated their golden wedding anniversary, but a month later he died at the age of 72. The *Western Times* of 31 January 1930 reported that 'the esteem and respect in which Mr William John Gibbings, for 30 years landlord of the Bridge Inn, Topsham, was held, was evidenced by the large gathering at the funeral which took place on Wednesday at Clyst St George church'. His widow, who was 77, took over the inn, establishing a tradition – of the inn being run by a woman – which continues today. The current licensee, Caroline Cheffers-Heard, is William Gibbings' great-granddaughter. She is the fourth generation, her daughter Riannon will be the fifth, and Amelia and Beatrice, born in 2008 and 2010 respectively, will be the sixth.

The Bridge has seen no major changes since William Gibbings took it over more than a century ago. Then as now, the heart of the inn is a cosy snug, with one side of the room formed by a high-backed settle with glazed panels above, and a grandfather clock, dated 1726, in one corner. At one end is a wood-burning stove – a daring innovation, less than a decade old – and at the other is a serving hatch, installed in the 1940s and the closest thing the Bridge has to a bar. Behind it is the inner sanctum, a serving area-cum-sitting room where honoured customers are allowed to sit while the

important work of fetching beer from barrels in the cellar goes on around them. Across the corridor is a tap room, hardly changed since Victorian times, where children and dogs are welcome, while outside is a serving hatch for customers sitting on benches overlooking the weir, where a lone heron always seems to be poised motionless, waiting for lunch to swim by.

The Bridge may not be everyone's idea of a great pub. True, there are always at least six real ales available, generally from West Country breweries, as well as cider, but there is not much in the way of lager, and wide-screen TVs, juke boxes and games machines are conspicuous by their absence. There is no piped music either, although there are regular live music sessions in the old malthouse. Phil Beer and Steve Knightley of Show of Hands live nearby and the Bridge is not only their local, but also one of their favourite performance venues.

If the Bridge is something of a museum piece, it is only because most other pubs have been gutted and revamped – often several times – in the name of progress. But, while so many of those revamped pubs have fallen by the wayside, the Bridge has gone from strength to strength. The secret of its success is not just that it harks back to times long gone, but that it works supremely well as a place for people to meet and chat and enjoy a beer or two in convivial company. It was a formula perfected by William Gibbings over a century ago, and it still works today because today's customers come to the Bridge for much the same reason they did back then. But perhaps the most ringing endorsement of the Bridge's unique character came in 1998, when the Queen, deciding it was high time she visited a traditional pub, chose to come here.

The Globe Inn on Fore Street has been one of Topsham's principal inns since the eighteenth century, although parts of the building are considerably older. On 6 October 1836, the *North Devon Journal* reported that the Duke and Duchess of St Albans, while touring the West Country, 'lunched at Harrison's Globe Hotel, Topsham, expressing themselves much pleased with the attention paid and the reception experienced by them'. The Globe was also a popular venue for meetings and celebrations associated with the town's maritime trade. On 20 June 1839, the *North Devon Journal* reported that 'a public meeting of merchants, ship owners and others ... which was numerously attended by parties from Exeter, Topsham, Exmouth, Starcross and the neighbourhood' had been held at the Globe to protest against the duties imposed by the corporation of Exeter on vessels using the port. On 27 December 1865, the *Exeter Flying Post* carried news of a more agreeable occasion:

> The Messrs Holman launched a fine vessel of 500 tons burthen from their yard [at Topsham] on Wednesday morning. The launch was a complete success, and when the ship glided into the 'untumultuous foam', the spectators vouchsafed their approving shouts. Mrs Thomas Holman was the sponsor, and the vessel was named the Hugh Fortescue. She is intended for the China trade. In the evening an excellent supper was provided by Mr John Harrison of the Globe Hotel, for more than 300 of the friends and workmen of the Messrs Holman ... The bands of the Woodbury and Topsham volunteers and a glee party were in attendance; and it is quite superfluous to say that human enjoyment was at its highest pitch.

Music is still very much associated with the Globe, as Topsham Folk Club meets regularly in the old malthouse at the back. The inn was recently refurbished, and reopened in May 2011 with boutique-style bedrooms and a stylish restaurant, as well as a bar serving ales from local breweries.

On 30 July 1869, the *Exeter & Plymouth Gazette* advertised the sale of

> all those three undivided fourth-part or shares of and in all that freehold messuage or tenement, brewhouse and cellars called the Passage House Inn; and also of and in all that ferry called the Passage House Ferry, situate, lying and being at Topsham ... and now in the occupation of Mr Charles Hall, as tenant thereof.

The Passage House Inn, seen here on an early twentieth-century postcard, is essentially a seventeenth-century building with eighteenth-century additions, but, as the nearby ferry dates back to medieval times, the chances are that there has been some sort of alehouse here for the reception of travellers for centuries. The Passage House has traditionally been one of the favourite haunts of Topsham's fishermen. On 28 November 1873, the *Exeter & Plymouth Gazette* reported that the landlord, Charles Hall, had applied to the magistrates to 'open his house two hours before time in the morning, during the fishing season, for the accommodation of fishermen'. The request was granted. The Passage House remains popular, and not just with fishermen. Inside, it is cosy and traditional, with a good choice of beers and wines and an extensive menu, while the large riverside patio across the way, with barbecues in summer, is justly celebrated. It also hosts popular annual events, such as a hotly contested tug-of-war and a mile-and-a-half swimming race across the estuary to the Turf Tavern.

The Passage House and Ferry from the west bank of the Exe

In 1954, WG Hoskins wrote that 'Topsham is one of those ancient, decayed estuary ports which are perhaps the most fascinating kind of town that England can show, with their colour, smells, and strong sense of past life everywhere in the streets and alleys and along the waterfronts.' His words are just as true over half a century later. At the heart of maritime Topsham is the Lighter Inn, which, when it was advertised for sale in the *Exeter & Plymouth Gazette* on 16 August 1828, was described as 'that old, well-established and desirable public house, situate on the quay at Topsham, called the Lighter, now in possession of Sarah Ireland'. On 25 April the following year, it was advertised for sale again, in the *Western Times*, along with 'that good vessel or lighter called the Mary, burthen per register 32½ tons, with all the stores now belonging to her'. So, in the same way that ownership of the Passage House Inn was combined with that of the Passage House Ferry, the original owner of the Lighter Inn also owned a lighter to offload cargoes from ships moored in the estuary.

When the inn was offered for sale again – in the *Western Times* on 29 August 1857 – the advertisement included a comprehensive description of the premises:

> The property comprises excellent dining and tradesmen's rooms, parlour, bar, tap room, kitchen, and seven good bedrooms, brewhouse, underground cellars, stable and other convenient offices attached, well supplied with pump and other soft water, in excellent repair, situated in the most populous and business part of the town, adjoining the custom house and on the quay. The present owner, Mr Thos Stancombe, successfully carried on an extensive business thereon for 23 years, and the present occupier continues to do the same.

In 1886, the *Exeter & Plymouth Gazette* reported that plans for rebuilding the inn had been approved. Although it is not clear how extensive the rebuilding work was, on 4 May 1971 fire swept through the inn, necessitating a major restoration project. Externally, the building was restored magnificently. Inside, although the labyrinth of rooms listed in 1857 has given way to an open-plan layout, wooden beams and a log-burning fire preserve the illusion of continuity, while photographs of Topsham quay in days gone by pay tribute to the inn's illustrious past.

WG Hoskins also considered 'the inns and taverns of Topsham ... as varied and excellent as those of any old river-port. Best of all is the Salutation (1720) with its former assembly room, bowling green, and all the other attributes of a good eighteenth-century inn.' It is seen here in the 1940s, with its assembly room extending out over the pavement. Underneath it, a magnificent single-leaf door – one of the largest in the country – which once led through to the inn yard, presents something of a mystery, for it looks far older than the building, yet where it comes from no one knows. As the town's principal inn, the Salutation was the venue for balls, assemblies and civic functions, as well as more dubious gatherings, such as one reported in the *Exeter & Plymouth Gazette* on 18 January 1851:

A day or two since, a party of young sportsmen having been out all day with the hounds, met in the evening at the Salutation Inn. After sundry spirited proceedings, one of the party placed a £5 note on the table, and, having had his horse brought into the room, offered to back him to the amount to leap over the table, but Mr Lake very prudently interposed and prevented such a foolish freak.

When the Salutation was offered for sale in the *Western Times* on 28 October 1837, it was described as

that capacious and long-established inn, called the Salutation Inn, together with the brewhouse, cellars, extensive stables, and coach houses, large bowling green, gardens, and numerous outhouses and offices ... now in the occupation of Mr William Lake. The house comprises, on the ground floor, excellent commercial and sitting rooms, tap room, kitchen, and larder, a tradesman's room, and a large dining room, with an extensive billiard room, and other convenient apartments behind; on the first floor, a good dining room, a sitting room, and six bedrooms; and a closet, and several good attics over. Topsham is situated at a convenient distance between Exeter and Exmouth, a favourite watering place, having the advantage of the London steamers frequently calling at the port, and coaches and omnibuses passing the house daily.

By the beginning of the twenty-first century, however, the Salutation was somewhat the worse for wear. In 2008 it closed, and for the next two years stood empty, until, on New Year's Eve 2010, Punch Taverns sold it to a local company. Two years later, after a lengthy refurbishment, it reopened. Facilities in the revamped inn include a restaurant, an informal café in a glazed atrium, a banqueting-cum-function room, and several guest bedrooms and suites. What they do not include – even though the Salutation is still styled an inn – is a bar, so you cannot just wander in for a drink. It may seem churlish to complain, after the Salutation has been saved so decisively, and its future so handsomely assured – especially in a town as blessed with good pubs as Topsham – but, even so, it seems a pity that future generations will not be able to stand and sup where so many drinkers – and their horses – have supped before.

Torbryan

The Church House Inn at Torbryan is not only one of the least changed inns in Devon; a wealth of historical artefacts – including an admiral's bunk from a Tudor man-of-war, Elizabethan bowling pins, and a sundial embedded in the floor – give a sense of continuity with generations long gone. It was built in the late fifteenth century, at the same time as the church, and has been at the centre of community life ever since. In the nineteenth century, sheep-shearing contests and steeplechases, held in the field at the back, attracted entrants and spectators from miles around. There were more refined entertainments as well. The *Western Times* for 23 January 1847 reported that 'the Torbryan Annual Ball took place at Mr R Pawley's Church House Inn on Monday last. It was attended by many respectable persons from Torbryan and the adjoining neighbourhood. The evening was spent in the greatest harmony.' At one time the inn belonged to the Kingskerswell Brewery. When the brewery closed in 1927, the inn, with over an acre of land, was bought at auction by the tenant, Mr WH Thomas, for £550.

In 1939, when it was offered for sale again, the premises were described as consisting of a 'lounge bar, lounge, bar-dining-room, excellent living accommodation, together with about one and a half acres of garden, orchard and pasture field, and car park'. It was bought by Howell Paine, whose sympathetic stewardship and restoration secured the future of one of Devon's most evocative buildings.

DEVON'S CHURCH HOUSE INNS

Devon's Church House Inns are among the glories of the county, yet their origins are shrouded in mystery, with myth and legend filling the vacuum left by lack of documentary evidence. The majority seem to date from the fifteenth or early sixteenth centuries, when many of Devon's churches were rebuilt, although some may have been converted from older buildings, such as monastic granges.

They started life not as inns but as church houses, built to accommodate secular gatherings which had previously been held in the nave of the parish church. They were not owned by the church, however, but by the community, and were usually managed by the churchwardens. The principal gatherings held in them were church ales. Until the seventeenth century, ale not only signified the drink still known as ale today but also social occasions at which it was drunk. Church ales were held several times a year to celebrate feast days. Ale was specially brewed, a lavish spread was laid on, and people from far and wide were invited to eat, drink and make merry. They paid for the privilege, of course, and the money raised was used to maintain the fabric of the church. By the end of the sixteenth century, ecclesiastical disapproval of these events led to them being proscribed, and they died out in the early seventeenth century. With a major part of their function gone, many church houses were converted to private houses, schools or, in some cases, inns, although some continued to be owned and used by the community.

In contrast to the elaborate masonry and architectural embellishments that characterise many late medieval churches, church houses were unadorned, built for function rather than show. Given the modifications many of them have since undergone and their similarity to other secular buildings of the period, it seems likely that some surviving church houses have not been recognised as such, but, in the absence of documentary evidence, it is not always possible to determine whether a particular building was a church house or not.

It may seem strange to us that, before there were church houses, all this drinking and merrymaking went on in the church itself, but the early medieval church was nothing if not inclusive. While the sanctuary at the east end of the church was kept sacred, the nave was regarded as a communal space which alternated between sacred and secular use according to the occasion. Here the community met not just to worship but also to deal with parish business, attend social events and, on feast days, celebrate with dancing, drinking, singing and the staging of plays. There must always have been some who disapproved of God's house being sullied in this way, and as time went on they became more vocal. Not only bishops and those within the church hierarchy but also local dignitaries came to feel that churches should be preserved from profane use. Rising affluence in the fourteenth and fifteenth centuries, as fortunes were made from the wool trade, was accompanied by a growing sophistication. New-found wealth was used to build magnificent new churches, proclaiming the piety and worldly success of the benefactors.

The Chaucerian rough-and-tumble of former days was no longer considered becoming by the nouveau riche. It was decided that such festivities would be

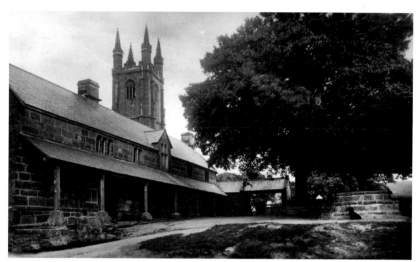

The church houses at South Tawton (above) and Widecombe (below) are among those which have continued to be used by the community

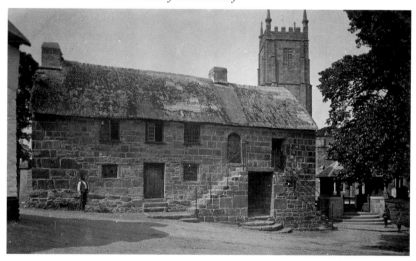

better housed in separate buildings, near the church and under the control of the churchwardens. Such buildings were not erected because of a sentimental attachment to old customs, but to make money. It was essential that communities continued to maintain their churches, and to get people to part with their hard-earned savings it was necessary to hold fund-raising events.

There is a persistent legend that many of Devon's church house inns were built by the masons who built the village church in order to have somewhere to live while they were doing the work. Although this is disputed by some historians, who maintain that church houses were built solely for the use of the community, such claims crop up so often that it would be strange if they had no foundation. Moreover, there is no reason why church houses could not have been built to fulfil both functions – housing the masons while they built the church and becoming prototype community centres once the work was done. There is even the possibility that the community may have used them – or at least a part of them – while the masons were still there. When you consider how many men would have been engaged for long periods on building the county's grander churches, it is clear that they would have needed somewhere to lodge. It is also likely that, as church building was going on all over the country, skilled craftsmen were very much in demand, with neighbouring parishes vying for the most highly-regarded. One way of persuading them to work on a particular building would have been to ensure that there was a comfortable, well-appointed place for them to stay. But, while there is

Church House Inns at Rattery (above) and Harbertonford (below)

ample reason to suppose that the legends connecting them with the masons who built the churches are true, until documentary evidence turns up, this conjecture must remain just that.

Church houses were not like inns, open on a daily basis for the sale of ale. Although they may have been used regularly for transacting parish business or holding meetings, only on special occasions would ale be brewed and served up. Between four and six 'church ales' a year, open to all comers, seem to have been the norm. In addition, there would have been 'guild ales' and other functions only open to invited guests, along with 'bid ales' to raise money for those who had fallen on hard times, and 'bride ales' to raise money for newly-weds. These latter celebrations have given us the word 'bridal'.

Just as church houses came about as part of a campaign to improve public morality and place more emphasis on religious observance, so they eventually fell victim to it. Henry VIII's break with Rome in 1534 marked the beginning of a process in which idols and stained glass were smashed, wall paintings whitewashed over, and anything that hinted of superstition or excess was suppressed. Po-faced piety – or Puritanism as it was more commonly known – saw anything that tended to people having fun, rather than contemplating the fallen state of mortal man, as deeply suspicious, deeply sinful and deeply unwelcome.

Holding church ales to raise funds for the upkeep of the church must always have been regarded by some as a necessary evil. As time went on, such killjoys devised new ways of raising money, such as installing pews in the church and renting them out to wealthier families. Before long, the reverence accorded to the church was extended to the day on which people went to church, sanctifying the Sabbath – the only day most people did not work – and purging it from all secular use. The strait-laced, miserable British Sunday was born.

Although church houses themselves were not abolished, they fell out of use because they lost their function. Although they survived the Reformation, by the 1590s the church ales which were their *raison d'être* were coming increasingly under threat. At the Quarter Sessions in the Chapter House of Exeter Cathedral in July 1595, for example, it was declared that

> church or parish ales, revels, May games, plays and such other unlawful assemblies of the people of sundry parishes into one parish on the Sabbath Day and other times, is a special cause that many disorders, contempts of law, and other enormities are there perpetrated and committed to the great profanation of the Lord's Sabbath, the dishonour of Almighty God, the increase of bastardy and of dissolute life, and of many other mischiefs and inconveniences of the commonwealth.

It was ordered that no such gatherings should hitherto take place on the Sabbath, that no ale should be 'used, kept or uttered' while services were being held in the church, and that 'mynstralsy of any sort, dauncying, or such wanton dallyances' should in future be prohibited. Four years later, the justices went a step further, ordering that 'parish ales, church ales, and revels' should be 'utterly suppressed'. As church houses were not owned by the church but by the community, this diktat, along with later ones, was widely ignored. Eventually, though, civil war and the reign of Cromwell saw the end of all such festivities, and the final death of the church houses. The restoration of Charles II saw some return of revelry, but for the church houses there was no reprieve.

Church houses were not just built in Devon: they were common in the other south-western counties, and to a lesser extent throughout the rest of the country. With a few isolated exceptions, however, only in Devon did a large number of them become inns. Even so, the majority of Devon's church houses found other uses, such as parish meeting places, schools or private houses. It is in Devon's Church House Inns, though, that the memory of a time almost unimaginably remote still lingers, a time when sacred and secular were one, and the seasonal round was nourished by communal celebration, washed down with locally-brewed ale.

Torcross

The Start Bay Inn at Torcross dates from the seventeenth century, if not earlier, but has been extended many times over the years. White's 1850 *Directory* listed two inns in Torcross – the Anchor, kept by William Pepperell, and the Dartmouth Inn, kept by Betsy Crispin. By 1853, the Dartmouth Inn had been renamed the Torcross Hotel, and by 1861 the Anchor had become the Fishermen's Arms, with John Pedrick – mason, brewer and victualler – in charge. On 4 January 1886, he and his family thought the inn was about to collapse around them, as the *London Standard* reported two days later:

> A severe shock of earthquake was felt in South Devonshire on Monday morning, at twenty minutes past ten. It was felt along the route between Dartmouth and Kingsbridge, as well as at other places lying more inland ... In the Green Dragon public house [at Stoke Fleming], kept by Mr Martin, the shock caused a quantity of plaster to fall down from the ceilings ... The phenomenon appears, however, to have been most severe at Torcross. The occupants of the Fishermen's Arms, which house stands on the beach, were so frightened that they rushed out of the place, thinking, as they said, that the building was going to fall. Mr TR Vickary, of the Torcross Hotel, gives several particulars of the severity of the shock. It appears to have been felt by almost everyone in the village.

In 1902, the landlord of the Fishermen's Arms, William Perrott, applied to the magistrates to rename it the Start Bay Inn, and his request was granted. Over a century on, the Start Bay is one of the most popular inns along the South Devon coast, with a reputation for fresh fish.

Torquay

The bar of the Castle Inn on Union Street in Torquay in the late 1940s. Opened in the late 1830s, it remained a free house until taken over by Heavitree Brewery in 1974. It was renamed Chaplin's in 1992 and closed in 2008. Two years later it reopened after a substantial refurbishment – complete with knights and dragons – as the Castle.

The Devon Arms on Park Lane is one of Torquay's more traditional pubs, and famous for its weekly jazz sessions. It is seen here in the 1920s when RW Burridge was the landlord.

A Victorian family on the lawn in front of the Cary Arms at Babbacombe around 150 years ago. The Cary Arms started life as a thatched inn for fishermen – and for the smugglers that haunted this isolated stretch of coastline. Respectability came with the discovery of Tor Bay by fashionable society in the early nineteenth century. One of those who settled here was Emma Keyse, a maid of honour to Queen Victoria, who lived in the house with three first-floor windows which can be seen behind the party on the lawn, and in the photograph below. Queen Victoria and other members of the royal family visited her here, giving the area a social cachet which, combined with its spectacular setting, made it one of the most celebrated places in Devon.

In 1884, it achieved notoriety of a different kind, when, on the night of 15 November, the elderly Miss Keyse was brutally murdered. John Lee, one of her servants, was convicted of the crime, but, although he was led to the scaffold at Exeter prison no less than three times, on each occasion, when the hangman pulled the lever to release the trapdoor, nothing happened. His sentence was eventually commuted to life imprisonment and he

was released in 1907, still proclaiming his innocence. The story of 'Babbacombe' Lee, or 'The Man They Could Not Hang' has inspired a book, a play, a film and a folk opera by Fairport Convention.

Emma Keyse's house was demolished in 1904, and two years later the Cary Arms suffered a disastrous fire, the aftermath of which can be seen below. It was rebuilt to re-emerge as one of Devon's most popular inns. In 2006 – exactly a century after being burnt down – it was bought by Lana and Peter de Savary, who have converted it to a stunning boutique hotel which still operates as an inn, with a bar where, as in all the best inns, dogs are welcome.

For centuries, Cockington, near Torquay, belonged to a family who resisted development, seeking to preserve its bucolic charm. When the estate was sold in 1932, it was acquired by a trust who commissioned Sir Edwin Lutyens to design a model village with an inn as its centrepiece. In the event, only the inn was built, in a vernacular style with characteristic Lutyenesque touches.

There was opposition from those who thought an inn would destroy Cockington's character; licence applications were turned down in 1934 and 1935, and it did not finally open until 23 May 1936. It was originally going to be called the Forge, but, as it was thought that visitors would confuse it with the nearby thatched forge, it was decided to call it the Drum. The renaming was taken seriously, as the *Western Morning News* for 20 May 1936 reveals:

> The celebrated artist Dame Laura Knight RA is painting a drummer boy in the eighteenth-century uniform of the Devon Regiment, and this painting will be a model for the Drum Inn sign, which will be in the form of a drummer boy. An eminent firm of clockmakers are preparing working designs for mechanism which will cause the model drummer boy to roll his drums each quarter of an hour and chime the hours.

There was also, according to the *Western Morning News* for 23 October 1946, a pane of glass in the saloon on which Laurence Whistler engraved the following poem:

> Drake left a drum to Englishmen
> And bade them beat and wake him when
> Perils upon his England come –
> But now where can we find that drum?
> You who stand and closely peer,
> Curious to read what's written here,
> And see the light of English skies
> Silver and glass and bless your eyes,
> Think of the England old and green
> You wander and are happy in.
> And if the hour of perils come
> Find, in your own loud heart, that drum.

Torrington

The rainwater heads on the Black Horse in Torrington High Street bear two dates – 1681 (when it was built) and 1931 (when it was restored). These two photographs, showing the Black Horse before and after restoration, indicate how mock-Tudor features were used to underline the inn's antiquity – doubtless destroying many original features in the process. Nevertheless, it remains an impressive building and a traditional popular hostelry, where beams and wood panelling provide a backdrop for the enjoyment of local ales and home-cooked food.

Just around the corner from the Black Horse stands the New Market Hotel, originally known as the New Market Inn, and dating from the early 1850s. On 27 April 1854, the *North Devon Journal* carried an advertisement:

GREAT TORRINGTON,
DEVON

To Innkeepers
To be let,
with immediate possession,
all that commodious and
newly-erected house,
known as the
NEW MARKET INN
or
COMMERCIAL HOUSE
situate in the centre part of
the town of
Great Torrington, now in
the occupation of
Mrs Dart.

This house is contiguous to the New Market, with a good business, and neatly furnished. It consists of six bedrooms, two front parlours, dining room 25 feet long, tap room, bar, kitchen, larder, two brewing houses, underground cellar, two six-stalled stables, one other stable, lock-up gig house, hay lofts, two walled gardens, spacious courtlage, and a small dwelling house attached, with a back entrance from Castle Hill.

The grates, bodley [sic], stove, furnaces, cupboard, shelving, and fittings of the bar, being the property of the proprietor, will be let with the house.

Also, an excellent plot of ground, about 1½ acres.

These premises afford every accommodation for carrying on an extensive business. Any respectable person who is desirous of commencing trade with a small capital will find this an advantageous undertaking.

This is a genuine advertisement and most satisfactory reasons can be given for disposing of this business.

Part of the furniture and stock to be taken at a valuation.

For viewing the same, apply to Mrs Dart, on the premises,
or to Mr Lee, auctioneer, Great Torrington,
and, for further particulars, to the proprietor, Mr Martin, Great Torrington Mills.

The photograph above shows the New Market Hotel in the 1920s. Its yellow Marland brick has since been painted cream and the building looks much more cheerful. In May 2012, it reopened after being closed for more than year, but is since reported to have closed again.

Over on Well Street was the Old Inn, long one of Torrington's best-known and busiest pubs. It was a popular venue for auctions and celebratory dinners, and the Buffaloes held meetings there. On 1 May 1930, the *Exeter & Plymouth Gazette* carried an advertisement for the Old Inn, which had 'wines, spirits and ales of the finest quality, excellent accommodation for tourists, football and cricket teams, and charabanc parties'. In the 1930s, the landlord was William Bament – presumably the gentleman seen standing by the door in this photograph – and it was known as Bament's Old Inn. Although the building survives, it has been converted to residential units and renamed Old Inn Mews.

At the bottom of Mill Street, with a wide flight of steps beside it, is the Torridge Inn, a splendidly traditional sixteenth-century inn serving local ales, hosting regular music sessions, and looking over the old bridge across the Torridge. Seen here in the 1920s, it reopened in February 2012 after being closed for some time, and has since become popular for its excellent Thai food.

Tuckenhay

The Maltster's Arms, famous in the early 1990s for having Keith Floyd as its landlord, dates from the late eighteenth century. At the front, it presents a modest two-storey façade to the world, but at the back it drops down a further two storeys to a quay once busy with boats shipping goods in and out. One of Tuckenhay's main exports was malt – hence the name of the inn – and the former malthouse, seen on this early twentieth-century postcard to the left of the inn, still survives. On 25 January 1841, the *Sherborne Mercury* reported that

> about ten days since, the floor of the malthouse at Tuckenhay belonging to Messrs Manning, maltsters, on which were upwards of two thousand bushels of barley in the process of being converted into malt, broke down with the weight. The greater part of the barley was taken up and removed into a loft over a coal cellar belonging to the Maltster's Arms adjoining, and on Sunday night the tenth inst., that floor also broke down and the barley falling among the coals was nearly all spoiled.

On the other side of the inn was a lime kiln, which featured in a report in the *Western Times* on 4 February 1843:

> A few days since, a youth, about 16 years of age, son of Mr W Walters of the Maltster's Arms, Tuckenhay, accidentally fell into the lime kiln adjoining, it being then about one-third full of hot lime. His younger brother, who stood on the edge, immediately ran for assistance, which being obtained he was quickly set free. Had he not been timely extricated, he would, without a doubt, have been suffocated in a very few minutes.

Since this postcard was published, the extensions at quay level have been replaced by a three-storey extension running the length of the building, so that only the upper floor of the old inn can still be seen from the river. More recently, a new extension has been built on top of the lime kiln. Despite – or perhaps because of – the changes, the Maltster's remains one of the most atmospheric and popular inns in this part of Devon – superb location, splendid food, and regular beer festivals.

Turnchapel

There were shipyards at Turnchapel at least as far back as 1637, but it was not until the late eighteenth century, when Lord Boringdon started expanding them, that the New Inn opened. It is believed to have occupied a building on the hill behind the current inn, before the licence was transferred in the nineteenth century. Until around 1910, however, the inn occupied only the middle of the three buildings seen here. The building on the corner was a dairy, into which the inn expanded when it closed. This photograph dates from the 1920s when Harry King was the landlord. Today, renamed the Clovelly Bay Inn, it is, thanks to its vibrant blue and yellow colour scheme, one of the most memorable pubs in the area. It is also one of the most popular – the local branch of the Campaign for Real Ale like it so much they have voted it Pub of the Year three years running.

A few doors along is Turnchapel's other pub – the Boringdon Arms, dating from 1808 – less colourful (possibly because it's a listed building) but offering no less traditional a welcome and excellent beer. It can just be seen near the far end of the row in this Edwardian postcard, which features in the foreground a pub which is now a private house – the Shipwright's Arms.

Just west of Turnchapel is the Mount Batten peninsula. An archaeological dig in 1988 found evidence that there was a port here trading with the continent as early as the eighth century BC. It also seems to have been the first major settlement in the Plymouth area. The ease with which it could be defended against attacks from the land by marauding tribes would have recommended it as a secure place to live; when attacks from the sea became a greater threat, however, the settlers moved inland. Long before Charles II ordered a tower to be built on its highest point as part of the nation's coastal defences, Mount Batten had been abandoned by all but a handful of boat-builders and fishermen. In the nineteenth century, however, it became popular with day-trippers and the Castle Inn was built to cater for them.

In September 1913, the government announced that Mount Batten would be used for seaplane trials, and four years later a permanent seaplane station, RNAS Cattewater, was established. Mount Batten's residents were forced to leave and the Castle Inn, renamed Greenleaf House, became the residence of the station commander. RNAS Cattewater was taken over by the newly-formed RAF in April 1918 and was renamed RAF Mount Batten ten years later. After several changes of role and heavy bombing in World War Two, the base closed in 1986. Since then a marina and sea-sport centre have been established on Mount Batten, along with a hotel, pub and apartment complex. Of the Castle Inn, however, there is no trace: it was demolished to build a sergeants' mess in 1962.

Tytherleigh

The Tytherleigh Arms – originally known as the King's Arms – lies in the far east of the county, a couple of miles from both Somerset and Dorset. It probably dates back to the sixteenth century, although its first recorded landlord was Richard Coxe in the 1620s. Until 1928, it formed part of the Tytherleigh Estate, but, when this was broken up, the Dorsetshire Brewery Co paid £1,750 for it at auction. In 2007 it was runner-up in a countywide contest for Dining Pub of the Year, and its stable block has been converted to letting rooms, opening onto a paved courtyard.

Uffculme

Uffculme, hard up against the Somerset border, provides a graphic illustration of how the fortunes of Devon's inns and pubs have fluctuated since the mid-nineteenth century. In 1850, White's *Directory* described Uffculme as 'a decayed market town' with 2011 inhabitants and two main employers – Fox Brothers' woollen factory and Furze's brewery. Nevertheless, it had no less than five inns – the Commercial, the George, the Half Moon, the London and the Star – with another – the Lamb – a mile to the north, in the hamlet of Appledore. The Star had only received a full licence two years earlier, despite objections from Mr Furze. The *Exeter & Plymouth Gazette* for 9 September 1848 describes how

> Thomas Sparks, of the Star Inn, a beer shop in Uffculme, applied for a licence, and was opposed by Mr Furze, brewer of that town, who stated that he was the owner of two of the four inns situated in the town, on the high road from Wellington to the Tiverton Road station, and which were sufficient for the accommodation of all the travellers who might come into the town. The business of the town had not increased, nor had the

population. The applicant lived near the factory, where there was a tolerable amount of population, but they were the poorer classes, who couldn't afford money for spirits, and required only the malt liquor and cider to sustain them in their work, and which the applicant already sold. His house was on a road which led to nowhere except the village of Kentisbeare. The Messrs Fox, who were the owners of the factory, had a room in it for their own accommodation, and stables for their horses. Besides, these gentlemen were Quakers, and known to be strong advocates of teetotalism, therefore they would not require accommodation of this sort. It appeared that Sparks brewed his own beer. Mr Hole observed that many of the signatures to the applicant's testimonials were those of Quakers, or of persons connected with them. The applicant called out that Mr Furze was 'augmenting too fast', and required to be 'criticised a bit'. If he had his beer of him, he should have been a clever chap. The magistrates retired to consult, and on their return granted the application.

Unfortunately, we have not found an archive photograph of the Star. By the time the 1878 *Directory* was published, however, another beerhouse had opened at the far end of the High Street, on the corner of Clay Lane. Its landlord, Thomas Jones, not only sold beer; he was also a veterinary surgeon and the name he chose for his beerhouse – the Farmer's Hotel – indicates the type of clientele he hoped to attract. In 1900 he was succeeded by his son, Sidney Jones, who is seen on the Edwardian postcard below standing outside the Farmer's Hotel on a glorious summer's day. By this time, both the Half Moon and the Star had closed. In September 1918 the licence of the Farmer's Hotel was revoked on grounds of redundancy, and it became a private house.

One of the inns that William Furze owned was the London Inn, which stood next to his brewery. The brewery, which was rebuilt in 1858, closed in 1918 after it was acquired by Starkey, Knight & Ford, but the London Inn remained open. In April 1987, English Heritage designated it a Grade II listed building, declaring it to be

an unspoilt small Victorian public house with its internal arrangement intact of small bar (to the left of entrance), tiny snug (to the right), kitchen to extreme right, with private rooms above, all intact. To the rear is the yard, entered through a wagon entrance to the right of the pub, and the yard is enclosed on the right by an outbuilding which, although not built as such, has served as a skittles alley since before the First World War. (The skittles and the return gulley are original).

If the listing was an attempt to save this piece of Devon's pub heritage – seen above in the 1920s – it failed, for three months later permission was granted to convert it to three houses. That left Uffculme with just two inns – the Commercial (now renamed the Ostler) and the George, both on Commercial Road.

Uffculme had one other inn, the Lamb, a mile north of the town in the hamlet of Appledore. The origins of this wayside alehouse, which was part of a working farm, went back to the eighteenth century, if not earlier, and it was popular for hunt meetings and other gatherings. On 8 September 1899, the *Western Times* reported that 'the Lamb Inn and land recently offered by auction and withdrawn has since been disposed of at a good figure to Mr W Furze, the Brewery, Uffculme'. Less than six months later, on 19 February 1900, the *Western Times* featured the inn again:

> The Lamb Inn, an old-fashioned hostelry on the Wellington main road, but in the parish of Uffculme, was destroyed by fire early on Friday morning. A cow, four pigs and some poultry were destroyed in the outbuildings. The owners (Messrs Furze, Uffculme), and the tenant (Mr Follett) were insured.

The photograph on the left shows the rebuilt Lamb shortly after it was taken over by Starkey, Knight & Ford in 1918. The building survives, but is no longer an inn, having been converted to residential accommodation and renamed Appledore Court.

Umberleigh

Umberleigh Rising Sun Hotel

The Rising Sun at Umberleigh in the Taw Valley has long been a popular fishing centre, and has a reputation for food. It is also one of North Devon's most historic inns, as a report from the *North Devon Journal* of 3 May 1866 indicates:

> The annual manorial court of AD Bassett, Esq, lord of the ancient manor of Umberleigh, was held on Tuesday last, at the Rising Sun Inn. As usual, an excellent dinner was provided, with a plentiful supply of punch. The son and heir of the worthy lord (AC Bassett, Esq) presided; and in a suitable speech gave the health of his father's tenantry. In reply, the health of the liberal and kind-hearted landlord was given, and drank with hearty expressions of goodwill. After which followed the health of the chairman, Miss Bassett, and Mr and Mrs Williams, which were proposed and drank by our sturdy yeomanry in a manner which showed the respect in which they are held by their tenantry. The manor of Umberleigh extends over the parishes of Umberleigh and High Bickington, and comprises about 2,000 acres, with a rental of about £2,000.

Since this postcard of the Rising Sun was published in the mid-twentieth century, the building has been extended to the left, while the cottage whose garden can be seen on the right has been demolished for road widening.

Uplyme

On 15 September 1832, the *Hampshire Advertiser* reported that a new road from Lyme Regis to Hunter's Lodge (now the B3165) had opened three days earlier and that 'the inn erected at Uplyme is named the Talbot Arms'. It was named after Admiral Sir John Talbot, who lived at Rhode Hill, just north of the village. In 1834, he presided over a trial of smugglers at the inn, which was reported in the *Western Times* on 1 March:

On Saturday last, William Rattenbury, Robert Orley, and two Frenchmen were landed from the Swallow, revenue cutter, and taken to the Talbot Arms at Uplyme, where they were tried before Sir John Talbot and John Hussey, Esq, on information laid against them, under the 49th section of the last smuggling prevention act. Mr Rutherford appeared on behalf of the crown, and called a number of witnesses for the purpose of proving the guilt of the prisoners by a chain of circumstantial evidence. Some papers, which were said to have been found in a jacket lying on a heap of tubs of smuggled spirit on the beach, were then offered in evidence by the learned gentleman. Mr Flight, who with Mr Hillman defended the prisoners, objected to these papers being received in evidence, they not having been shown to be in the handwriting of either of the prisoners, or at all connected with them. Sir John Talbot decided that the papers could not be received in evidence. After a patient hearing the prisoners were acquitted.

The Talbot Arms, as a new and well-appointed inn, soon became popular for all manner of events and celebrations. In the early hours of 24 June 1926, however, a lorry parked in the garage of the inn caught fire, and the blaze soon spread to the bar. As water supplies were limited, the contents of beer and cider barrels were poured onto the flames, retarding the progress of the fire until the fire brigade arrived from Axminster. Although the garage was destroyed, the rest of the building was saved. Hardly had cleaning-up operations got underway, however, than disaster struck again, as reported in the *Evening Telegraph* on 2 July:

The Talbot Arms Hotel, a well-known country hostelry at Uplyme near Lyme Regis, was burnt to the ground in the early hours of this morning. The occupier, Mr Tomlins, his wife and two children, and two visitors, had to escape in night attire. Villagers kept the fire from spreading with buckets of water until the brigade arrived. The garage of the hotel was destroyed by fire last week.

The following January, plans for rebuilding the Talbot Arms were approved and the new inn opened later that year, with further alterations carried out in 1937. Even though the Talbot Arms, seen here shortly after it reopened, is one of the newest inns featured in this book, it offers a traditional welcome amid the traditional ambience of a village pub dedicated to good beer, good food and serving the needs of locals and visitors.

The Hunter's Lodge at Raymond's Hill, two miles north of Uplyme, still looks much as it did when this postcard was published around 1930. Situated high on the Axminster-Bridport road near the border with Dorset, the Hunter's Lodge has been a well-known landmark since coaching days, and is believed to date from the sixteenth century. Mitchell, Toms & Co of Chard, whose sign can be seen receiving attention from the man on the ladder, merged with Brutton & Sons of Yeovil in 1936, eventually becoming part of Charrington's in 1960.

Wembury

On 14 February 1885, a picture of the Jubilee Inn appeared on the cover of the *Illustrated Police News,* which specialised in sensationalised accounts of the most shocking crimes and murders. The inn's sudden notoriety was not due to an uncharacteristic outbreak of violence in this peaceful community, but because of a drama on the high seas. On the evening of 28 January, a Nova Scotian barque, the Wellington, anchored in Wembury Bay and, after sending up distress signals, was towed into the Yealm estuary. On board was the horribly mutilated body of the captain. The crew said that three days earlier, after a bout of heavy drinking, the captain had run amok with a revolver, firing indiscriminately at members of the crew, whom he accused of trying to poison him. He seriously wounded two of them, one of

whom later died. With great difficulty, four of them managed to restrain him, but not without using considerable force, and he subsequently died of his injuries. The four who had overpowered him were arrested and appeared at an inquest convened at the Jubilee Inn. Among the newspapers which covered the story was the *Portsmouth Evening News*, whose reporter observed that the inn 'was crowded to excess by the farmers of the neighbourhood'. The four men were later tried and acquitted at the assizes in Exeter.

In the late 1940s, the Jubilee hosted gatherings of a more convivial nature, when the local vicar was invited to hold harvest festival and carol services there. These events, for which a harmonium was brought from the parish hall, proved so popular that many people had to stand outside.

The inn dates from the mid-eighteenth century, and once had its own cider orchard. It was known as the Old Inn until renamed to commemorate George III's Golden Jubilee in 1810. Around 1890, it was bought by Alfred Perring, and it remained in his family until Lottie Perring sold it to Watney's in the 1960s. Now renamed the Odd Wheel, it reopened after a major refurbishment in July 2010, retaining a two-room layout – on one side, a bar with sofas, juke box, pool table and a selection of local beers; on the other, a restaurant specialising in locally-sourced food.

West Anstey

White's 1850 *Directory* for Devon described West Anstey as 'a small scattered village on the acclivities of a lofty eminence, near the source of the River Yeo and the borders of Somersetshire'. Despite having a population of only 279, it was served by two inns – the Partridge Arms, kept by Thomas Shapcott, and the New Inn, kept by John Venner, a miller and baker. Among the functions held at the New Inn was the annual dinner of the West Anstey Agricultural & Labourers' Friend Society. On 13 October 1860, the *Exeter & Plymouth Gazette* described how, after the eighth annual agricultural meeting and ploughing match had been held in incessant rain the previous Wednesday, 'the dinner was provided by Mr Venner of the New Inn ... and was served up in the club room, which was very tastefully decorated for the occasion with floral devices, mottoes, and a number of Chinese lanterns. About 70 persons sat down, and many others, owing to the smallness of the room, could not be accommodated.'

In 1864, the Devon & Somerset Railway Company received approval to build a line from Norton Fitzwarren to Barnstaple, which would pass through West Anstey. Two years later, as work on the line got under way, the New Inn was the scene for an unfortunate incident, which was reported in the *North Devon Journal* on 7 June 1866:

> Mr Superintendant Wood summoned John Venner of Anstey for an offence against the tenor of his alehouse licence ... It appears that two or three navvies called at Mr Venner's house and seeing a couple of respectable (?) yeomen present begged to be treated to some ale; their request was complied with on condition that they would drink of a quart each at a draught; and nearly three quarts were thus disposed of by one of the unfortunate navvies, who became intoxicated and, having been placed in an outhouse, he was found some time afterwards there dead!! The defendant was fined 5s, and costs £1 3s.

In February 1912, the New Inn was destroyed by fire, and the owners, Hancock & Sons of Wiveliscombe, replaced it with the building seen on the previous page. By now the population of West Anstey had dwindled to 202, and it soon became apparent that the new New Inn was not only too large but in the wrong place. On 8 February 1935, the *Western Times* reported that the brewery had applied to transfer the licence to a new building a mile away:

> For some time it had been obvious ... that the community was not served as it should be by the premises at the New Inn and it was considered a very opportune time, being the King's jubilee year, to erect fresh premises and call them the Jubilee Inn, on the main South Molton-Taunton road. There was an increasing demand for what were known as road houses, and in motoring from South Molton to Taunton, with certain exceptions, there was no accommodation for tourists or travellers, and ... it would be serving a very useful purpose if these new premises were erected and licensed. The New Inn would then be shut down.

The Jubilee Inn, seen on the left in the 1940s, opened a few months later. Today, the New Inn is a private house, while West Anstey's other inn, the Partridge Arms – now Partridge Arms Farm – offers bed and breakfast, with a bar open to residents. The Jubilee, after being closed for some time, was sold in 2013. Since then, it has been extended as part of a major refurbishment, still underway at time of going to print. It is understood that the plan is to reopen it as an inn.

West Buckland

The man seen in the distance on this Edwardian postcard, standing outside the door of the New Inn at West Buckland, is presumably the licensee, Charles Nott, whose name can be seen above the door. He took the inn after replying to an advertisement in the *North Devon Journal* on 16 September 1880:

> Wanted, at Michaelmas, a man and wife, to manage the New Inn, West Buckland. Advantages offered. 15s a week. Furnished house, garden and stables rent free, with certain trade profits. Testimonials and references for man and wife to be forwarded, by Sept 23rd, to the secretary of the New Inn Committee, West Buckland, South Molton.

More information on this committee comes from a report in the *Western Times* of 19 February 1904:

> At South Molton County Sessions yesterday, Charles Nott, of the New Inn, West Buckland, was charged with selling whiskey more than 25% under proof ... Mr BT James defended. The house is carried on under a committee, consisting of a couple of clergymen, the churchwardens, and others. The defendant is only a manager and licensee under the committee. Mr James said the committee carried on the business on philanthropic and public grounds, and the manager was not responsible for the blending of the spirit. The profit after payment of reasonable interest on capital was devoted to local objects. The offence, if any, was not committed with the object of obtaining extra profit, or to the prejudice of the customer. The water was put in in a hurry, and had not been properly mixed. The Bench imposed a fine of 10s and costs 10s.

The administration of the inn by a committee of churchmen, and its location next to the church, suggest that it may originally have been a church house. When it closed in the 1930s, having been allowed to deteriorate to such an extent that demolition was all but inevitable, the local landowning dynasty, the Fortescues, offered the landlord the lease of a nearby farm. The site is now used as car parking for the church.

West Down

Information on the history of the Foxhunters' Inn near West Down is scanty, but it seems to have opened as a beerhouse in the early 1830s when the turnpike road from Braunton to Ilfracombe was built, and may originally have occupied one of a row of cottages. By 1850, the landlord was John Phillips. He was subsequently granted a full licence, and White's *Directory* for 1878 lists him as 'farmer and victualler, Fox & Hunter'. Four years earlier, in 1874, the railway from Barnstaple to Ilfracombe had opened, killing the coaching trade on which the inn relied for much of its custom. The railway ran past the Foxhunters', however, and on 14 January 1886 the *North Devon Journal* reported that

> the inhabitants of West Down are petitioning the directors of the London & South Western Railway Company for the construction on the Ilfracombe line of a station at Foxhunters' Inn, near that village. At the time the line was constructed, a level was made at the spot named in anticipation of the erection of a station. The petition has been very numerously and influentially signed, and the seals of the Board of Guardians, the Highway Board and the Corporation of Barnstaple have been attached to it. The desirability of erecting a station at the point named cannot possibly be questioned, and it is to be hoped that the directors will return a favourable answer to the application.

They didn't, but the Phillips family stayed on at the inn long enough to see its fortunes revive with the growth of motoring in the early twentieth century. Roadhouse-style half-timbering – similar to that on the St George & Dragon at Clyst St George – was added, and a thoroughgoing 'olde-worlde' makeover was carried out, as the postcard above shows. Not only were the bars adorned with over 450 pieces of brass, along with hunting trophies and coaching lanterns, but the old Bude to Newquay stagecoach was installed across the road. After being closed for some time, the Foxhunters' was sold in January 2014, but, at the time of writing, plans for the building had yet to be announced.

Whiddon Down

Its thatch and corrugated iron have been replaced by tiles, its walls have been painted white and shutters flank the windows, but the Post Office Inn – its name now shortened to the Post Inn – has otherwise not changed that much since this postcard was published in the 1920s. In common with many other inns, it once housed a post office. White's 1850 *Directory*, which lists Thomas Hooper as the landlord, also lists a 'post office at Thomas Hooper's, Whyddon–Down. Letters despatched at 10 morning via Exeter, and 8 night to Okehampton, etc'. When the inn was advertised for sale in the *Exeter Flying Post* on 4 July 1860, it was described as 'that well-known public house, called the Post-office Inn, with stables, wheelwright's shop, offices and garden'.

In 1942, an amateur theatre company was formed in Whiddon Down, and on 27 November the *Western Times* announced that the Whiddon Down and District Pig Club would present the Turnpike Players in Bernard Shaw's *Androcles and the Lion*. Among the other plays they staged at the inn were Shaw's *The Man of Destiny* and *Arms and the Man*, Shakespeare's *Hamlet* and *Macbeth*, and Wilde's *The Importance of Being Earnest*. In April 1944, the inn hosted a 'concert of music from the operas', presented by CEMA – the Council for the Encouragement of Music and the Arts. With peace, came a return to more accustomed delights, such as the Mid-Devon Hunt Ball, held at the inn on 8 December 1950, but its role as a beacon of culture in the dark days of World War Two must have lived long in many people's memories.

In 2008, the inn closed and an application was submitted to convert it to residential use. Following widespread protests, the application was withdrawn. As with the Old Swan at Monkokehampton, that could have been the beginning of a long stand-off, with the inn left empty and slowly deteriorating. At Whiddon Down, however, the decision was taken to refurbish and reopen. Today, the Post Inn is more popular than ever, a traditional pub with a proper bar area as well as a restaurant and a newly-opened beer garden at the back. All of which goes to prove that, with the right management, a pub can come back from the dead.

Whitestone

A superbly atmospheric postcard of the Traveller's Rest at Whitestone, four miles west of Exeter on the old A30, in the days when motorists were tempted to stop not just for refreshment but also for petrol. It was petrol that got the Traveller's Rest's landlord into trouble in the straitened times after the Second World War. The *Western Times* for 14 February 1947 named him as one of those who had bought petrol on the black market from a clerk at RAF Chivenor, and he ended up with a hefty fine. Such things were

---

MURDER AT WHITESTONE

'Exeter, August 4. About seven o'clock on Monday evening, one Henry Bloins went into a publick house at Whitestone, about three miles from this city, kept by Mrs Mortimore, a widow woman about 74 years of age, and called for some beer which he paid for, and then, there being no one in the house but the old woman and himself (some people who were there when he went in, being going home) he took up a hatchet, with which he gave her several blows on the head, and after robbing her, left her weltering in her blood. Soon after, a neighbour's servant passing by the door, heard dreadful groans, and alarming the neighbours, they went in, and found her lying on the ground, wounded in a shocking manner. A surgeon was immediately sent for, but she expired before he could come. Bloins having been left alone with the old woman, he was suspected; diligent search was made for him, and about ten o'clock he was found under a hay-rick, covered with hay, and on Tuesday morning was carried before John Baring Esq. who committed him to the High Gaol. He is a lad about 18 years of age, and was lately a drummer in Lasauselle's [Lascelle's] Regiment.'

Bath Chronicle & Weekly Gazette, 18 August 1763

---

untypical, as news from the Traveller's Rest usually featured events such as ploughing matches, celebratory dinners or sporting gatherings like the one reported in the *Exeter & Plymouth Gazette* on 29 June 1839:

> On Monday a grand pigeon match came off at the Traveller's Rest Inn, on the Okehampton road. Two matches were shot for, and several sweepstakes and single matches took place. The birds, which were best Blue Rocks, died game; and those that escaped, or were out-bounders, fell to the lot of the usual body of sporting characters who haunt these places for amusement.

Visiting the Traveller's Rest today, you won't find any petrol pumps, and, while the main building looks much the same, the tea hut has been replaced by a large restaurant extension. It remains, however, a traditional, friendly inn, with its own sweetshop, a doggie corner and a beer garden with a brook burbling away in the background.

Widecombe in the Moor

The aptly named Old Inn at Widecombe in the Moor, parts of which are believed to date back to the sixteenth century, if not earlier. Writing in the 1880s, John Lloyd Warden Page, a chronicler of the moor, described it as 'a very humble inn'. That was before Sabine Baring Gould set this remote moorland village on course to become a tourist honeypot by popularising the song 'Widecombe Fair'. On 8 August 1906, the *Western Times* reported that

> to accommodate visitors to Widecombe, which are increasing in number year by year, Mr Foot, the licensee of the Old Inn, where space is limited, proposes erecting a sort of nest [sic] – one-storey iron building, 24ft by 17ft or 18ft – to accommodate visitors who come there.

Since then, the numbers of visitors – and the accommmodation available at the Old Inn – has continued to grow. It is now owned by Hall & Woodhouse, who carried out a major refurbishment in 2006.

Willand

An Edwardian view of the Halfway House at Willand, a couple of miles north of Cullompton on the old A38. A sign on the front wall of this greatly extended inn lists some of the places it is halfway between, such as Taunton and Exeter, and Bristol and Plymouth. It is also midway between junctions 27 and 28 of the M5 – a distinction its original owners certainly did not have in mind when they named it, but one that has proved very useful, as motorway travellers in the know regularly drop in to sample the food. Its Sunday carvery is renowned, while for drinkers there is not only a large bar with widescreen TV but also a large garden at the rear.

Winkleigh

White's 1850 *Directory* listed five inns in Winkleigh – the Barnstaple Inn on the corner of Fore Street and Barnstaple Street, the Clotworthy Arms on the corner of Exeter Road and Torrington Road, the King's Arms in Fore Street, the Ring of Bells by the church, and the Seven Stars in the High Street. Around 1863, another inn – the Butcher's Arms – opened opposite the King's Arms. Three years later, on 21 September 1866, the landlord of the Clotworthy Arms placed an advertisement in the *Western Times* announcing an auction of

> all the handsome and valuable household furniture, a first-class four-pull beer engine and pipes, spirit kegs, kitchen stove, dairy and culinary requisites, an excellent and roomy posting carriage well adapted for a mourning coach, a well-bred and handsome mare, four years old with her foal, corn in ricks, and other effects of Mr George Edwards, declining business.

The inn became a private residence called Clotworthy House, which now offers bed and breakfast accommodation.

So Winkleigh was back to five inns, and, for an idea what the village was like in the late nineteenth century, we can do no better than to turn to a somewhat effusive article in the *Western Times* for 4 June 1880:

> Come with me, gentle reader, this bright and joyful May morning, to Winkleigh, and you shall taste of pure North Devon rural pleasures. For this is a red letter day ... It is the anniversary of the Working Men's Association in that elevated and ancient village, when the members meet to dine and make proselytes to their order ... The dinner was held at the Butcher's Arms Inn, where host Smale served up an excellent repast. The vicar presided. Upwards of 200 sat down to dinner, and praised the catering of the landlord. During the afternoon the band discoursed music of various kinds, they and the crowd of listeners filling the not very ample space between the Butcher's Arms and the King's Arms opposite. Sports seemed at a discount, the only one I saw being football, which was played by some active youths just without the village. Great conviviality prevailed in the several inns.

Sadly, as far as the Butcher's Arms was concerned, the conviviality came to an abrupt end 16 years later, on 6 May 1896, when the inn was destroyed by fire, along with two adjoining houses. The report in the *Exeter Flying Post* concluded with the observation that 'the disaster is likely to quicken the movement for the provision of a fire engine'. The Butcher's Arms was rebuilt as the Winkleigh Hotel, which in Kelly's 1902 *Directory* advertised 'first-class accommodation for visitors and cyclists, hot & cold baths, good shooting, golf links in adjoining parish and within easy distance of meeting points of four packs of hounds'. The *Directory* added that the landlord, Charles Hill, was 'an agent for Goulding's manures and seed merchant'. After closing in the 1990s, the hotel was extended and converted to housing.

Looking west along Fore Street around 1905, with the Winkleigh Hotel on the left and the Barnstaple Inn in the distance. The sign of the King's Arms can also be seen on the right.

The Winkleigh Hotel was not alone in having a landlord with an interesting sideline. In 1878, Charles Williams, the landlord of the Barnstaple Inn on the other side of Fore Street was not only a saddler but also the parish clerk. In 1914, its landlord was John Carter, an 'agricultural implement merchant, cart & van builder and wheelwright'. The Barnstaple Inn's licence lapsed in 1916.

The next to go was the Ring of Bells, originally built as a church house. As long ago as 1883, the magistrates objected to the renewal of its licence – due to unspecified reports of bad conduct – but, as the postcard below shows, it survived

into the twentieth century to be taken over by Simonds of Reading and renamed the Ring O'Bells. On 23 April 1954, it was sold, along with a number of other West Country inns, at an auction in Exeter. Two years, later, it made national headlines when the *Daily Sketch* offered it as the first prize in a competition. It survived for another twelve years, before being destroyed by fire in 1968.

Then there was the Seven Stars, whose story is even more unusual, for this was an inn that effectively ceased trading for around 40 years but never lost its licence and survived to become one of the two inns left in Winkleigh today. First recorded in 1815 with Joseph Ashton as landlord, by 1850 it was being run by a butcher called Nathaniel Hammett. When we get to the 1878 *Directory*, however, there is no mention of the Seven Stars, although there is a listing for a James Francis, grocer and wine & spirit merchant. We know that this was the Seven Stars because of a report of a licensing session in the *Exeter & Plymouth Gazette* on 24 August 1883:

> The Seven Stars Inn, Winkleigh, kept by James Francis, was objected to. Mr Sparkes of Crediton appeared for Mr Francis. PC Phillips stated that there was no room for lodgers, and no stable room. The house was well conducted. Population 572, and five licensed houses. The landlord kept a grocer's shop besides. Mr Sparkes said that the information given was wrong. There was stable accommodation for three horses. The two objections raised against the house were not supported by the facts, as there was ample accommodation for man and beast. The landlord was 84 years of age, had lived in the house a good many years, and other houses had been licensed since his, and if any were to be deprived it certainly should not be the oldest, which first met the wants of the public. It was one of the best-conducted houses in the place, and if the old man were turned out he could not get a livelihood in any other way. He produced a memorial signed by a large number of respectable people, and it would have been signed by the vicar, only he said that if he signed one there was a kind of obligation to sign all. The Bench decided to grant the renewal.

Two years later, James Francis died and the licence was transferred to his daughter Annie. Kelly's 1889 *Directory* listed Miss Annie Francis and Miss Sarah Francis as 'grocers and agents for W&A Gilbey, wine and spirit merchants'. Sixteen years later, when the licence came up for renewal, the status of the premises was once again queried, as reported in the *Exeter & Plymouth Gazette* on 8 February 1905:

> In connexion with the Seven Stars, Winkleigh (tenant, Mr W Farleigh), the place is held on a six days' licence. There is also a grocer's business attached. There is no accommodation. Mr Farleigh is the sole agent for a wine and spirit firm. Very little was consumed on the premises. Mr Henry said his client was prepared to close the bar, and to sell off the premises only. The superintendant did not object to the off licence. Mr Farleigh asked to hold the same licence on the undertaking that nothing was consumed on the premises. This was granted.

This gentlemen's agreement meant that eventually the Seven Stars could resume selling alcohol on the premises, a role it continues to fulfil admirably today. Few pubs can have such a history of resurfacing after such a period of prolonged hibernation – and, as if that wasn't enough, in the 1950s the building almost shared the fate of the Ring O'Bells, losing its top floor to fire and having to be rebuilt, which is why the inn today looks very different to the thatched building seen in the 1930s' photograph opposite.

Finally, just across the road from the Seven Stars, is the King's Arms, Winkleigh's other surviving inn, with thatch intact. Inside are wood-burning stoves, inglenooks, oak settles, flagstone floors, beamed ceilings ... and an enigma. In 2002, members of the Winkleigh Cave & Mine Exploration Group took themselves down a well shaft in the inn to investigate persistent rumours that it led to a network of tunnels. At the bottom they found two passageways, each about 20 feet long, which appeared to be exploratory adits, possibly a legacy of an attempt to find a seam of silver. There were silver mines in other parts of Devon, so this is not as far-fetched as it may seem. The shaft was originally in the yard, before the building was extended over it, so did an innkeeper here fancy having his own silver mine, or is there another explanation for this underground mystery?

The King's Arms around 1920, with the Winkleigh Hotel on the right

Witheridge

The Hare & Hounds at Witheridge – the epitome of the village inn, with its thatched roof, windows half-curtained to preserve its patrons' modesty, and one of the coachyard gates standing invitingly open. Sadly, although it looks much as it did when this photograph was taken in the 1920s, it closed in 1967 and is now a private house.

Woody Bay

Station Hotel. Woody Bay.

This unassuming hotel is, like the nearby Hunters' Inn, a legacy of one of Devon's biggest development scams. When Colonel Benjamin Green Lake acquired vast tracts of land in North Devon in the 1890s, he drew up plans to transform a secluded cove called Wooda Bay into a resort to rival Ilfracombe and Lynton. A narrow-gauge railway from Barnstaple to Lynton was being built, opening up the area to mass tourism for the first time, and, to encourage daytrippers to visit by boat, he even built a pier. The railway opened, with a station at Wooda Bay, in 1898, and on 23 November 1899 the *Bath Chronicle* informed its well-heeled readers that

> visitors to the delightful neighbourhood of Lynton and Wooda Bay will be interested to know that a fine hotel is to be built at the Wooda Bay station of the Lynton Railway. Wooda Bay has a future. There are now some ten houses with two hotels at Wooda Bay, the last building being a post office. All the work, including the new hotel at the station, is being done by Colonel Lake, who has spent many thousands on the estate.

The problem was that the money wasn't his; it belonged to his clients. The following year, he ran out of luck, was arrested and imprisoned, and the estate was put up for sale. At the auction, in October 1900, the 'nearly completed' Station Hotel failed to reach its reserve, but was subsequently acquired by Starkey, Knight & Ford. No one who knows this spectacular corner of Devon will shed a tear over the failure of Colonel Lake's plans, although the closure of the Lynton & Barnstaple Railway, a mere 37 years after it opened, is for many a source of regret to this day. After the station – by then renamed Woody Bay – closed in 1935, the Station Hotel became the Moorland Hotel. Now known as Moorlands, it is still there, and the station has been reopened by a group intent on restoring as much as possible of one of England's most legendary lost lines.

Woolfardisworthy – or Woolsery

Woolfardisworthy, near Hartland, is pronounced – and usually spelt these days – Woolsery. The Farmer's Arms in the centre of the village was first recorded as The Hotel in White's 1850 *Directory* with Thomas Friendship as landlord. It became the Farmer's Arms around 1930, and this photograph was taken shortly afterwards. The door seen here has since been converted to a window, and the entrance is through the thatched part of the building to the right. In 2007, a 20-foot well and a bread oven were discovered during building work, and there have been suggestions that the building is much older than previously thought, possibly having started life as church house. Whatever its origins, it was a friendly, traditional and popular local, at the heart of the community – until it closed in December 2012. It rapidly fell into disrepair, with part of its thatched roof covered with a green tarpaulin. In 2014, villagers persuaded Torridge District Council to declare it an asset of community value, a decision the owner subsequently persuaded them to reverse. In October 2014, however, a couple who had founded – and subsequently sold – the social networking site Bebo bought the inn, along with the derelict manor house, and announced that, after a major refurbishment, the manor house would become a hotel and the Farmer's Arms would reopen as a proper pub..

Yarcombe

Before the Honiton & Ilminster Turnpike – now part of the A30 – was authorised in 1807, Yarcombe was very isolated. As the largest village on the 14-mile stretch of road between Chard and Honiton, it was inevitable that its inn should become an important calling point for coaches. The annual auction of the franchises for the turnpike gates along the road was also held at the Yarcombe Inn. The building predates the road by many centuries, however. Believed to have been the church house, it has been suggested that, unlike most church houses, which date from late medieval times, it was built by monks from France in the ninth century. To enhance its historical credentials even further, it was once owned by Sir Francis Drake. When advertised for sale in the *Exeter Flying Post* on 13 October 1853, the accommodation consisted of a 'dining room, parlour, bar, kitchen, four good bedrooms, brewhouse, cellars, stables, a good skittle alley, garden, etc'. The inn was – and had been 'for many years past' – in the occupation of Mrs Rebecca White, as yearly tenant.

Perhaps it was something to do with Mrs White's influence, but events and celebrations at the Yarcombe Inn seem always to have been marked by a gaiety and a lack of the aggravation that dogged less fortunate houses. Take this report from the *Sherborne Mercury* of 19 June 1855:

> On Tuesday last, the members of the Yarcombe Friendly Society celebrated their annual meeting by dining together under a special marquee in a field contiguous to the Vicarage House, the Rev P Gilpin, Vicar of Yarcombe, in the chair. The dinner, and subsequently tea for the ladies, was provided for by Mr Harry White of the Yarcombe Inn, in a very creditable style. The present condition and future prospects of this society are encouraging. The Churchstanton band was in attendance, and the 'merrie dance' on the green was duly honoured. A number of visitors from the neighbouring parishes were present, the weather was beautifully fine, and the day's proceedings terminated much to the satisfaction of all present.

We do not know what relation Harry White was to Rebecca White, but, having taken over the inn sometime between 1853 and 1855, he was still there on 21 January 1862 when the *Sherborne Mercury* reported that 'the annual ball was held at the Yarcombe Inn on Thursday evening last. About 70 attended. The dancing commenced at seven o'clock and was kept up with spirit until an early hour.'

The following year, a Mr Colman took over the inn, and on 31 March 1863, the *Sherborne Mercury* reported that

> the annual Lady Day meeting was held at the vestry room ... on Thursday ... The general business of the day having been gone through, the parishioners adjourned to the Yarcombe Inn, where a good substantial dinner, in the old English style, was provided by host Colman, our new and much respected landlord. Upwards of 20 of the most influential inhabitants of Yarcombe partook of its bounties ... The healths of the new and outgoing officers having been drunk and responded to, the vice chairman, in a very neat speech, proposed the health of their worthy host and hostess, Mr and Mrs Colman, wishing them every prosperity in their new undertaking, and Mr Colman responded. The remainder of the evening was spent in discussing the general topics of the day, and the party did not break up till a late hour.

By 1878, Mr Colman had been succeeded by Thomas Wright, who was still there in 1902. He was succeeded by William Wright (probably his son), who in 1912 handed over to Thomas Farrant. On 24 January 1913, the *Exeter & Plymouth Gazette* reported that

> an invitation dance took place at the Yarcombe Inn, which proved an immense success. Over 150 persons attended and danced until 4am to the strains of Messrs Pymm and Pidgeon's violins. This was the first dance under the new management of Mr and Mrs T Farrant, and the result must be highly gratifying to them.

By 2008, it looked as though this historic inn, the hub of the community for centuries, had reached the end of the road. Fortunately, the community decided otherwise, and, after being closed for over a year – and being featured by Jay Smith in a TV series called 'Save Our Boozer' – the Yarcombe Inn was reopened by a dedicated group of local people who soon won plaudits for the quality of their beer, food and that all important welcome. In 2011 the local branch of the Campaign for Real Ale voted it their Pub of the Year. In March 2013, however, it was acquired by new owners, and in August 2014 closed again. In June 2015, when it was sold again, the buyers declared their intention of applying to convert it to residential use. The parish council responded by applying to have it listed as an Asset of Community Value. A decision was being awaited as the book was published.

An inconclusive and downbeat note to end on perhaps, but one that sums up the plight of many of Devon's pubs. On our journey through the county, we have come upon many success stories and many superb traditional pubs; we have also come upon many tales of woe, of steady decline or sudden closure, of battles lost and communities bereft, for the first time since records began, of a place to meet in convivial cheer. Much of the blame for this, despite talk of changing social trends, cheap supermarket booze, the smoking ban and so on, can be laid at the door of the long-term trend towards more and more pubs being owned by larger and larger organisations – first breweries and, since the 1990s, 'pub companies' – or 'pubcos'.

On the opposite page is a description of a long-forgotten grand day out, lubricated by visits to several hostelries. This light-hearted interlude leads into the story of how Devon's breweries grew ever larger, swallowing up ever more pubs in the process, before themselves being swallowed up by even larger players, leaving most of the county's pubs at the mercy of multinational companies.

THE CORPORATION OF CRABTREE

The members of this ancient and loyal corporate body gave themselves, their wives and friends, a treat on Monday last, having hired a special train to bring the body corporate, and merry souls, to Exeter from Plymouth; and after due time spent in the ancient city, to take them back again for the charge of 4s 6d each. The Corporation of Crabtree ... like the Corporation of Ide, near [Exeter], is a self-constituted body, created, so far as we recollect, by force of imitation of the old defunct Corporation of Plymouth ... These extra-constitutional bodies were doubtless of great influence in their day, keeping the greater corporates within bounds by sound and practical teaching. At Exeter, when the people used to be mocked with a narrow election, they were amused by the Corporation of Ide, who chid the practice by a broad and farcical election. At Tiverton, the junta of thirteen, who abused the nation by sending up two members of parliament in the name of the town, were, if our memory serve us, gravely rebuked by the more earnest and constitutional solemnity of the 'mock' election at Bolham – an election, however, which was conducted with less hypocrisy and less corruption, than the genuine sham at the Guildhall. So with the Crabtree Corporation; whatever the Plymouth Corporation did, the Crabtree Corporates overdid. If the Plymouth Corporates stuffed, the Crabtree Corps all but bursted; if the constitutional body got drunk, the extra-constitutional body got drunker – there was but this difference between them: the one committed its excesses in the name of the constitution, and the other in abatement of constitutional pretensions – the one body got drunk in earnest, and went to church with the mace – the other got drunk in fun, and made no parade of their religion afterwards. But the latter had no mace for state occasions: granted but they were at all times spicy.

The Corporation met at early dawn and regaled themselves with white ale, Mr Recorder Tutton having first suck. The Right Worshipful Phil Davis, the mayor, issued an address to the disorderlies of Crabtree, to be temperate and discreet, and not take advantage of the absence of the constituted authorities. Town Clerk Elliott then proclaimed the closing of the shops not yet opened, and the body departed. Arrived at Exeter, they were greeted at the St Thomas station by a deputation of Grecians who wished to meet them at dinner at Ager's White Horse; a dutiful address and a gracious answer being the ceremonies observed. The distinguished visitors then proceeded up the High Street with a band of music and corporate insignia, colours flying, etc. They did not go to the cathedral in state – the corporation seats not being reserved for them. But the several members proceeded on a tour of inspection of the city – but shirked an invitation to see the gaol; and his worship fainted at the sight of the stocks under the Guildhall porch – such barbarous appliances are not tolerated in the enlightened borough, where inebriation is a pastime and not an offence. The corporate body then left its card at Paul Measor's, and inspected the post office – the surveyor of the body, who does the architecture, being directed to prepare plans for a similar structure for the accommodation of the Crabtree correspondence – the Exeter post office being deemed a fitting model for such a borough. Several distinguished topers visited the corporaters at their hostelry, and when the train started 57 were left behind, reported invalided by the journey, having been in the sun too much throughout the day. The report in the borough was that a jolly lot had been left behind drunk, but this was false, for they looked anything but jolly the next morning.

From the *Western Times*, 9 September 1848

Starkey, Knight & Ford, Ltd.,

————BREWERS &————
WINE & SPIRIT MERCHANTS,

Bottlers of the
FINEST IRISH & SCOTCH WHISKIES.

Shippers of the finest brands of
WINES & SPIRITS,
Which are well matured in the Company's own Bonded Stores.

BRILLIANT PALE ALES

IN BOTTLE 2/6 PER DOZ.
IN CASK 1/- PER GAL.

PERFECT PURITY INSURED.

Tiverton.

Devon's Lost Breweries

As anyone who frequents Devon's free houses will know, the county's drinkers are spoilt for choice, with around 30 breweries producing an ever-changing range of beers. It is a sobering thought, though, to realise that the oldest of those breweries is only 32 years old. Devon's brewing heritage is a rich and diverse one, yet it had to die before it could be reborn.

The last of Devon's historic breweries – Plymouth Breweries – closed in 1984 after being taken over by Courage. Its closure meant that virtually all the beers on offer in the county's pubs were not only brewed elsewhere but came from a handful of large breweries. Worse still, those same breweries owned most of the county's pubs, which they effectively waged war on by gutting and rebranding, ripping out anything old and distinctive to impose the bland uniformity of corporate pub design.

It might have seemed that things could not get worse, but in the early 1990s, in the wake of the government's 'Beer Orders', these large breweries offloaded their pubs to pub companies or 'pubcos'. This meant that, for the first time, vast swathes of Britain's pubs were owned not by breweries but by companies with real-estate portfolios. Counties like Devon, with no regional breweries left, were particularly badly affected. Although the pubcos maintained links with the big brewers, supplying their beers – with a hefty mark-up – to the pubs they owned, they had no direct interest in selling beer, and, as the property market boomed, it was inevitable that they would increasingly seek to realise the assets tied up in their portfolios. As a result, many pub closures are due not to the inherent non-viability of the pubs concerned but to the imperative to maximise investment. And, while free houses can choose from the ever-increasing range of beers brewed in the county and further afield, the majority of pubs are obliged to serve a limited range of the same predictable beers.

Although this may seem a modern phenomenon, its roots go back centuries. It is tempting to think that, until comparatively recently, country pubs were largely self sufficient, serving their local communities, and relatively unaffected by larger economic forces. In some cases they were, but, then as now, these tended to be the free houses, owned by their landlords, who either brewed their own ale or bought it from whom they chose. And, as time went on, the number of free houses slowly dwindled, as the breweries grew ever larger and more acquisitive.

By the eighteenth century, brewing was England's biggest industry, with huge breweries being established. Although many pubs continued to brew their own beer, technological advances, and the ability to brew newly-popular styles of beer, especially porter, meant that, from the mid-eighteenth century onward, the larger breweries had the advantage over small producers. And, as breweries grew ever bigger, vast fortunes were made, fuelling ever greater expansion and centralisation. According to the historian Peter Haydon, 'not only was brewing the largest industry in the country, it was intrinsically and umbilically linked with the evolution of capitalism. Brewing was the first truly modern capitalist industry and shared many of the characteristics associated with modern industrial capitalism.'

As time went on, local breweries were gradually bought up in a process of amalgamation. Craft gave way to profit and economy of scale. To comprehend how this process worked in Devon, and how it led to the loss of all the county's historic breweries, the following listings give an overview of the major breweries operating from the mid-nineteenth century onward, and indicate what happened to them.

These listings, arranged alphabetically by town or city, have been compiled from various primary and secondary sources. Information, in many cases, has not only been difficult to come by but also contradictory regarding dates and other details. Where bankruptcy, high finance and general wheeler-dealing came into play, the process of merger, takeover and so on was not only extremely complex but accompanied by the minimum of publicity. Hopefully, however, the following overview – which we have tried to ensure is as error-free as possible – should give a broad idea of the process of takeover and amalgamation that led to the state we are in today.[1]

BARNSTAPLE

Taw Vale Brewery, Litchdon St. Established as the Barnstaple Brewery in 1851 by John Kay, a London brewer. The *North Devon Journal* of 3 May 1851 was fulsome in its praise: 'Barnstaple, which is celebrated for its shipbuilders, is now likely to be celebrated for its native porter; and the beverages of this kind, produced by Mr Kay, are of such excellence as will render it almost unnecessary to send to more distant places for similar preparations.' Three years later, due to 'the unprecedented support and success he has met with', John Kay expanded the brewery, but this led to cash flow problems. In April 1855, he brought in another London brewer, Edwin Oliver, as a partner, but in January 1856 the receivers were called in and the brewery closed. It reopened in May 1856, with John Kay as manager, but in September it was bought by JE Barlow and became the Taw Vale Brewery. In 1889, it was acquired by Arnold, Perrett & Co of Wickwar, Gloucestershire, with a substantial number of tied houses; in 1896 the estate was sold on to Starkey, Knight & Ford of Tiverton. Brewing ceased in 1900.

> BARNSTAPLE BREWERY, LITCHDON STREET.
>
> JOHN KAY begs to announce the completion of his Premises, which are constructed on the most scientific principles, with regard to the London treatment and fermentation of Porters and Family Ales.
>
> J. K. respectfully informs the Nobility, Clergy, Gentry, and Inhabitants of Barnstaple and its vicinity, that he will be prepared by the end of the present month to execute any orders with which he may be favoured, on the following terms. viz.,—
>
> | | s. | d. | | | s. | d. | |
> |---|---|---|---|---|---|---|---|
> | Stout | 1 | 6 | per gallon. | XX | 1 | 1 | per gallon. |
> | Porter | 1 | 0 | ,, | XXX | 1 | 4 | ,, |
> | Pale Ale | 1 | 3 | ,, | XXXX | 1 | 6 | ,, |
> | Table Ale | 0 | 8 | ,, | | | | |
>
> In casks of 4½, 9, 18, and 36 Gallons.
>
> N.B.—In carrying out the London mode of business, J. K. will, within a reasonable period, change or credit the return of any Beer or Porter.
>
> Drays will attend the Vicinity and neighbouring towns.
> Barnstaple, March 7th, 1851.

---

1 Breweries outside Devon that acquired breweries in the county – and did not subsequently dispose of them – are indicated by an asterisk; an account of what later happened to them appears in a separate list at the end of the county listings. Where the names of the tied houses sold with breweries are known, they are listed in a footnote. Generally, however, their names are only readily available when breweries were offered at auction, not when they were taken over as part of a private deal.

BARNSTAPLE BREWERY.

THE PROPRIETOR, in returning his Thanks to the Inhabitants of *Barnstaple* and its vicinity, for the unprecedented support and success he has met with in Establishing a Local Brewery, begs to Advertise the GREAT INCREASE HE HAS MADE in the PLANT and STORES; and respectfully calls the attention of the Neighbouring Families and PUBLIC TRADE to the Largest STOCK ever held in the North of Devon, of

LONDON PORTER, BEERS, PALE ALE, & TREBLE STOUT.

Families supplied in SMALL CASKS in the Neighbouring Towns with PORTER, BEER, STOUT, AND PALE ALE, of the Best Quality, at Prices from 8d. to 20d. per Gallon.

BREWERY PRICES.—IN CASKS OF NINE GALLONS AND UPWARDS.

PER GAL.		PER GAL.	
PORTER, LONDON	15d.	X ALE	8d. to 10d.
Ditto, ditto	18d.	XV ditto	10d. to 12d.
Ditto, EXTRA STOUT	20d.	XX ditto	13d. to 15d.
PALE ALE	18d.	XXX ditto	16d.
BITTER ALE	18d.	XXXX ditto	18d. & 20d.

ANY BEERS DISAPPROVED OF CHANGED WITHIN SIX DAYS OF DELIVERY.

THE PUBLIC TRADE

Supplied with the best Porter in *EIGHTEEN GALLON KILDERKINS, warranted full to the Bung, and Fresh. Delivered Carriage Free.*

Depôts for the Supply of Families in Small Casks, at Bideford, Torrington, Holsworthy, Southmolton, Northmolton, Chulmleigh, Braunton, Ilfracombe, Linton, &c.

☞ DRAYS attend the above Towns every Fortnight.

Dated July, 1854.

JOHN KAY, BARNSTAPLE BREWERY,
Late Brewer, Anchor Brewery, *Chelsea.*

Opposite page: John Kay announces the opening of the Barnstaple Brewery in the North Devon Journal *of 13 March 1851*

Above: Expansion announced in the North Devon Journal *of 6 July 1854*

Right: The receivers take over, and the brewery gets a new name – from the North Devon Journal *of 15 May 1856*

Below: Under new ownership, and henceforth known as the Taw Vale Brewery – from the North Devon Journal *of 25 December 1856*

BARNSTAPLE AND TAW VALE BREWERY.

THE TRUSTEES of the above Estate respectfully acquaint the Public of the North of Devon, that they have made arrangements for

RE-OPENING THE BREWERY,

And are now enabled to supply

THE PUBLIC AND PRIVATE TRADE

With ALES and PORTERS of very superior qualities.

The Trustees beg to call attention to the new arrangements they have entered into, combining the advantage of a supply of Water of First-rate Brewing quality from the Barnstaple Water Company, together with Malt purchased from the best Markets, which enables them confidently to solicit Public support.

List of Prices :—

X	8d. per Gallon.
XX	12d. ,,
XXX	16d. ,,
XXXX	18d. & 20d. do.

DOUBLE X PORTER, 21s. per Kilderkin of 18 Gallons.

BEER not approved of, changed within Eight Days of Delivery.—Drays attend all the Neighbouring Towns.

☞ All Orders or Communications to be addressed to the Manager, Mr. JOHN KAY, Brewery Office, *Litchdon, Barnstaple.*

TAW VALE BREWERY, BARNSTAPLE.
J. E. BARLOW,

HAVING in September last Purchased the above BREWERY from the Assignees of KAY and OLIVER, begs to inform the Inhabitants of North Devon, that he is now prepared to execute any orders they may be pleased to favour him with in BEERS AND PORTERS, of a superior quality, at the following Prices:—

X ALE, Brewed to supply the deficiency of Cider				8d. per Gallon.
XX " " "				12d. ,,
X K, a Mild Pale Ale, brewed expressly to suit the wants of Private Families				14d. ,,
XXX " " " "				16d. ,,
XXXX, extra Strong				20d. ,,
PORTER				14d. ,,
EXTRA STOUT, for Winter drink				20d. ,,

J. E. BARLOW, in quoting the above Prices, respectfully solicits the favour of an Order, feeling convinced that from his long experience in one of the Largest London Breweries, combined with buying (for CASH) Malt and Hops in the best Markets, he is enabled to give, for the Price, an Article superior to any yet introduced into this district.

☞ *BEERS, in Casks of 9 Gallons and upwards, delivered Carriage Free.*

Dated Barnstaple, December 16th, 1856.

Anchor Brewery, Boutport St. Established by Edwin Petter in 1881; acquired by William Hancock & Sons* of Wiveliscombe, Somerset in 1918, with seven tied houses; two other tied houses were sold to Starkey, Knight & Ford of Tiverton; one was sold to the Yeo Vale Brewery.[1]

ANCHOR BREWERY,
BARNSTAPLE.

EDWIN PETTER,
MALTSTER, CORN, SEED, MANURE,
AND GENERAL MERCHANT,

BEGS to inform the Public of Barnstaple and its neighbourhood, that he has just completed the construction of a Brewery, adjoining his Malting Premises in Boutport-street, replete with all the best appliances and newest improvements, and that he is now prepared to supply

GENUINE ALES,
BREWED ENTIRELY FROM THE BEST MALT AND HOPS.

The well-known character of the Malts manufactured by E. P. for the last twenty-seven years will, he believes, be a guarantee that the Ales sold by him will be of the Best and Purest Quality, and equal, if not superior, to any sold by the Largest Brewers in the Kingdom.

N.B.—These Ales will be entirely the product of Malt and Hops, and no Saccharine derived from any other source, or any other ingredients whatsoever, will be introduced therein.

MILD, PALE, BITTER ALE, STOUT AND PORTER,

Supplied in 4½ to 54 Gallon Casks, at from 10d. to 1s. 6d. per Gallon.   [4727

Above: The opening of the Anchor Brewery, announced in the North Devon Journal on 5 May 1881

Below: Barnstaple's last surviving brewery, from the North Devon Journal of 26 May 1927

Yeo Vale Brewery, Bear Street. William Pugsley established a brewery in Boutport Street some time before 1894. In 1900 he moved to new premises at the Yeo Vale Brewery in Bear Street. The brewery closed in 1930. Three years later Henry Williamson mourned its loss:

W. PUGSLEY'S BREWERY,
BEAR STREET,

The only Brewer in Barnstaple, is still using Malt and Hops only in his Brewings. Pure Beers can be obtained at 9/. and 12/- per 4½ Gallon Casks upwards. Also at the "Curriers Arms," Vicarage Street, at 4d. and 5d. per pint. WHY PAY MORE.

There used to be another place in North Devon where one could get real ale, and that was in a one-man brewery in Barnstaple. A pin, or a 4 gallon cask, cost 12s. Lovely stuff it was, a nutty flavour, yet not cloying. One could drink the whole pin in an evening without having that horrible morning taste on the tongue which the American dialect, with its present richness akin to that of the Elizabethan age, calls the 'hangover'. Good beer should have no hangover, either in the head or the palate. But the world is full of bad beer, and it's too late to protest. The townsman likes the heavy immature adulterated stuff; and the one-man brewery in Barnstaple is closed for lack of business.

---

1 The seven tied houses sold to Hancock & Sons were the North Country Inn and the Swan Inn, Barnstaple; the Rock House Inn, Georgeham; the Coach & Horses, Appledore; the New Inn, Abbotsham; the New Inn, Torrington; and the Rising Sun, Appledore. The two tied houses sold to Starkey, Knight & Ford were the Ebrington Arms, Knowle and the Bell Inn, Chittlehampton. The tied house sold to the Yeo Vale Brewery was the Plough Inn, Bickington.

BRIXHAM

Lakeman's Brewery, Fore St. Established by Stephen Lakeman in 1780, the brewery remained in the Lakeman family until 1901. It was acquired by Simonds* of Reading, Berkshire in 1938, with 50 tied houses. Brewing ceased in 1950.

A Lakeman's delivery lorry in the 1920s

DARTMOUTH

Bartlett & Co., Warfleet Brewery, New Rd. Established in a former paper mill in 1840. Inspired by Queen Victoria declaring that the River Dart reminded her of the Rhine, the company declared its beer to be 'the Barley Wine of the English Rhine' and also claimed that its Warfleet Pale Ale was 'the finest beer in Britain'. It was acquired by Heavitree Brewery of Exeter in 1926. Brewing ceased in 1929.

DAWLISH

Dawlish Brewery, High St. Established in 1817; acquired, with around 30 tied houses, by Heavitree Brewery of Exeter in 1926.

EXETER

City Brewery, Commercial Rd. The City Brewery was established in 1760, but has links with a much earlier brewing tradition. On 1 February 1563, the council, clearly fed up with the way the city's brewers were carrying on, ordered them 'to brew henceforth a more wholesome drink, or else order [would be] taken for the setting up of a common brewhouse'. It seems that the brewers did not mend their ways, for in 1657 a benefactor called Dr Robert Vilvaine 'purchased of the Mayor and Chamber, for a term of 999 years, a piece of ground in Exe Island, on which he built a large Brewhouse, with a Malthouse adjoining, called the Public Brewhouse, which he gave to the Chamber ... for the maintenance of four poor Scholars, to be taken out of the Free Grammar School here, and sent to Exeter College in Oxford; and for allowing 8/- per annum for a Schoolmistress, to teach poor Children freely, in the Parish of St Sidwells.'[1]

In 1760, Richard Densham leased land adjoining the brewhouse to build a cellar and warehouse to carry on the brewing trade, and subsequently went into partnership with Samuel White. Whether he initially used the public brewhouse is unclear, but, if he did, he had long abandoned it by 1822, when Daniel and Samuel Lysons wrote, in their *Additions and Corrections to the Magna Britannia*, that 'it is long since the buildings were used as a brewery: they were very convenient for the woollen manufacture, and have decreased in value in consequence of its declension.'

Densham & White's Brewery was first referred to as the City Brewery in a deed of 1801. The partnership later changed to White & Crockett, and on 5 October 1833, the *Western Times* announced that 'Messrs White & Crockett ... have disposed of their business to Messrs Salter & Owens of the St Thomas Brewery, whom they confidently recommend as their successors. Messrs Salter & Owens, in taking possession of [this] long-established and respectable business, beg to announce that their trade will in future be carried on at the City Brewery.' In 1845, Benjamin Salter sold his interest in the company to John Norman. Twenty years later, in 1865, Walter Pring became a partner, and it was as Norman & Pring that the brewery was henceforth known. It became a limited liability company in 1911. In 1944, Norman & Pring Ltd acquired St Anne's Well Brewery (see listing on page 343) and concentrated brewing there in 1956. The company was acquired by Whitbread* in 1962 with 102 tied houses, and it was merged with Starkey, Knight & Ford, Tiverton. According to WG Hoskins, in *2000 Years in Exeter*, the cellars of the City Brewery contained two arches of the old Exe Bridge, part of which has been revealed following demolition of the brewery and nearby buildings in the 1970s. Another link with the past is the St Thomas Brewery, from which production was moved to the City Brewery in 1833, but which survives as the Harvester Malt House on Haven Road.

Heavitree Brewery, Church St, Heavitree. Established 1790 by John Wolland. His son, Thomas Wolland, and his nephew, William Wolland, later took over. His daughter, Elizabeth, married Thomas Baker, and it was the Baker family who eventually inherited the business, which became Baker & Son in 1860. In 1890 Robert Baker formed Heavitree Brewery Ltd, and embarked on a campaign of buying up other breweries to acquire their tied houses and closing the breweries down. By the time Heavitree closed its own brewery in 1970, it had 135 tied houses, and henceforth operated as a pub company. The brewery was demolished in 1980, and a year later the company became the Heavitree Brewery PLC.

Eagle Brewery, North St. Established in 1850 by Frederick Pinder, who later leased the brewery to WH Wilkinson. After Pinder died in 1876 it was sold to George & Charles Finch, who already operated as wine & spirit merchants in Fore Street. In 1892, they sold out to Heavitree Brewery, whose interest was not in the brewery – which they closed – but in the tied houses that came with it. According to the *Exeter & Plymouth*

---

1 Alexander Jenkins, *History and Description of the City of Exeter*, 1806

Gazette for 25 November 1892, Heavitree paid around £40,000 for the business, which, 'besides the brewery and the premises in Fore Street and public houses in Exeter and the neighbourhood', included 'freehold hotels and inns at Crediton, Cullompton, Lapford, North Tawton, Ottery St Mary and other places'.

HOME BREWED ALE.

THE restorative, tonic, and invigorating properties of SOUND ALE, when carefully Brewed from the best Malt and Hops, are proverbial. Every one would be glad to get this beverage if attainable. But it is not customary in this part of England, as is the case in others, for families to brew their own Beer. Many complaints consequently arise as to the difficulty of getting a really genuine article. To provide for this want,

FREDERICK PINDER, Eagle Brewery, St. Sidwells,

has completed arrangements to prepare HOME BREWED ALE, expressly for the use of private families, pure, sound, and economical. He supplies five different sorts :—

	s.	d.	
XXX.—The finest Ale that can be brewed	1	6	per gallon.
XX.—Excellent Ale for family use.	1	1	per gallon.
X.—A very good Ale—light, pleasant and palatable	0	10	per gallon.
Pale Bitter Ale, of Matchless Quality	1	1	per gallon.
Table Beer, for Schools, Frugal Families, &c.	0	6	per gallon.

Further particulars, and directions for the management of Beer, in Casks, will be found in Circulars, to be had at the Brewery.

Advertisements for the Eagle Brewery (above) from the Western Times *for 16 March 1850, and the Windsor Brewery (right) from the* Exeter Flying Post *for 9 April 1862. Both breweries were later acquired by the Heavitree Brewery and closed.*

LONDON PORTER BREWERS.

ALGER & CROWSON,

WINDSOR BREWERY,
HEAVITREE.

IN returning our sincere thanks to our numerous supporters in Exeter and neighbourhood for the liberal favours bestowed on us during the past three years, while regretting the disappointment at being unable, through the vast and unexpected influx of trade, to supply all the orders entrusted to us last season, we beg to assure them that every effort will be used to prevent a recurrence thereof. The better to ensure this we would be grateful to those who propose honouring us with orders for

PORTER OR STOUT

to do so at their earliest convenience.
Ship Inn, Heavitree, April 1st, 1862.

Windsor Brewery, Heavitree. Established in 1860 by Messrs Alger & Crowson; five years later, William Crowson was in business on his own and, according to an advertisement in the *Western Times* for 19 May 1865, looking for builders and bricklayers to build him a new brewery and malthouse. Among the first beers he brewed in the new premises was 'Crowson's Edinboro XXXX Ale, a 'superior ale, of extra strength and fine flavour, suitable especially for the festive season' of 1867. He had other business interests as well. The *Exeter & Plymouth Gazette* for 9 August 1878 carried two advertisements from him: one for 'harvest beer supplied in farmer's own cask, at 7d per gallon, delivered to Exeter stations'; the other for 'several houses at Heavitree ... to let: £10, £19, and £25 a year'. William Crowson died in 1885 at the age of 52; the business was carried on by his widow and later by his son. On 26 April 1898, the *Western Times* reported that

> the Heavitree Brewery Company has acquired the Windsor Brewery ... which, since Mr Crowson succeeded his late father in the management of the business, has been considerably improved and developed, has a good many houses in the city, and a few elsewhere. It is said that overtures for purchase were made by the Heavitree Brewery Company some time ago, and were not entertained, but on the present occasion the price offered was sufficiently tempting. The amount to be paid is reported to be over £30,000. It is not unlikely ... that the company will go in for brewing stout, and the manufacture of aerated waters, for which their newly acquired premises will afford scope.

The reported price was a serious underestimate. At a shareholders' meeting in 1901, it was revealed that the price paid was £50,526. The Windsor Brewery closed the following year.

Well Park Brewery, Alphington Rd. Opened in 1882 by Stevens, Pidsley & Co. It later became Ross & Pidsley and Ross & Son, before Messrs Aylwin & Snowden took it over in 1914. When war broke out, Snowden enlisted, leaving Aylwin to run the business. When conscription was introduced, he was called up, and, although he was given temporary exemption, he did eventually have to serve, and the brewery closed. In the summer of 1919, they placed advertisements in local papers announcing that, as they had returned to civil life, the brewery would reopen. In 1925 it was acquired by Devenish's* of Weymouth, Dorset, with 22 tied houses, who used it as a depot until 1958. The building has since been converted to residential accommodation.

Above: A Well Park Brewery delivery lorry, seen in 1927 after the brewery had been taken over by Devenish's.

Left: An advertisement in the Exeter & Plymouth Gazette *of 27 June 1919 announcing the reopening of the Well Park Brewery*

Opposite page: The opening of the Well Park Brewery announced in the Exeter & Plymouth Gazette *on 2 November 1862*

THE WELL-PARK BREWERY, EXETER.

STEVENS, PIDSLEY, & CO.

BEG to notify the completion of their NEW BREWERY, which has been erected on the most improved principles.

Their Senior Partner's 20 years' experience at BURTON-ON-TRENT and other large Breweries, and the fact of their possessing a WELL of WATER reported on as being of the highest possible purity, gives them confidence in being able to produce

ALES OF UNDOUBTED QUALITY.

	PER GALL.		PER GALL.
AK FAMILY ALE,	1s. 0d.	WELL PARK BURTON,	1s. 3d.
XX MILD ,,	1s. 2d.	INDIA PALE ALE,	1s. 6d.

DOUBLE STOUT, 1s. 4d. PER GALL.

Supplied in Casks of 4½ Gallons and upwards.

COMPARISON OF PRICE AND QUALITY RESPECTFULLY SOLICITED.

ORDERS RECEIVED AT THE BREWERY,
OR THROUGH AGENTS.

West of England Brewery, Okehampton St. Established by William Mortimore of the Okehampton Inn around 1878. In 1906, after his death, it was sold at auction, along with seven tied houses[1], to WH Morton of the Turk's Head for £10,000; in 1909, it was sold to Messrs Carr & Quick, wine merchants of Queen Street, for £6,300. Brewing ceased in 1927, but Carr & Quick continued to use the premises for bottling beer.

St Anne's Well Brewery, Lower North St. Established by Messrs Harding, Richards & Thomas in 1878; became a limited liability company in 1889; acquired in 1944 by Norman & Pring of City Brewery (see listing on pages 339-40) with 78 tied houses. Brewing ceased in 1968. The building has since been converted to mixed-used commercial accommodation.

Globe Inn, Clifton Road. Nicholas Lamacraft, a maltster and brewer, took the licence of the Globe in 1856; it was transferred to his son, Harry Lamacraft, in 1878. He was still there, and still brewing beer, in 1919. He eventually retired in 1925 and died, aged 80, in 1933.

HARBERTONFORD

Harbourne Brewery, Maltsters Arms. Recorded in 1861 with a Mr Ellis as brewer, the lease was advertised in the *Western Times* on 6 September 1878. It was taken by a Mr Fairweather, but in 1886, following the death of the owner, Philip Grills, it was offered for sale. It seems to have been acquired by a relative of the deceased with an eye for business, as this report from the *Western Times* of 16 April 1886 indicates:

> Considerable dissatisfaction having been expressed for some time at the price charged by the Totnes butchers for meat, and Mr Gidley Grills of Bourton Farm being unable to obtain what he thought a satisfactory price from the butchers for his bullocks at the recent Totnes market, decided to slaughter his own beasts and to open a stall for the sale of meat in the market on Saturdays. He accordingly made a commencement

---

1 The seven tied houses sold with the West of England Brewery in 1905 and 1909 were the Okehampton Inn; the Golden Ball Inn, Mary Arches St; the Blackamoor's Head, West St; the Alexandra Inn, Bonhay Rd; the New Inn, Silverton; the Railway Inn, Exminster; and the Golden Lion, Moretonhampstead.

on Saturday, selling his joints from ½d to 1d per lb cheaper than the other butchers, the result being that by four o'clock in the afternoon he had cleared out his stall. It is understood also that Mr Grills has opened a brewery at Harbertonford, expecting to get a larger profit from his barley by brewing. His beer is pronounced to be of good quality and has sold well.

William Gidley Grills died at the age of 80 in 1915, and in 1925 the brewery, along with six tied houses, was offered for sale as one lot. It failed to find a buyer and the estate was sold as separate lots.[1]

HONITON
Honiton Steam Brewery, Mill St. Established c1846; transferred in 1896 from James John Cuddon to John George Hann, and became JG Hann & Co Ltd; acquired by the Dorsetshire Brewery* in 1927 with ten tied houses.

KINGSBRIDGE
London Brewery, Church St. Established by 1866; acquired by John Kelland in 1884; acquired by the Bedford Brewery, Plymouth in 1904, with 11 tied houses.[2]

South Devon Brewery, Union Rd. Established next to the Exeter Inn around 1842. On 27 December 1856, the *Western Times* advertised for sale 'that Four Quarter Brewery, commonly called, or known as the South Devon Brewery, now in the occupation of Mr RH Fairweather, as tenant thereof ... The brewery was established about 14 years since; the brewhouse is newly erected, and is allowed to be one of the most convenient in the South Hams, the late proprietor having spared neither trouble nor expense in its erection.' It was bought by WH Prowse, and it continued to be known as WH Prowse & Sons until 1946, even though it had been acquired in 1934 by Charles Blundell, a wine and spirit merchant from Westwell Street in Plymouth. Pubs owned by the brewery seem thenceforth to have borne the name 'Blundells of Plymouth' on their signboards – see, for example, the Dolphin at Kingston (p 168) and the Seven Stars at Tamerton Foliot (p 267). Brewing ceased in 1948, and the 25 tied houses were supplied with beer from the Tamar Brewery, Devonport, until the business was acquired by Simonds* of Reading in 1951.

KINGSKERSWELL
Kingskerswell Brewery. Established in 1896 by John Earl and Charles Tayler. The business soon ran into financial difficulties, and a year later was being run under the supervision of the creditors. In 1898, it was acquired by William Henry Mortimer of the Ashburton Brewery, who moved his business to Kingskerswell and closed the brewery at Ashburton. The Kingskerswell Brewery was sold, with eight tied houses, in 1927.[3]

1 The six tied houses were the Maltster's Arms and the Red Lion, Harbertonford; the Globe Inn, Harberton; the Dartmouth Inn and the Kingsbridge Inn, Totnes; and the Waterman's Arms, Ashprington.

2 The 11 tied houses sold with the London Brewery were the Ship & Plough Hotel and Seven Stars, Kingsbridge; the Rose & Crown and London Inn, Dodbrooke; the Sportsmans' Arms, Hemborough Post, Blackawton; the Forces Tavern, Blackawton; the New Inn, Morleigh; the Globe Inn, Frogmore; the New Inn, Chillington; the King's Arms, Beesands; and the Royal Oak, Malborough.

3 The eight public houses sold – all to different buyers – when the Kingskerswell Brewery closed were the Railway Hotel, Exeter Inn and Town Arms, Ashburton; the Star Inn, Cold East, Ilsington; the New Inn, Ilsington; the Tavistock Inn, Poundsgate; the Rugglestone Inn, Widecombe; and the Church House Inn, Torbryan.

LITTLEHAM (nr BIDEFORD)

Apps Brewery. According to an article in the *Western Times* on 31 December 1859, this 'was established in 1850 by the late Mrs Harding, on property belonging to her son, the Rev Lymebeer Harding ... The reason for establishing the brewery was the quality of the water which had been analysed by Mr Herapath and found to be possessed of very valuable constituents for brewing. The first management took place under Mr T Barrow, Mrs Harding's butler, assisted by the Revs L Harding and C Padley.' The enterprise proved successful, but was brought to an end by a devastating fire in 1885.

A FINE TONIC FOR INVALIDS AS WELL AS THE ROBUST.

Brewed from a Spring Water adjoining the Brewery.

THE APPS BREWERY SPRING WATER ALES.

Highly recommended by the late eminent Chymist, WM. HERAPATH, Esq., of Bristol, and Dr. ANDREW URE, of London.

1s., 1s. 4d., and 1s. 6d. per Gallon.

In Pins, Firkins, Kilderkins, Barrels, or Hogsheads, fresh from the Brewery Weekly.

The Brewery Company respectfully solicits a trial of these wholesome Ales. Carriage Free to any Station on the North Devon Line.

T. JOCE, Agent,

Formerly with George and John Harris, Barnstaple, and Collier and Co., Plymouth.

STORES—54 AND 56, BOUTPORT-STREET, BARNSTAPLE.

An advertisement from the North Devon Journal *for 5 July 1877 extolling the benefits of drinking Apps Ales*

MILTON DAMEREL

Woodford Bridge Inn. Kelly's 1914 *Directory* listed William Vodden as a brewer at the Woodford Bridge Inn, but it seems to have closed the same year, for, when the inn was advertised for sale in March 1914, there was no mention of a brewery. For more information on the inn see pp. 188-89.

NEWTON ABBOT

Old Brewery, Wolborough St. When advertised for sale, along with a malthouse, in the *Exeter & Plymouth Gazette* on 27 December 1834, this was described as an 'extensive and long-established brewery, now and for many years past conducted, and carried on by the proprietor, Mr Edward Palk'. It consisted of 'capacious cellars, two furnaces, one containing 840, the other 370 gallons, pumps, mash fan, under back, backs, working fans, stillions, vats and casks, containing from four gallons and a half and upwards, to 120 barrels, and all other articles and conveniences necessary for the purpose of an extensive trade.' By 1878, it had been acquired by John Mills, and later became Mills Brothers. It was acquired by St Annes' Well Brewery, Exeter in 1924, with six tied houses.

MILLS BROTHERS,
*M*altsters, *B*rewers,
— AND —
SPIRIT MERCHANTS,
The **Old Brewery,**
WOLBOROUGH STREET,
NEWTON ABBOT.

An advertisement from 1914

Pinsent & Co (later Pinsent & Sons), Mill Lane Brewery, Highweek St. Although information is scanty, it seems that Edward Palk may have gone into partnership with Thomas Pinsent after selling the Old Brewery, and established a new brewery and malthouse. The first record of their having formed such a partnership comes in the report of a court case in the *Western Times* on 19 September 1840. Four years later, on 12 October 1844, the company placed a notice in the *Exeter & Plymouth Gazette*:

TO THE PUBLIC!!

It having been industriously reported by some designing Persons, that the late EXTENSIVE SEIZURE of DELETERIOUS DRUGS, and other PROHIBITED ARTICLES, which was made about a week since in a Brewery in Newton Abbot, were found and taken from the Mill Lane Brewery, Newton Bushel. Messrs PINSENT & Co consider it their duty thus publicly to contradict such a BASE and UNFOUNDED REPORT; and to assure the Public at large, that no such seizure, or even search, has been made on their Premises.

Unfortunately, it has not been possible to trace the report on which the malicious rumour was based. Pinsent & Sons was acquired by Heavitree Brewery in 1919, with 45 tied houses.

PAIGNTON

Paignton Brewery, Victoria St. Information on the complex and fraught history of this enterprise is sketchy, but it seems to have been established in 1854 by a maltster called John Distin. He was declared bankrupt in 1862. It later became the Paignton Brewing & Trading Company, but went into liquidation in 1880. It was acquired, along with 15 tied houses, by a spirit dealer called Ernest Gottwaltz for around £20,000. He subsequently went into partnership with a Mr Lind, and by 1890 held a total of 52 tied houses. In that year, a new company, the Torbay Brewery & Cider Company, was set up to acquire and amalgamate the Paignton Brewery and the Fordton Cider Works at Crediton. Three years later, in 1893, the new company was acquired for £48,000 by Arnold, Perrett & Co of Wickwar, Gloucestershire with 54 tied houses. Three years after that it was sold to Starkey, Knight & Ford of Tiverton. The brewery building survives.

PARRACOMBE

Crocombe & Son. Richard Crocombe, a maltster and corn merchant, starting brewing in the 1870s. The brewery closed in 1940 when his son, Frederick Crocombe, died at the age of 72. A few years earlier, Henry Williamson had written that, 'in the village of Parracombe there is an inn where you may get what now-a-days is very rare – genuine home-brewed beer. This home-brew tastes of *beer*. It has none of that metallic bitter taste which the townsman is said to approve, and which is only saltpetre, fermented glucose, and other chemicals. If you visit the inn in cold weather, when a fire is burning, get the poker red hot on the embers (avoiding tar-smoke) and plunge it into your beer. It's an old custom hereabouts.'

PLYMOUTH

Castle Brewery, Hoegate Street. Closed 1882. For more details see pages 353-6

Tamar Brewery, Tamar St, Morice Town. An advertisement in the *Exeter Flying Post* on 13 November 1800 alerted 'millers and others concerned in the corn and flour trade' that 'a windmill, in good repair, and capable of doing as much work as most mills in the West of England' was to let. They were advised to 'apply to Mr White, brewer, at Exeter; or to Messrs Dansey, White & Co at the Tamar Brewery, Plymouth Dock.' The Mr White referred to at Exeter was almost certainly the one at the City Brewery; as one of the partners in the Tamar Brewery was also called White, and both breweries were involved in the lease of the windmill, there may have been a link between the two businesses at this time. On 12 February 1814 the *Royal Cornwall Gazette* announced that the Tamar Brewery 'and various public houses in Plymouth Dock, Stoke, Stonehouse, etc' were for sale. According to the advertisement, 'the brewery has been in work several years [and forms] altogether a concern almost unequalled either for size or convenience of situation.' In the 1880s, Thomas Liscombe disposed of the brewery to George Crake, and in 1919 it was acquired by Simonds* of Reading with 28 tied houses. Simonds had had an agency in Plymouth since the 1890s, and made the most of their new acquisition: brewing continued and by the 1930s the Tamar Brewery had 70 tied houses. Brewing eventually ceased in 1975, long after Simonds had been absorbed into Courage, Barclay & Simonds.*

Devonport & Tiverton Brewery Co, New Passage Brewery, Morice Town. The New Passage Brewery was established by Thomas Husband by 1844. The Devonport & Tiverton Brewery Co was formed in 1876 to amalgamate it with the Old Brewery at Tiverton. The New Passage Brewery was acquired by the New Victoria Brewery of Plymouth in 1923, with 27 tied houses.

Eagle Brewery, Queen St, Devonport. Established c1878. When offered for sale with 11 tied houses, the *Exeter & Plymouth Gazette* for 22 July 1921 reported that 'the trustees of the estate, who had carried on the business for the last 30 years, thought that now was a good time to sell. For the past 15 or 16 years Mr Paull had run the brewery practically single-handed and the balance sheet had been satisfactory for many years past.' It was sold to Benjamin Letherby of Devonport for £29,850.[1]

Bedford Brewery, Alexandra Rd, Mutley. Founded in 1824 as Polkinghorne & Co in Bedford Street. Moved to Mutley in 1898, and registered in 1900 with 22 tied houses. In 1904 the company acquired the London Brewery, Kingsbridge. In 1908, it went into liquidation and the New Bedford Brewery Co was set up. This was acquired by Samuel Allsopp & Sons Ltd* in 1919 and business was transferred to the New Victoria Brewery.

Victoria Brewery, Hyde Park Rd. Registered in 1893. Acquired by Samuel Allsopp & Sons Ltd* in 1898 with 30 tied houses and renamed the New Victoria Brewery. Its closure was reported by the *Western Morning News* on 30 November 1948:

> Brewing is to cease at Messrs Ind Coope & Allsopp's New Victoria Brewery ... Messrs Ind Coope & Allsopp's houses in the Plymouth district will sell beers brewed by Messrs H&G Simonds at the Tamar Brewery, Devonport. In return, many of Messrs Simonds's houses will sell certain of Messrs Ind Coope & Allsopp's Burton-brewed ales.
>
> Nearly 50 men are employed at the New Victoria Brewery, which was built in 1892, but only a few are engaged in brewing. Not more than half a dozen men are likely to be discharged. About 600 barrels of beer were brewed a week. Messrs Ind Coope & Allsopp will retain their offices at the brewery and store and bottling stores, which will handle all ales brewed at the company's brewery in Burton on Trent.

1 The 11 tied houses sold with the Eagle Brewery were the London & South Western Railway Tavern, the Life Boat, the Avondale Arms, the Prince of Wales, the Millbridge Inn, the Butcher's Arms, the Lord Hood and the Steam Packet, Devonport; the Sir Francis Drake, Plymouth; and the Tamar Inn, Calstock.

Octagon Brewery, Martin St. Established by Joseph Godfrey in 1861. On 18 March 1898, the *Western Times* reported that it had been sold to 'Mr W Gilling of London, for £148,000, including 38 freehold and leasehold public and beer houses, seven rented houses, the goodwill of the trade, representing about 13,000 barrels of beer per annum, with a yearly rent roll of about £2,500'. The following year, the Octagon Brewery Ltd was registered as a limited liability company. It was acquired by Simonds* of Reading in 1954, with 48 tied houses. Brewing ceased in 1970.

Plymouth Breweries Ltd, Chapel Street, Stonehouse. Formed as a limited liability company in 1889 to amalgamate five breweries: the Regent Brewery, Chapel St, Stonehouse; the Anchor Brewery, Chapel St, Stonehouse; the Frankfort Street Brewery, Plymouth; the South Devon Brewery, Willow St, Plymouth; and the Saltash Brewery, Saltash, Cornwall. The *Exeter & Plymouth Gazette* of 30 October 1889, reporting the merger, ventured the opinion that

> the brewery trade of Plymouth and Stonehouse, although at present very remunerative, has somewhat suffered through being in so many hands, and the present amalgamation of breweries, which have hitherto worked more or less in competition, will undoubtedly prove of great advantage and will, while increasing the profits on the trade itself, greatly reduce the cost of production, the combined businesses being under one management.

Samuel Vosper of the Regent Brewery was appointed managing director, and in 1893 the Regent Brewery was enlarged, with the other four breweries closing a year later. Initially the company had 146 tied houses; although a number of these later closed, acquisition of three breweries in Torquay meant that the company still had around 150 tied houses when it was acquired by Courage Ltd* in 1970 and became Courage PB. It continued to operate on traditional lines, however, with wooden barrels and horse-drawn drays until closure in 1984.

CW Blundell & Co. See listing for the South Devon Brewery, Kingsbridge.

SIDMOUTH

Old Town Brewery, Fore Street. When advertised for sale at auction, together with the Ship Inn and a malthouse, in the *Exeter Flying Post* on 27 September 1849, the Town Brewery was described as a 'well-built stone and brick brewery recently erected in the most substantial manner, including all modern improvements, with its steam and water engines.' In the 1878 *Directory*, Arkell & Iles were listed as the owners, but by 1889 it had been acquired by Thomas Ford & Son of Tiverton. When it became part of Starkey, Knight & Ford's in 1895, it was closed and used as a depot until 1920, when it was sold.

Vallance's Brewery Ltd, Temple St. Established as the Sidmouth Brewery in 1832, by 1874 it had become Harvey & Vallance's, but was later taken over by John & George Vallance to become Vallance's. It was acquired by Woodhead's Brewery of London in 1946 with 35 tied houses, and sold to Devenish's* of Weymouth in 1957.

TAVISTOCK

Tavistock Brewery, Higher Market Street. On 19 August 1819, the *Exeter Flying Post* advertised the auction of the estate of William Sleman, deceased. This included 'a moiety or half part of and in the profits to arise from that long-established brewery, known as

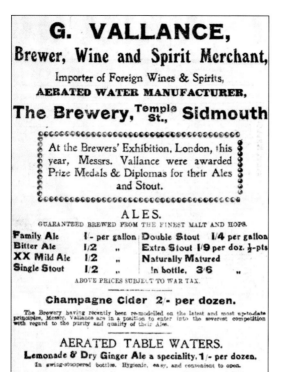

G. VALLANCE,

Brewer, Wine and Spirit Merchant,

Importer of Foreign Wines & Spirits,

AERATED WATER MANUFACTURER,

The Brewery, Temple St., Sidmouth

At the Brewers' Exhibition, London, this year, Messrs. Vallance were awarded Prize Medals & Diplomas for their Ales and Stout.

ALES.

GUARANTEED BREWED FROM THE FINEST MALT AND HOPS.

Family Ale	1 - per gallon	Double Stout	1/4 per gallon
Bitter Ale	1/2 "	Extra Stout	1/9 per doz. ½-pts
XX Mild Ale	1/2 "	Naturally Matured	
Single Stout	1/2 "	In bottle, 3/6 "	

ABOVE PRICES SUBJECT TO WAR TAX.

Champagne Cider 2/- per dozen.

The Brewery having recently been re-modelled on the latest and most up-to-date principles, Messrs. Vallance are in a position to enter into the severest competition with regard to the purity and quality of their Ales.

AERATED TABLE WATERS.

Lemonade & Dry Ginger Ale a speciality, 1/- per dozen.

In swing-stoppered bottles. Hygienic, easy, and convenient to open.

An advertisement from the Exeter & Plymouth Gazette *for 11 December 1914*

The Peter Tavy Inn, acquired by the Tavistock Brewery sometime before 1819. It was later transferred to another concern known as the Tavistock Brewery, but in 1927 this was acquired by Simonds of Reading

the Tavistock Brewery' and seven 'leasehold public houses'.[1] On 10 December 1853, when the lease of the Tavistock Brewery was advertised in the *Western Times*, 'an extensive and very lucrative business [had] for many years been carried on by the late Mr John White, deceased (formerly White & Skinner) as a general brewer and wine and spirit merchant'. White & Co were still listed as brewers and wine and spirit merchants in White's 1878 *Directory*, but, although the business was still listed in Kelly's 1889 *Directory*, it was now as a wine and spirit merchants only. The tied houses were transferred to the Bedford Brewery.

Bedford Brewery, Brook St. Established by 1877 by AM Richards & Co, and renamed the Tavistock Brewery after the original Tavistock Brewery closed. It was sold in 1899, with seven tied houses, for £13,730; in Kelly's 1902 *Directory* EB Gilbert was listed as the owner. In 1904, it was bought by Ernest Hilton and became Hilton & Son. In 1912, following a fire in the malthouse, he tried to sell, but the brewery failed to reach its reserve price.[2] In 1916, it was acquired by Kenneth Johnstone and Henry Soltau, two local solicitors. Brewing ceased in 1927 when it was acquired by Simonds* of Reading.

1 The seven leasehold tied houses included in the sale of the Tavistock Brewery in 1819 were the Buller's Arms, the King's Arms, the Ordnance Arms and the Dartmoor Inn in the parish of Whitchurch; the Dartmoor Inn in the parish of Lydford; the Peter Tavy Inn; and the Waterman's Arms in Calstock.

2 Advertised as part of the estate were two freehold public houses – the Tavistock Hotel and the Harvest Home, near Tavistock – and five leasehold properties – the White Hart, Chilsworthy; the Peter Tavy Inn; the New Inn, Horndon (now the Elephant's Nest); the Royal Standard, Mary Tavy; and the Forest Inn, Hexworthy.

TEIGNMOUTH

Teignmouth Brewery, Mere Lane. A report in the *Western Morning News* on 25 June 1886 described its destruction by fire. It was rebuilt and operated until 1909, when it was sold.

Teign Brewery, Teign Street. Established by 1878 by William Banbury; acquired by Simonds* of Reading in 1931.

TIVERTON

Devonport & Tiverton Brewery Co, Old Brewery, Bampton St. On 23 January 1830 the *Western Times* advertised a brewery and malthouse on Bampton Street in Tiverton, 'newly-built within a few years, the property of William Richards, a bankrupt'. The advertisement noted that there was 'no other brewery in Tiverton or within many miles of the place'. It was still Tiverton's only brewery in 1850, when Richard Snow was listed as the owner. The Devonport & Tiverton Brewery Co was formed in 1876 to amalgamate it with the New Passage Brewery in Devonport. The Tiverton Brewery was acquired by William Hancock & Sons* in 1919.

Thomas Ford & Son, Fore St. Established in 1852 by Thomas Ford. In June 1891, it was destroyed by fire, but was soon rebuilt, and in the *Brewing Trade Review* of 1 March 1895 it was described as the largest brewery west of Bristol, with branches and agencies in Plymouth, Sidmouth, Exeter, Torquay, South Molton and Truro, and 40 tied houses. In the same year it merged with Starkey, Knight & Co of Bridgwater to create Starkey, Knight & Ford Ltd. After being acquired by Whitbread* in 1962, with around 400 tied houses, the Bridgwater brewery was closed. Two years later, when Whitbread acquired Norman & Pring Ltd, Exeter, it was merged with Starkey, Knight & Ford and later renamed Whitbread, Devon. Brewing at Tiverton ceased in 1982.

TORQUAY

St Mary Church Brewery, Fore St. Established in the 1850s, it was taken over by John Greenslade around 1880 and renamed Greenslade Brothers, It was acquired by Plymouth Breweries in 1925. Brewing ceased in 1927.

Swayne & Co Ltd. Established by 1899 in Fleet Street, in 1900 Swayne & Co moved to the Ellacombe Brewery in Church Rd. It was acquired by Plymouth Breweries in 1925.

Torquay Brewing & Trading Co, Fleet St. Registered as a limited liability company in 1865 to acquire Matcham & Hussey's Brewery in Fleet St, Torquay. Acquired by Plymouth Breweries in 1897.

TOTNES

Castle Brewery, Fore Street. Established sometime before 1878 by William Sawyer. He was declared bankrupt in 1880 and the brewery was later owned by WO Dobree, who advertised 'the celebrated Totnes Stout' for sale. It closed in the 1890s, possibly after having been acquired by Walter & Phillips of the Lion Brewery.

Lion Brewery, South Street. Philip Condy is listed as an innkeeper and brewer at the Lion Inn in 1850; he had settled in Totnes in 1836 so his tenure probably dated from then. It still belonged to Condy & Co in 1889, but in June 1897, the *Brewers' Journal* reported that Walter & Phillips, the new owners, were planning to rebuild it. It closed in 1921 and the brewery and 16 tied houses were put up for auction.

Totnes High Street with the entrance to the Lion Brewery on the right. In 2013, 92 years after it closed, brewing returned to Totnes with the opening of the New Lion Brewery on Station Road.

UFFCULME

Furze & Co. Steam Brewery. William Furze was established as a brewer and maltster in Uffculme, with at least two tied houses, by 1848. In 1858, he built a new brewery, which was acquired by Starkey, Knight & Ford of Tiverton in 1918, with 26 tied houses. The building survives.

WOODBURY

White Hart. On 21 March 1894, the *Exeter & Plymouth Gazette* reported that

> a large company, including representatives of the brewery firms of the district, assembled at the White Hart Inn, Woodbury yesterday, when Mr A Thompson ... submitted to public auction this well-known hostelry, with its three-quarter brewery, malthouses,

An advertisement in the North Devon Journal *for 2 May 1861*

> **THE UFFCULM STEAM BREWERY ALES.**
> **WM. FURSE, PROPRIETOR.**
>
> THESE Unrivalled Ales are calculated to supersede the more expensive kinds, and to supply a superrior Article, where Ales of small and infeior Breweries have hitherto been used. Agents are appointed at many of the Towns in the Counties of *Devon, Somerset,* and *Cornwall,* through whom Families can be supplied *Carriage Free.*
>   The following ALES (which are warranted pure) are particularly recommended :—
>
>   s. d.
>
> THE UFFCULM STANDARD ALE, of a mild, brisk, and mellow palate, and suited to general Family use, is rcommended by Medical Men to invalids, andl argely patronised by the Public (per Galln) 1 0
> BEST MILD ALE.—To those who require a full rich Ale, this Article must please. It is of Burton flavour, and supplied mild or bitter (per Gallon).. 1 2
> X PORTER (per Kilderkin)..................... 18 0
> XX STOUT PORTER, equal to London, ditto 21 0
> XXX, OR OLD ALE, of prime October, 1859, Brewing. This is a first-class Ale for the Christmas festivities, in 1s 3d., 1s. 4d., and 1s. 6d. per Gallon, iu Casks of 9, 18, and 36 Gallons.
> AGENT, MR. M. SNELL, Wine and Spirit Merchant, *Barnstaple.* [1130

stabling, outbuildings, gardens, and premises attached, and which for over 80 years has been in the occupation of the same family, and is now only for disposal in consequence of the proprietress, Mrs Ebbells, retiring ... After spirited competition, the property was knocked down to Mr Robert Glanville, maltster, of Woodbury, for £1,200; he, in addition, takes the trade utensils, stock, and effects at a valuation.

Kelly's *Directories* for 1918 and 1923 listed Tom Glanville as a maltster and brewer in Woodbury; it is not known when the brewery ceased operation.

Breweries outside Devon which acquired breweries in the county

Samuel Allsopp & Sons Ltd, Burton on Trent, Staffordshire. Established in the 1740s, registered 1887. Merged with Ind Coope & Co Ltd in 1934 to form Ind Coope & Allsopp Ltd, which became Ind Coope Ltd in 1959. Merged with Tetley Walker and Ansells to form Ind Coope Tetley Ansell, later renamed Allied Breweries

Courage & Co Ltd, London. Founded 1787, registered 1888. Merged with Barclay, Perkins & Co to form Courage & Barclay in 1955. Merged with H&G Simonds to form Courage, Barclay & Simonds in 1960. Became part of the Imperial Tobacco Group in 1972.

JA Devenish & Co, Weymouth, Dorset. Established in 1742, registered 1889. Brewing at Weymouth ceased in 1985, but continued at Redruth Brewery, which had been acquired in 1934. In 1986 Devenish merged with Inn Leisure PLC. In the 1980s, the company was taken over by Greenall's. Brewing continued at Redruth after a management buyout.

Dorsetshire Brewery, Sherborne, Dorset. Established 1796; in 1951 acquired by Brutton, Mitchell & Toms of Yeovil, who were themselves acquired by Charrington's (later part of Bass Charrington) in 1960.

William Hancock & Sons, Wiveliscombe, Somerset. Established some time before 1807, registered 1896; merged with SW Arnold & Sons Ltd, Taunton in 1927 to become Arnold & Hancock Ltd. The company was acquired by Ushers Wiltshire Brewery, Trowbridge in 1955. Brewing ceased in 1959. Ushers was absorbed by Watney Mann in 1960.

H & G Simonds Ltd, Reading, Berkshire. Established in 1768; registered 1885. Merged with Courage & Barclay Ltd, London in 1960 to form Courage, Barclay & Simonds. Brewery closed 1979.

Whitbread & Co Ltd, London. Established 1742, registered 1889. New brewery opened in Luton 1969, London brewery closed 1976. In 2001, the company decided to dispose of its brewing arm to concentrate on its leisure interests.

*

We end this sad litany of amalgamation and merger on a brighter note. By the time Devon's last historic brewery – Plymouth Breweries – closed in 1984, the tide had already started to turn, with the revival of craft brewing. It was in 1977 that the Blackawton Brewery was established near Totnes. Although it has since closed, after a move over the border to Cornwall, the 1980s saw 16 more breweries open in the county. Most of them – including Devon's unlikeliest brewery on Lundy Island – have since closed. Three, however, have survived: the Beer Engine in Newton St Cyres, established in 1983; the Barron Brewery (now renamed the Exe Valley Brewery) in Silverton, established in 1984; and Summerskills, established at Bigbury in 1983, moved to Plymouth a year later and revived, after a two-year hiatus, in 1990. The 1990s saw 16 new breweries open in the county, of which eight are still brewing: Otter Brewery at Luppitt (established 1990), Branscombe Vale Brewery at Branscombe (1992), Princetown Breweries (now renamed Dartmoor Brewery) at Princetown (1994), Teignworthy Brewery at Newton Abbot (1994), Jollyboat Brewery at Bideford (1995), Barum Brewery at Barnstaple (1996), Country Life Brewery near Westward Ho! (1998) and Clearwater Brewery at Torrington (1999). Since then, around 40 more breweries have opened, and, although some have closed, there were, at the last count, at least 30 breweries operating in the county.

Plymouth's Hoegate Brewery

Partly because it is unusually well documented, partly because of the light it sheds on the early history of brewing in the county, and partly because of the people associated with it, the story of the Hoegate Brewery in Plymouth is worth featuring at some length.

It was established in 1764, when William Clark bought a former tavern known as the Pelican on Southside Street. The tavern had previously been owned by Richard Pett, a wine cooper who was a force to reckon with in mid-eighteenth century Plymouth. He had established the city's first playhouse in the garden of his great house, and, although a ramshackle affair, he managed to attract a company from Bath to perform there. Unfortunately, the company were already notorious in Bath for their dissolute and intemperate habits, and were no longer welcome there. They became known as the 'Brandy Company', and, after gaining an unenviable reputation for debauchery, fighting, squalor and indifferent acting, the Plymouth theatre closed in 1758. In 1766, two years after converting the former Pelican to a brewery, William Clark got his hands on the old theatre and converted it to a malthouse.

William Clark's acquisition of these properties was not fortuitous. It is possible that he had been apprenticed to or worked for Richard Pett; what is certain is that he married his daughter, and thus became part of one of Plymouth's most successful commercial dynasties. As the business prospered, he negotiated a contract to supply beer to the navy, acquired Efford Manor in Eggbuckland as his country retreat, and went into partnership with Philip Langmead, his sister's husband.

William Clark died in 1786 or 1787. His only son, who married Philip Langmead's younger daughter, died young, shortly after being appointed High Sheriff of Devon in 1795, and the brewery passed to Philip Langmead. Despite being in his mid-fifties, he rose to the challenge – as well as to several others – admirably. He expanded the brewery, and in 1797 bought a steam engine – the first in the city – from Boulton & Watt's Soho Foundry in Birmingham for £3,860. He retired in 1800, leaving his two sons – William Langmead and John Clark Langmead – in charge.

He went on to become Mayor of Plymouth, was elected MP for the city in 1802, and in 1808 became head of the newly-founded South Devon Bank. His two sons also became mayors of Plymouth, but, when John Clark Langmead tried, unsuccessfully, to follow his father into parliament, his candidature drew the following splenetic outburst from a naval officer called Thomas Byam Martin:

> Our brewers in this town, all wealthy purse proud fellows, and big pretenders to honour, but in fact rogues in grain, have been famously hauled over the coals, being detected in defrauding their customers, as well as the revenue, and they are defaulters to government to the amount of £6,400 between three of them, the mere duties only. The penalties if sued for will be three times that sum, and it will be a sin to spare them.

Quite what occasioned this attack is unclear, but Byam was no firebrand – he was later knighted and became Admiral of the Fleet – and there must have been some substance to his allegations. The opprobrium heaped on brewers like the Langmeads went hand in hand with the wealth, power and influence they enjoyed.

In 1823 the business was put up for sale, and advertisements appeared in newspapers throughout the country. The following, from the *Norfolk Chronicle* of 1 November 1823, is worth quoting at length because of the light it sheds on the operations of a large brewery in the early nineteenth century. Certain comments and pieces of information in the advertisement also suggest that, although the reason for the sale is not given, the brewery was in financial difficulties and needed substantial investment to get it back on its feet:

Mr WW SIMPSON of 24, Bucklesbury, London
has the honour to announce that he has received instructions from the proprietors
Messrs W and JC Langmeads, to submit for Sale by PUBLIC AUCTION
at Garraway's Coffee House, London,
in the month of November instant, in One Let

The FEE SIMPLE, and INHERITANCE of that
Most Valuable and OLD-ESTABLISHED BREWERY
which has been carried on during the greater part of a century, with very considerable success; consisting of an Ale, Porter, and White Ale Brewery, situated at Plymouth. The Plant and Utensils are fitted up on the most improved principle, and comprise two coppers, of 69 barrels each, and one of 18 barrels, mash tun, capable of wetting 30 quarters, steam engine, vats, coolers, and all other utensils appropriate to a concern of this magnitude.

There are attached to the Brewery and which will be included in the purchase, Seventy FREEHOLD and LEASEHOLD PUBLIC-HOUSES, situated in the towns of Plymouth, Plymouth Dock, Stonehouse, and in the immediate neighbourhood, which as well as the Beer Trade, are commanding a very large proportion of Business in the Wine and Spirit Trades.

The Proprietors let this Estate in 1822, with the privilege of supplying the public-houses with Beer, Porter, and Spirits, at an increased rental of £1200 per annum, which added to the present rental amounts to £3200 and at the period above referred to, the Trade was upwards of 8000 barrels, independently of Table Beer and White Ale.

Mr Simpson takes leave to offer it as his decided opinion, arising from an actual survey, that the amount of sale might be doubled immediately by good management, and the introduction of an article brewed on the London plan.

Plymouth, Plymouth Dock, and Stonehouse include a population of upwards of 60,000 inhabitants, exclusive of the Army and Navy, and the neighbourhood is rising every day from the immense public works which are going on. The consumption arising from the number of licensed houses belonging to the concern must always be very considerable, and in the event of a war would doubtless be at least quadrupled.

The Public Houses are let from year to year, at very low rents, and in the hands of a tenantry highly respectable. The whole of the estate is in a substantial state of repair.

It seems that the business failed to find a buyer, and, almost four years later, on 3 April 1827 a further auction was held. Two lots were on offer. The first consisted of 'all those capital new-built MALT HOUSES, Malt Kilns, Stables, Cellars, Store Rooms, and Lofts, situate on the western side of Broad Hoe Lane, otherwise Hoe Gate Street ... late in the occupation of Messrs Langmead and Company.' The second consisted of 'all those large and commodious BREWERY PREMISES, comprising Brew-houses, cellars, Store-rooms, Malthouses, Lofts, Malt-kilns, Stables, and yards, together with an inexhaustible well of fine water, situate on the eastern side of Broad Hoe Lane, otherwise Hoe Gate Street ... late also in the occupation of Messrs Langmead and Company.' It is not clear what had happened to the tied houses, which were not included in the sale. From subsequent information gleaned from local newspapers, it seems that the first lot went to a maltster called John Putt, while the second lot went, for £4,782, to two naval officers, Robert and Edward Scott, who had amassed a small fortune from prize money during the Napoleonic wars.

The enterprise did not get off to a good start. On 30 June 1828, the *Hampshire Chronicle* reported that 'very early on Thursday morning a most alarming fire broke out in the brewery of Mr Scott at Plymouth, which nearly destroyed the whole of the buildings and stock.' Fires at breweries were common, although arson was an ever present danger as well. Brewers, growing rich when many people were starving because of lack of work and soaring food prices, were seen as fair game for radical activists. On 18 December 1830, for example, the *Royal Cornwall Gazette* reported that several of Plymouth's breweries had been threatened with destruction unless they got rid of their horse mills:

> At Plymouth Dock, Devonport and Stonehouse several individuals have received letters signed 'Swing', threatening them with the destruction of their premises by fire. The following is a literal copy of a letter received by each of the principal brewers, Messrs Liscombe of Devonport, Scott of Plymouth, and Mr Hare of Stonehouse, all evidently written by the same hand, and bearing the Plymouth postmark:
>
> From Resadence, December 3 1830.
> We now inform you to destroy your horse-mill in your brewery emedently, eals it will be destroyed by fire. We have a plan, and it will only take a few minuents.
>
> 'Swing'

Robert Scott, who seems to have been the driving force behind the brewery from the start, bought a house called Outlands in Stoke Damerel, which he extended in a style befitting a new-made country gentleman. He had five sons, one of whom died young, while two went into the Indian Army and one became a naval surgeon. It was left to the youngest son, John Edward Scott, to follow his father into the brewery trade.

For a time, all went well, and the company started acquiring and building tied houses. One of the most prestigious was the Millbay Pier Hotel, the lease of which was advertised in the *Exeter Flying Post* on 1 August 1854:

> This hotel has been occupied three years, was erected from plans prepared expressly to meet the trade of the locality and is replete with every convenience for first-class as well as other visitors. Its immediate proximity to the pier ensures the custom of persons embarking and disembarking from the numerous foreign coasting and Irish steamers which call periodically. A very large business has been done which may be greatly increased ... For further particulars and terms of letting apply to ... Messrs Scott & Son, the proprietors, Hoe Gate Brewery.

After his father's death, John Edward Scott took over management of the brewery – which at some stage was renamed the Castle Brewery – and in 1862 settled into life as a country gentleman at Outlands. By the late 1870s, however – whether because John Edward Scott had neglected the business or whether through the exigencies of the brewery trade – it was clear that the Hoegate Brewery was becoming increasingly unviable. Efforts were made to turn the business around, and new equipment was installed, but in 1882, bowing to the inevitable, it was put up for sale. The sale particulars, however, which appeared in the *Exeter & Plymouth Gazette* on 11 August 1882, described it as a business opportunity that was too good to miss:

> Skardon & Sons are instructed to sell by auction ... in one Lot, or in such Lots as may be determined at the time of Sale, all that old-established, extensive FREEHOLD BREWERY known as the CASTLE BREWERY ... in Hoegate-street and Southside-street, Plymouth, in the county of Devon, for many years carried on by Messrs Scott and Co, comprising a well-arranged and commodious Brewery, convenient in every respect for carrying on the business, with offices, valuable steam appliances, bonded and other cellars, and extensive stabling, cart sheds, yards, etc, plant, machinery, vats, etc, together with 16 valuable and well-frequented FREEHOLD and LEASEHOLD INNS, situated in the best parts of Plymouth, Devonport, Stonehouse, and Tamerton Foliot, and POLICIES of LIFE ASSURANCE.
>
> Within the two last years the plant has been thoroughly renovated and the brewery premises and business much improved, and the whole of the Inns are well situated, in excellent repair, and respectably tenanted. The whole property, as a going concern, offers to any company or capitalist an opportunity for investment of rare occurrence.

No one came forward to take over the brewery, however. A deed in the Plymouth & West Devon Record Office records that, in November 1883, 'part of the brewery premises known as the Castle Brewery' was sold to a dairyman called FJ Gloyn.

John Edward Scott retired to live the life of a country gentleman at Outlands, but in 1894, with the money received from the sale all gone, he was forced to let the house and, at the age of 63, look for a job in order to support his family. He was appointed manager of Holcombe Brewery, near Shepton Mallet in Somerset, and moved into Holcombe House. Three years later, he died, leaving his family effectively penniless. Although the means by which they overcame their problems lies outside the scope of this chapter, mention has to be made of one of John Scott's sons, Robert Falcon Scott, who was serving as a naval lieutenant at the time of his father's death, and who went on to achieve immortality by leading an heroic expedition to the South Pole in 1912.

Devon White Ale

In recent years the growth of microbreweries has led to the revival of many long defunct beer styles. One legendary Devon brew has yet to be resurrected, however, which, given its long-standing popularity, seems something of a missed opportunity.

The history of Devon white ale is shrouded in mystery and confusion. One thing is clear, however: it had absolutely no connection with Dutch witbier or German weissbier, which are brewed with wheat. Devon white ale, in fact, seems to bear no relation to any other known beer style. It has frequently been claimed that it was confined to the South Hams, yet in the mid-nineteenth century it was brewed in at least 44 Plymouth pubs.

Another bone of contention is the so-called secret ingredient essential for brewing this elusive liquor. Some sources state categorically that the recipe was known only to the members of one family and handed down from generation to generation; others imply it was common knowledge. And as to where it was first brewed, although Dodbrooke (now part of Kingsbridge) is the name that most frequently crops up, Dartmouth, Plymouth and even Germany have also been suggested.

The first, albeit rather dubious, reference to white ale is said to come in Andrew Boorde's *Dyetary of Health*, published in 1542. Boorde is chiefly remembered today for his intemperate attack on the use of hops in beer. He was rude about other things as well, including Cornwall, which he described as

> a poor and very barren country of all manner thing, except tin and fish. Their meat, and their bread, and drink, is marred and spoilt for lack of good ordering and dressing ... Their ale is stark nought, looking white and thick, as pigs had wrestled in it.

Although he added that Cornish ale 'will make one to cack, also to spew', he gave no details about how it was brewed, which suggests this may have been simply a conventional unhopped ale marred by careless preparation. And, as this is the only time that Cornwall features in the story of white ale, we will move swiftly on to 1736 and the first unequivocal reference to it.

This comes in William Ellis's *London & Country Brewer*, a compendious tome in which we are told that 'the Plymouth people ... are so attach'd to their white thick ale, that many have undone themselves by drinking it'. Unlike Boorde, Ellis gives details of how this seductive tipple was brewed:

> Their white ale is a clear wort made from pale malt, and fermented with what they call ripening, which is a composition, they say, of the flour of malt, yeast, and whites of eggs, a nostrum made and sold only by two or three in those parts, but the wort is brewed and the ale vended by many of the publicans, which is drank while it is still fermenting in earthen steens, in such a thick manner as resembles butter'd ale, and sold for twopence-halfpenny the full quart. It is often prescribed by physicians to be drank by wet-nurses for the increase of their milk, and also as a prevalent medicine for the colic and gravel.

Two years later, in the third volume of *The London & Country Brewer*, Ellis returned to the subject of white ale,

> in order to set forth its excellency, and pave a way for its general reception in the world. To this end I write with an eager pen, by the inducement of the best qualities belonging to a public

liquor, viz. pleasure and health. About 60 years ago (as far as I can learn) this drink was first invented at or near the town of Plymouth ... This liquor is brewed from pale malt, after the best method known in the western parts of this county; and as it is drank at Plymouth, in particular by the best of that town, the alewives whose province this commonly falls under to manage from the beginning to the end, are most of them as curious in their brewing it, as the dairywoman in making her butter; for as it is a white ale, it is soon sullied by dirt, and as easily preserved in its frothy head ... And, though the wort is brewed by the hostess, the fermentation is brought on by the purchase of what they call ripening, or a composition (as some say) of the flour of malt mixed with the whites of eggs. But as this is a nostrum known but to a few, it is only guessing at the matter; for about 30 years ago, as I am informed, there was only two or three masters of the secret, who sold it out as we sell yeast, at so much for a certain quantity; and that every time a new brewing of this sort of ale happened a great ball or lump of it was generally sufficient to work four or five steens of wort, and convert it from a very clear body into a thick fermenting one, near the colour and consistency of butter'd ale, and then it was only fit to be used; for if it was let alone to be fine or stale, it was rejected as not worthy of buying and drinking. Yet some out of curiosity have kept it in bottles, rack'd it off clear, and made of it flip and other compositions very good. Now this white ale being fermented into such a gross body, becomes a sort of chyle ready prepared for digestion in the stomach, and yet so liquid as to pass the several secretory ducts of the animal system soon enough to give room for new supplies of this pleasant tipple, even at one common sitting in a public house: For though this drink is not so thin and clear as the brown sorts, yet by its new, lubricious slippery parts, it is soon discharged out of the stomach; and notwithstanding such evacuations, it leaves a very nutritious quality behind it in the body, that brings it under a just reputation for preventing and recovering those who are not too far gone in consumptions; and therefore would be of extraordinary service to labouring people. In short, this famous liquor is of such a salubrious nature, as renders it a most agreeable drink both to the sedentary and active person; which plainly shows the transcendent quality peculiar to this white ale, beyond all other malt liquors whatsoever. For who dare, nay who can make so free with any new beer or ale, while it is under fermentation, as with this, and that by reason of the poisonous quality of the yeast, and the fulsome, nauseating, unwholesome nature, that such working drinks are endowed with; whereas this invites one to drink it as fast as any of the common brown or pale ales, and at the same time administers to the body such medical assistance, that no other malt drink, wine, nor any potable liquor now in use, as I know of, comes up to it, not only for the aforesaid intention, but it is likewise usually prescribed by physicians as a remedy in the colic and gravel by its lubricating, diuretic nature ... Its strength also is so great, that though it is drank while working, it is as intoxicating as the common ales or beers; for by the time a man has drank a quart or two to his share, he will find it enough to go off with; and if anyone thinks fit to make it stronger (as is often done) it is only adding half a pint of sherry with a little loaf-sugar and nutmeg, and then it will not only be strong, but very pleasant; and sometimes entertaining to a fault; insomuch, that several have been enticed by its luscious, stimulating taste and cordial quality, to a degree of extravagance, by their too frequent expense of money and time in the enjoyment of this delicate improv'd ale.

Given such a ringing endorsement, it is surprising that white ale did not catch on elsewhere. Perhaps this had something to do with the availability of that secret ingredient, although strangely enough this was not mentioned by the next writer to sing its praises, the anonymous author of *Every Man His Own Brewer*, an early home-brew manual published in 1768:

This drink is prepared from pale, slack dried malt of the lowest quality, and without the use of any hop, or other alkaline preservative, as being for spending immediately after fermentation, which is brought about without yeast, in the following manner:

When the extract is drawn off into the wort tun, a paste is prepared from wheat flour, bean flour or malt flour, it matters not which, except as to body; either of these flours are made into a paste with white of eggs, and being thrown into the wort sets it a fermenting, whence arises a fine white froth, which no sooner falls than the liquor becomes drinkable, tho' not fine, nor is usually permitted so to be, as it then turns stale, but is for the present extreme brisk and agreeable.

This is not cleansed into casks as other ales, nor is a wort tun, as above mentioned, commonly employed; but as great neatness is requisite, it is most usually let down from the mash into glazed jars called steens, and worked in, and drawn from them for use.

Charles Vancouver, the progenitor of the myth that white ale could only be found in the South Hams, was in no doubt about the importance of ripening, however, which he called grout. In his *General View of the Agriculture of the County of Devon*, published in 1808, he wrote that

the brewing of a liquor called white ale is almost exclusively confined to the neighbourhood of Kingsbridge: its preparation, as far as could be learnt by the surveyor, is 20 gallons of malt mashed with the same quantity of boiling water; after standing the usual time, the wort is drawn off, when six eggs, four pounds of flour, a quarter of a pound of salt, and a quart of grout are beat up together, and mixed with this quantity of wort, which, after standing twelve hours, is put into a cask, and is ready for use the following day. This beverage possesses a very intoxicating quality, and is much admired by those who drink not to quench thirst only. A mystery hangs over the ingredient called grout, and the secret is said to be confined to one family in the district only. No difficulty however could arise in ascertaining its component parts, by submitting a certain portion of it to the test of a chemical examination. That this liquor is of considerable antiquity is plain, from the terrier of the advowson of Dodbrooke, and which expressly calls for the tithe of white ale. The present worthy incumbent commutes this claim, for half a guinea annually from every house in the parish where this ancient beverage is retailed.

Dodbrooke was also cited as the birthplace of white ale in White's 1850 *Directory of Devon*, which added that 'it is said to have been introduced by a German regimental surgeon, some centuries back, at Dodbrooke'. This German connection is intriguing, but, as this seems to be the sole reference to it, it may be as much of a red herring as Vancouver's claim that white beer was only brewed in the South Hams.

A correspondent in the *Exeter & Plymouth Gazette* for 12 January 1856 gave further details of Dodbrooke's claim to be the place where white ale was first brewed:

Dodbrooke is certainly the first known as the first place where white ale was brewed. I think this is borne out by the fact that a tithe ... is paid by all innkeepers who brew this ale. It has been gradually raised from tenpence until it has reached the present sum of a guinea. It is also further proved by some old papers still preserved in the parish church of Kingsbridge, from which Dodbrooke is only separated by a small stream of water which runs below the pavement, bearing the date of 1528 ... in which mention is made of this ale ... What I consider the strongest proof of the claim of Dodbrooke to the invention of white ale is that a family, who have resided here and in Kingsbridge in a direct line of descent for years before 1528 to the present date, are the only persons who possess the receipt for making the mixture which produces white ale, and this receipt is or has been preserved by the family as an inviolable secret. This mixture, which is known by the name of grout, is, at a particular stage of the brewing, put into, and mixed with, the wort, and as soon as the process is finished the result is white ale, a truly delicious beverage. All innkeepers are obliged, previous to brewing, to send to the representatives of this family for the necessary quantity of the mixture, without which no ale could be made.

Not everyone was convinced by the claims surrounding this so-called secret ingredient. In 1828, for example, Samuel Gray published a recipe for white ale in *The Operative Chemist*:

> Pale ale wort 25 gall, hops 2 handfuls, yeast 3lb, grouts 6 or 8lb. When the fermentation is at its height, bottle in strong stone half pints, well corked and wired; it effervesces when opened. The grouts here mentioned are made by infusing 6 or 8lb of malt in a gallon and a half of water, covering it warm by the fire side, stirring it often: when in full fermentation it is to be boiled down to a thick paste.
>
> This is a singular instance of a supposed secret which has been published upwards of a hundred and fifty years. The natives of Kingsbury [sic], in Devonshire, pretend that they alone can make white ale, and there is one family that pretends to the exclusive possession for the secret of making grouts. Now the method of making grouts, and from it white ale, was published in Bauhin's Historia Plantarum, being then the common English ale.

In 1850, a more detailed recipe appeared in *The Publican, Innkeeper & Brewer's Guide*:

> Mash one sack of pale malt or pale and amber malts with sufficient liquor at 170 degrees to draw off 30 gallons. Stand two hours and a half; set tap and turn over as much liquor at 180 degrees for second mash as will draw off 30 gallons more. While the second mash is standing, lade or pump the first wort into the copper; add half a pound of hops and increase the heat gradually while the second wort is running off, which add to it. Boil the wort very slowly for 20 minutes or half an hour. When it begins to get cloudy, or to break, which may be seen by dipping out a little in a basin, it is then boiled enough, for this must not be boiled so long as for beer. Run it off into the coolers with the hops, and cool down as speedily as possible to about 80 degrees in winter and about 60 in summer, and pitch the tun or square. While it is running into the square, mix a portion of the wort with 24 pounds of fine wheaten flour and 24 fresh eggs into a thin smooth batter, and then put it into the whole with one pound of salt, and set to work with one pound of ripening ... Cover it well up. In ten hours a fermentation will be visible all around the sides of the tun or square, which will increase until it forms a thick head over the whole surface, about as thick as a penny piece. It will then break into little white heads which will fall back, at which point it should be cleaned by passing it through a fine wire sieve into twelve or fourteen-gallon casks with the heads out. Put them in a place where there is no draught, that the liquor may not chill, and let it be well covered, that it may continue fermenting for eight or ten hours longer, when it will be fit to drink. A thin brown head will then be formed on the top, which should remain undisturbed, to keep the ale fresh under it. Should this head begin to break away, and fall through the liquor, it may be skimmed off, or it will be drawn off with the ale and spoil its appearance.

All of which seems straightforward, apart from that reference to ripening. This was, you will not be surprised to learn, that secret ingredient, although the author of the Guide seems unsure about just how secret it was. He starts by telling us that the recipe has been 'held by one or two families for many years, no one else in the neighbourhoods where the ale is drank but these knowing how to prepare it'. He then explains that 'the ripening, sold at Plymouth, for causing the fermentation, is a mixture of malt, hops and wort, which is quite sour, and without any appearance of fermentation, and is evidently a preparation in which a natural state of fermentation has occurred.' He goes on to say, however, that, if ripening is not available, some of the first wort, mixed with malt and hops, or the first mash, should be 'close corked' for three or four days in a warm place. This will, he claims, produce 'the same result ... without having recourse to the ripening'.

More light was shed on the mystery of the secret recipe for grout or ripening in a paper presented to the Devonshire Association at Kingsbridge in 1877 by a local historian called Paul Q Karkeek:

> By what means grout in the South Hams became a secret I cannot explain: doubtless someone devoted attention to it, and so was enabled to produce a ferment that could be relied on; and consequently was in a position to leave the method a secret for his children. This secret came into the Randall family with a Miss Grace Stentiford, who married the grandfather of the present generation of Randalls, about the year 1770. At one time its manufacture produced a very good income, but the railroads, and other destroyers of old-fashioned ways and doings, introduced the clear ale and beer of today; and it has not been made by the Kingsbridge Randalls for some years. It is still sold by a person of the same name, living in Plymouth; but others have set up claims to possess the secret, and have produced a ripening or grout which has answered all the purposes of the original.

Mr Karkeek was determined to get to the bottom of the mystery. He obtained a sample from John Randall, the 'white ale ripening maker' at 38½ Old Town Street, Plymouth, alluded to above, and sent it to an analytical chemist in Yorkshire, who prepared the following report:

> The sample had a peculiar odour and very acid reaction, and contained ground malt and hops, plainly visible to the naked eye. As it is composed of a very complicated organic mixture, it is next to impossible to make a proximate analysis of its constituents chemically; and, as such is the case, I had to depend on microscopical examination ... The fine deposit, when separated from the malt and hops, and which I may term the yeast, is made up of yeast cells (torulae) and wheat starch granules, in about equal proportions. In treating it with iodine, this was plainly proved without the microscope, and under its power, much albuminous matter, small scales of hops, etc, were very easily distinguished.
>
> The great peculiarity in the grout was the shape and size of the yeast cells, which are quite different to any that I have ever seen, being smaller in diameter and more ovoid than either German or any other English yeast. It is not so much the ingredients mixed with it, as the peculiarity in the yeast itself, which makes it different to other yeast; and you may rely on it that this is the whole secret. It was also greatly contaminated ... and is not calculated to produce a sound-keeping ale; in fact, any brewer's chemist would condemn its use in the brewery, and, as you remark that the grout ale only keeps one month in the winter and a few days only in summer, this plainly carries out what I say. Yeast so contaminated will produce lactic acid, in preference to alcohol; moreover, it is a well-known fact, that the lactic fermentation is more quick in its action than alcoholic. Besides the above, I discovered ... that common cane-sugar was present. We may then consider that grout consists of — first, yeast (torulae) cells, having a very uncommon appearance, and contaminated greatly by bacteria, vibrios, penicillum glaucum, and the putrefactive ferment preponderating; second, wheat starch or flour; third, albuminous matter in large quantity, probably eggs; fourth, chloride of sodium; fifth, common cane-sugar; sixth, ground malt and hops.
>
> As I before remarked, there is nothing very peculiar in grout, excepting the torulae cells. Bakers from time immemorial have, in out-of-the-way places, been used to make their own ferment, and the products agree very much with your grout. At best it is a very poor mess, and not to be compared with German yeast, neither do I consider that it is a proper or safe

thing to administer, especially in the summer; and I think it very probable that if you can trace it back where it has been largely consumed in ale, sickness would be far above the average in that locality ... The grout fermentation is what we should consider very quick, and I attribute its quick action not particularly to any constituent of the yeast, or to the peculiarity of the torulae cells itself, but to the action of lactic organisms, with which the yeast is greatly contaminated ... If it were considered desirable to imitate grout ale, I have not the least doubt it could be done with ordinary yeast; but with this difference, that in all probability it would be an immense improvement.

None of which would have come as welcome news to the white ale brewers, or indeed to their customers, especially as Mr Karkeek was not only a noted local historian, but also medical officer for Torquay. Given his influence, it may be no coincidence that it was around this time that white ale started to disappear, so rapidly, in fact, that less than 20 years later it had disappeared almost entirely.

He did, however, give details of two recipes passed on to him by two white ale brewers, which provide a vivid insight into the brewing process. The first explained that

the ale is always prepared in small quantities, and three bushels of malt to be used at one time is found a suitable quantity. From these three bushels from 30 to 36 gallons of worts are taken, just as the brewer wishes to give a more or less fair quality. About the same quantities or 'lengths' of worts are then taken as for sixpenny ordinary or common beer; but instead of using one pound of hops to the worts for each bushel of malt mashed, only about two ounces are used for white ale, and the hops are boiled with the worts in the copper in the usual way. After the worts are cooled down in the cooler they are run into a tun to ferment, and at the time of turning, 14 lbs of wheaten flour, a number of eggs at discretion, and the ferment called grout (half a pint) are added. Ordinary white ale can be used four days from the brewing, and will keep a month in winter, but not more than a week in summer, and the good or bad quality of the grout appears to very much affect the keeping properties of the liquor. Hundreds of hogsheads are drawn on the third day of brewing, but the fourth day is usually the first of perfection. Many successful brewings occupy a period as follows — the quality of the grout again appearing to materially regulate the time after it has been added: Mash on Mondays at seven; brewing over and worts cooled down by six pm., when the grout, flour, and eggs are added. On Tuesday morning, about eight, the ale can be turned into small open wooden vessels, called ale cans, and at any time in the following day (Wednesday) the ale can be sent into consumption in any vessel and used. The fermentation still goes on in the ale cans.

The second brewer described the process as follows:

The water for the first mash (170 degrees) being put into the mash tun, I put into it two bushels of malt — the mash-stick would then stand without holding. Cover the mash tun with sacks to keep in the steam; remain three hours; draw off, measuring the liquor that you may know what quantity of boiling water is required — I made about thirty gallons — for the second mash, allowing for reduction in steam, etc. Cover this as before, and stand two hours; put the whole into the copper, boiling gently two hours; put 1lb. of hops in at the same time, that all may boil together; then draw off through a strainer into the cooler. When cooled down to 100 degrees, put in one quart of grout, and stir it well; then take 15lbs. of best flour, and strew it evenly over the liquor; of course this is in a cask, being transferred from the cooler, which I had omitted to mention; the mash tun will do after the grains are removed; cover up well with sacks, it must be kept warm. The following day lift up the sacks gently; don't allow a rush of cold air to chill it. If you find it bubbling too much — experience must guide you — withdraw some of the sacks. The next day it will be fit to draw off, and put into jars. We do not always put eggs, but it improves it very much, and we sometimes call attention to the number of shells lying about the courtlage as a proof. It is generally understood, but as yours would be for your own consumption, a dozen well beat up with a little of the liquor, and put in at the same time as the grout, would do it a deal of good.

Despite the mystery – real or imagined – surrounding the use of ripening, it is clear that white ale differed fundamentally from anything we would recognise as ale today, due to the use of eggs and the imperative for it to be drunk within a few days. It was this – linked almost certainly with health concerns – that led to its demise. By the late nineteenth century, home-brew pubs were dying out as breweries bought them up and supplied them with their own beer. White ale did not lend itself to production on an industrial scale; the logistics of brewing, distributing and selling it within a limited timeframe would have been intractable. White ale had to be brewed in – or very close to – the places where it was going to be drunk; as home-brew houses disappeared, it was inevitable that white ale would disappear as well.

That said, it took a long time to die out, although it nearly succumbed in 1855 when new legislation was introduced. On 30 October 1855, the *Sherborne Mercury* reported that

> one of the favourite liquors with many persons in the south and west of Devon is white ale. The brewing of this liquor is now prohibited, as it contains other ingredients besides malt and hops. At this the brewers and drinkers of white ale are much displeased. The makers of the grout or ripening will be great losers by the prohibition, as its composition is known but to a few, who obtained a good profit thereby.

Faced with the loss of their livelihood, white ale brewers organised a petition. This forced a change of heart, and on 17 November the *Exeter & Plymouth Gazette* published a letter from the Board of Trade, acknowledging 'the receipt of an application from brewers of white ale in Devonport and other parts of Devonshire' and informing them 'that it is not the board's intention to interfere with the process as at present practised'.

White ale brewing was an important business in Plymouth at the time. Of the 122 inns listed in the 1852 *Directory for Plymouth, Stonehouse, Devonport, Stoke & Moricetown*, 29 brewed white ale, while of the 126 beerhouses, 15 were also white-ale brewers. White ale was brewed at some of the best inns in town, such as the Old Four Castles in Old Town Street (a picture of which appears on page 215). One visitor described arriving there on Christmas Eve 1847 to find 'bowls of hot punch, or egg flip mulled from the white ale for which this locality is famed ... steaming on the table of every guest room in the inn'.

By the time of the 1895 *Directory*, however, only two white-ale brewers were left in Plymouth – William Rawlings at 1 Well Street and James Mitchell at 103 Exeter Street. When James Mitchell died in 1930, an obituary recorded that, 'as the last brewer of the famous white ale in South Devon [he] was well known in the licensing trade. After being in business for 36 years he retired in 1922.'

Although we are fortunate in having a record of the extent of white-ale brewing in Plymouth in the mid-nineteenth century, there are no similar records for the South Hams or for Tavistock, where it was also popular. The following selection of newspaper reports from across the area, however, will give some idea of how deeply white-ale drinking was woven into the fabric of everyday life:

> Kingsbridge: An inquest was held here on Monday, touching the death of Richard Wildman, who died in consequence of falling into a lime kiln, when in a state of intoxication. The

deceased was a dealer and hawker of earthenware, and had been drinking white ale on the night of the 7th instant, with a companion called Lakey, until both became inebriated; it being late, instead of returning to their lodgings, they reeled to Mr Steer's lime kilns, where both of them fell in; the kiln was 16 feet deep. Mr Steer, hearing a noise, left his bed and got them out of the kiln but Wildman was so much injured that he died on Saturday last. Verdict: Died by falling into a lime kiln when in a state of intoxication.

Exeter & Plymouth Gazette, 25 March 1837

Kingsbridge, Prize Ploughing & Spade Husbandry Match: This match (or rather an apology for one) came off on Wednesday last. The attendance was meagre in the extreme, four ploughs only were set to work, and the company altogether consisted of about 150 to 200 persons – a dozen of them only being yeomen or tradesmen. The dinner took place at the Golden Lion Inn; thirteen only sat down, and though a few tradesmen joined in the evening, there was great difficulty in keeping the steam up. No prizes were awarded, but the ploughmen and boys had a good dinner of beef and pudding with white ale to wash it down.

Western Times, 11 March 1848

Dartmouth [from a report of a smuggling trial]: William Blight, landlord of the Ship in Dock Inn, Dartmouth, deposed that in December last he took an empty hamper from the Commercial Inn to Mr Nichols, and which he took back to the same inn filled. He could not say what were its contents, but he believed one of the parcels contained loaf sugar. The defendant rewarded him with a pint of white ale.

Exeter & Plymouth Gazette, 1 February 1851

East Allington: The hay has been saved in a very bad condition in this neighbourhood. The harvest here is likely to be very late; the crops have been materally injured by the heavy rain, consequently they will now be below an average. A new game has been got up in this village by the lovers of white ale, called the Ted-dle-ey-wirk, which is likely to prove beneficial to the landlord.

Western Times, 6 August 1853

Loddiswell: Died April 2nd at Loddiswell, Miss Betty Taylor, aged 89 years. She was landlady of the Church House Inn, upwards of 50 years, and was celebrated for keeping good white ale, so much so, that for the last 20 years strangers frequently visited Loddiswell to have a pint of Aunt Betsy's white ale.

Sherborne Mercury, 15 April 1856

Salcombe: The Fifth of November was duly regarded here on Friday last in rather an amphibious manner. A 'guy' having been prepared and a bonfire lighted, the figure was taken off in a boat to the middle of the harbour, where it was placed on planks and ignited. The night was dark, and the burning effigy produced a brilliant effect, to the delight of some 300 persons who assembled to witness it. The funds for these celebrities [sic] are collected by public subscription. One of the items in the expenditure is for 'cakes and white ale', which latter is of an entirely local character, being unknown beyond twelve miles in this place and Kingsbridge. The said ale, the old people say, was formerly brewed as a medicine; it is now the general drink of the district.

Western Times, 13 November 1858

Kingsbridge: On Monday Joseph Welcome was charged ... with brawling in the church on Sunday morning. The defendant pleaded ignorance of the affair altogether. He had taken a little too much white ale, and therefore was unconscious of what was laid to his charge. As the case was not pressed the magistrates fined him in the mitigated penalty of £1 including costs.

Western Times, 14 April 1870

Dartmouth: A visitor in an interesting article published in a Kidderminster paper records his impression, from which the following is an extract: 'On the cliff, at the mouth of the river, which is remarkably narrow, is what remains of Dartmouth Castle, a building from whence many a stirring scene has been viewed ... Looking up at the weather-worn tower of the old castle, where I expected to see the lady looking out for the return of him who would never see her more, I beheld the word 'Refreshments'! It was painted in great flaring yellow letters on an immense signboard that seemed to smother and overpower the grey time-honoured pile. Sick at heart, and dreading lest a closer examination should reveal the inevitable illuminated card, whereon a frisky clown is knocking out the eye of a clerical-looking gentleman with the cork from a bottle of 'Bang-up Pop', I fled. My companion followed me and arriving at an inn earnestly entreated me to try a glass of white ale; or, as he poetically and playfully put it, 'to drown my sorrow in the flowing bowl'. I had never before had an opportunity of tasting the celebrated white ale of Dartmouth, and I shall survive my grief if a second opportunity does not occur. It is a thick, light mixture, and looks, but doesn't taste, like egg-flip; and I was informed by the landlord that the manufacture of the article with which it is fermented is a profound secret. It is to be hoped that the present member of the family who possesses it will die without committing the recipe to paper. The ale is drawn from an open, deep tub, and will only keep a few days; a rapid draught is therefore necessary, and, in reply to a question as to whether he obtained this, mine host said he sold three times as much of it as of the ordinary ale. A chemist's shop next door would, I should imagine, be a good speculation.

Western Times, 3 May 1872

Tavistock: Two inhabitants of Tavistock, better known than valued, have this week passed away for ever. 'Barnicott's Ghost' will never more shuffle through our streets, stick in hand, in clothes 'a world too wide' for his shrunk form, and mutely appealing by his poverty-stricken aspect to the compassion of the charitable. Often have we seen him, made almost mad by tormenting fiends in the shape of boys, brandishing his faithful staff, and attempting, uttering much strong language the while, to bring it swiftly on the backs of his tormentors, who, however, generally eluded his vengeful pursuit, and turned with fresh jibes on the pursuer. Wretched as the poor fellow's life was, he only very recently surrendered the freedom of the streets, with all its sorrows, for the confinement of the workhouse, with its comparative comforts. What a cheerless, melancholy thing life must have been to him! And no less pitiable was the life of that other well-known inhabitant named 'Mad Martin'. Nature had not been kindly to him in the bestowment of her gifts; certainly she did not give him the charm of personal beauty. Perhaps his most conspicuous characteristic, after his face, was his ceaseless thirst, and his deepest sorrow that the supply of white ale was limited. Life for him presented only two objects worth striving for – ale and tobacco. What to him, and to such as him, was all our boasted civilization, our arts, our letters, our churches, and our chapels – nay, the very idea of religion itself? To this poor creature getting drunk was the highest form of enjoyment, the one thing needful, without which life was but a dreary blank. Verily, the lives of such men as these should make us reconsider some of our smug conclusions, and force us to think that there are still a few moral problems beyond the range of our philosophy.

Exeter Flying Post, 6 January 1875

Blackawton: Henry Hambling of Blackawton was charged by PC Toms with keeping open the Dartmouth Inn during prohibited hours on the 27th ult. The officer stated that he saw several men in the house on the night named at a quarter to eleven, and also saw a pint of white ale carried to a man named Cole, who paid 2½d for it. Mr W Davies, who appeared for defendant, said his client was now ill in bed, and was unwell on the day in question. Mrs Hambling locked the bar at ten, told the servant to clear the house and went upstairs to her husband. This being the third conviction against Hambling, he was fined £3 and 15s costs.

Western Times, 10 May 1878

East Prawle: On Saturday afternoon an inquest was held at the Providence Inn, East Prawle, by Mr Sidney Hacker, District Coroner, on the body of Joseph Partridge, 73 years of age, who met with his death in somewhat peculiar circumstances on Wednesday. It appeared from the evidence that the deceased, who resided at East Portlemouth, went to Chivelstone and recorded his vote on Wednesday. He afterwards went to the inn, and remained two or three hours, but the only drink he took was two half-pints of white ale. On leaving the inn he was met by two boys, who called him an Old Tory, but deceased declared they were mistaken, as he had voted for Mildmay. A few yards from the point where the boys met him the deceased fell down, his head resting in a pool of water which was collected at the side of the road. Deceased was afterwards found quite dead ... The jury, after considering the evidence, returned a verdict of accidental death.

Exeter & Plymouth Gazette, 7 December 1885

That report from East Prawle is the last reference we have found to white ale being sold outside Plymouth. When white-ale brewing finally died out is, like so much connected with this elusive beverage, a mystery. Occasional references to it continued to crop up long after its demise, however, in books and local newspapers. Some of them perpetuated old myths, others came up with new ones. None were as bizarre, though, as those which featured in an exchange of letters in – of all places – *The Times*, as Britain braced itself for war in 1939. On 22 April 1939, a Mr HE Vickery, the editor of a magazine called *Bottling* from Guildford, wrote that

white ale ... was discovered by chance about the middle of the eighteenth century. A farmer who lived near Loddiswell had a sick cow, and he called in the local farrier to prescribe for her. The farrier gave her a drink which contained, among other ingredients, malt and flour. Some of this drink was left over and it began to ferment. A curious person tasted it, found it good, and after a few experiments white ale was produced. It was brewed from malt and hops, wheaten flour and eggs, and then a curious ferment called grout was added.

This prompted a reply from Mr E Kerry Cox, Senior Ale Conner of the City of London:

I have always understood that the beverage was an ancient one and subject to tithe for many years. As with so many home-made beverages, however, the manufacturing processes seem to have become much simpler in course of time. Fifty years ago it was still being brewed, but only of ordinary ale with eggs and flour mixed, although it was even then so nutritious that Devon labourers regarded it as 'meat, drink and cloth combined'. Earlier, as Mr HE Vickery's letter suggests, more trouble was taken with the concoction, malt, hops, flour, spices, and a mysterious compound known as grout or ripening being used.

At which Mr JI Mosley from Shaldon weighed in, declaring that

white ale is a thing of the past. A few years ago I made inquiries in the Kingsbridge district and found that it had been made at one of the inns at Marlborough [Malborough]. There is a local tradition that its thickness and colour were due to a mysterious ingredient called grout, which was really pigeon's dung. I was told that the last manufacturer, who died without passing on the secret, did indeed keep a number of pigeons.

You can almost imagine the roar of laughter that greeted Mr Mosley's anonymous informant, when he told his cronies what he had said to the snooper from Shaldon who had come asking a lot of damn-fool questions. They would have been even more delighted had they known the story would one day appear in *The Times*.

Strangely enough, no one from Devon could be bothered to refute the story about the pigeons. That was left to Sir Garrard Tyrwhitt-Drake of Cobtree Manor in Maidstone:

> When I was a pupil at Messrs Fox's Brewery at Farnborough, Kent, in 1900 the firm was celebrated for its white ale. This beer was brewed the same as any other beer, but from the very palest coloured malt and sugar, it was the colour of pale straw, but tasted just like any other ale of similar strength. There certainly was no question of grout or pigeons connected with it!

And there, sadly, with reference to a white ale that bore no relation to the white ale of Devon, this Beachcomber-like exchange of letters came to an end.

Over a century after white ale finally died out, given the advances in brewing technology and the growth of microbreweries, a revival would seem well overdue. It is a pity that something that was so much a part of Devon's heritage for well over 200 years, and had such passionate adherents, should have disappeared so totally. With the current level of interest in heritage beers and rare beer styles, there seems no reason why a home-brew pub serving Devon white ale, either in Plymouth or the South Hams – and subject to the quality control standards so conspicuously absent when Mr Karkeek carried out his investigations – should not be a magnet for beer-lovers from across the world. Penpont Brewery over the border in Launceston have already stolen a march on brewers in Devon by brewing a traditional – and reportedly very palatable – white ale in 2011, and home-brewers as far afield as Portland in Oregon, have blogged their success in coming up with something akin to this most recondite of tipples.

So the gauntlet is down. We surely cannot be alone in wanting to try this most tantalising of lost beers. It was the most popular drink in the South Hams for generations, as well as the staple tipple of many drinkers in Plymouth. If nothing else, we owe it to them to give it a go and see what all the fuss was about. The time has come for Devon's brewers to revive a unique part of the county's brewing heritage.

Acknowledgements

Thanks to Phil Beer and Steve Knightley of Show of Hands for permission to quote from the lyrics of 'Country Life'; to Anne Williamson, manager of Henry Williamson's literary estate, for permission to quote from *On Foot in Devon* and *Devon Holiday*; thanks also to the many pub landlords throughout the county for their hospitality and their help while we were researching this book, and especial thanks to Caroline Cheffers-Heard and family of the Bridge Inn, Topsham, and Roger and Carol Cudlip and family of the Tom Cobley Tavern, Spreyton, for their support and encouragement during the time the project was taking shape. Thanks also to Caroline Cheffers-Heard for permission to reproduce the painting of the Bridge Inn which adorns the back cover. An earlier version of the chapter on Devon White Ale appeared in *Brewery History: The Journal of the Brewery History Society*, 156 (Winter 2013).

Bibliography

A Dean Prior Miscellany, Dean Prior, 2000
The History of Widecombe Fair, Chudleigh, 2007
The Story of Hatherleigh, Hatherleigh, 1991
Barber, Chips, *The Story of Hallsands*, Pinhoe, 2001
Barber, Norman, ed. Mike Brown & Ken Smith, *A Century of British Brewers: 1890 to 2004*, New Ash Green, Kent, 2005
Baring-Gould, Sabine, *An Old Home and its Dependencies*, London, 1898
Baring-Gould, Sabine, *Further Reminiscences, 1864-94*, London, 1925
Baring-Gould, Sabine, 'Introductory Essay on English Folk Music', in *English Minstrelsie*, Vol 7, H Fleetwood Shepherd & others, Edinburgh, 1896
Brown, Cynthia Gaskell, *The Church House at South Tawton, Devon*, South Tawton, 2006
Burton, SH, *Devon Villages*, London, 1973
Courtney, Cyril, *Beesands & Torcross of Yesteryear*, Pinhoe, 2001
Cowley, Patrick, *The Church Houses: Their Religious and Social Significance*, London, 1970
Denham, Chris, *The Local: Ales & Tales of the West Country*, Kingsbridge, 1999
Gale, AW & others, *The Building Stones of Devon*, Trowbridge, 1992
Green, Cyril Wallington, *The Parish of Sampford Arundel, 1800-1914*, no date
Haydon, Peter, *The English Pub: A History*, London, 1994
Hemphill, Ian, 'The Lost Inns of Teignmouth,' in *News & Brews: South Devon CAMRA Magazine*, Spring, Summer & Autumn 2008
Hoskins, WG, *Devon*, London, 1954
Manco, Jean, 'The History of the Distillery, Southside Street, Plymouth.' Unpublished report. 2011; accessible via Plymouth City Council planning wesbsite (www.plymouth.gov.uk)
Norris, Gerald, *West Country Rogues & Outlaws*, Newton Abbot, 1986
Quick, Tom, *Dartmoor Inns*, Tiverton & Exeter, 1992
Richmond, Lesley & Alison Turton, *The Brewing Industry: A Guide to Historical Records*, Manchester, 1990
Robinson, Chris, *Plymouth: As Time Draws On*, Plymouth, 1985
Robinson, Chris, *Victorian Plymouth: As Time Draws On*, Plymouth, 1991
Slade, Pat, *Bideford*, Stroud, 1996
Tanner, Kathy & Peter Walsh, *Hallsands: A Pictorial History*, Kingsbridge, 1984
Thomas, David St John, *A Regional History of the Railways of Great Britain: Volume 1, The West Country*, Newton Abbot, 1960
Tierney-Jones, Adrian, *West Country Ales*, Tiverton, 2002
Trump, HJ, *Teignmouth*, Chichester, 1986
Vesey, Barbara & Peter Long, *Hidden Inns of the West Country*, Aldermaston, 2003
Webb, Pete, *The Pubs and Inns of Ashburton*, Pinhoe, 1995
Williamson, Henry, *On Foot in Devon*, London, 1933
Williamson, Henry, *Devon Holiday*, London, 1935

General Index

Brewery Index

Some other pub titles from Akeman Press

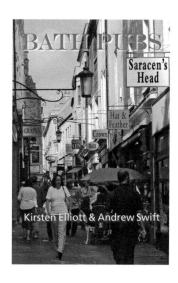

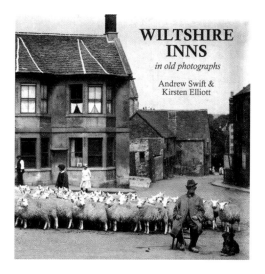

Visit our website
www.akemanpress.com
for details of all titles or to place an order